Campus Life
in the Movies

Campus Life in the Movies

A Critical Survey from the Silent Era to the Present

JOHN E. CONKLIN

McFarland & Company, Inc., Publishers
Jefferson, North Carolina, and London

LIBRARY OF CONGRESS CATALOGUING-IN-PUBLICATION DATA

Conklin, John E.
  Campus life in the movies : a critical survey from the
silent era to the present / John E. Conklin.
      p.   cm.
  Includes bibliographical references and index.

  ISBN 978-0-7864-3984-3
  softcover : 50# alkaline paper

  1. College life films—United States—History and criticism.
  1. Title.
  PN1995.9.C543C66   2008
  791.43'63557—dc22   2008038152

British Library cataloguing data are available

©2008 John E. Conklin. All rights reserved

*No part of this book may be reproduced or transmitted in any form
or by any means, electronic or mechanical, including photocopying
or recording, or by any information storage and retrieval system,
without permission in writing from the publisher.*

On the cover (top to bottom): Images from *Class of '44* (1973,
Warner Brothers); graduation cap ©2008 Shutterstock; film reel
©2008 Photodisc; *Where the Boys Are '84* (1984, TriStar) and
Revenge of the Nerds (1984, Twentieth Century–Fox)

Front cover by TG Design.

Manufactured in the United States of America

McFarland & Company, Inc., Publishers
  Box 611, Jefferson, North Carolina 28640
    www.mcfarlandpub.com

For my mother,
who introduced me to the
college campus as a toddler

TABLE OF CONTENTS

Preface   1

Introduction   3

1—Getting In   13
2—Freshman Year   35
3—Higher Learning   53
4—Teacher's Pet   72
5—Love Story   95
6—Going Greek   122
7—The Big Game   143
8—The Activist   169
9—Those Were the Days   186

Chapter Notes   203
Filmography   208
Bibliography   214
Index   217

Preface

Hollywood films have presented audiences with stories of campus life for nearly a century, shaping popular perceptions of our colleges and universities and the students who attend them. I first became aware of the power of films to distort, or at least accentuate, certain aspects of campus life when I saw *National Lampoon's Animal House*. Perhaps the most popular of all college movies, it is set at fictional "Faber College," but is based on the experiences of one of its screenwriters, Chris Miller, at Dartmouth College's Alpha Delta Phi fraternity in the early 1960s. In 1961, I joined the chapter of the same fraternity at Cornell University, also an Ivy League school, yet I failed to recognize much in the film that looked familiar. Though it was many years before I began to explore systematically how the movies portray undergraduate life, whenever I watched a film set on a college campus I inevitably compared it to my own observations as a student and a professor.

Fifteen years ago I began to collect lobby cards, which are 11 x 14" movie posters; ten years ago I started to look for cards from movies that had a college theme. The illustrations in this book are from that collection. I began to seek out movies about campus life and discovered it had been the subject of hundreds of Hollywood films over the years. In 2002 I composed a list of movies dealing with college life from the American Film Institute's *Catalog of Motion Pictures Produced in the United States* and the Internet Movie Database and tracked down as many of them as I could. Eventually I located and watched 589 of the 681 films on my list. This is more than the number of movies used in two previous books, 237 in Wiley Lee Umphlett's *The Movies Go to College: Hollywood and the World of the College Life Film* (Rutherford, NJ: Fairleigh Dickinson University Press, 1984) and 55 in David B. Hinton's *Celluloid Ivy: Higher Education in the Movies, 1960–1990* (Metuchen, NJ: Scarecrow Press, 1994). Some of the difference in numbers is because the college movie has become a more popular genre since 1990, and some is because I include movies that deal with campus life even when it is not the main theme. From my detailed notes on the 589 movies I watched and from other sources of information for the 92 I was unable to see, I developed a narrative about the aspects of undergraduate life that repeatedly appear in the movies.

Cinematic depictions of campus life can alter attitudes and behavior. High school students, a major audience for college movies, develop ideas about what the future holds from watching Hollywood portrayals of the undergraduate experience. Some probably join fraternities expecting them to be "animal houses," and a few even behave in ways the movies suggest is typical of Greeks. College administrators' responses to students can be affected by attitudes that are shaped by what appears on the screen. Alumni who reminisce about their college years are influenced by what they see in the movies; a student romance might evoke a happy recollection of a long-ago love affair or stir up an unpleasant memory of a past breakup. By suggesting what campus life is like today, the movies might even make some parents reluctant to foot the high cost of a college education if they think they are paying for their children to spend four years hooking up and binge-drinking.

I would like to thank Tufts University for its support in acquiring some of the films and lobby cards used in this book. I also appreciate the encouragement and support offered by my wife, Sarah Belcher Conklin, throughout the years it took to complete this book.

INTRODUCTION

A grocery store worker in *Small Town Girl* (1936) realizes "there's so much more" to life as she watches a parade of cars carrying Harvard students and alumni to their traditional football game with Yale. Unlike Dorothy in *The Wizard of Oz* (1939), who is sure "there's no place like home," Janet Gaynor's character feels that college offers an opportunity for a better life, one more exciting than her dull job and the friends and relatives whose every word she can predict. For Anne Shirley in *Sorority House* (1939), college has a different meaning: "It means friends I'll keep all my life. Memories. Oh, I've got lots of memories already. It means learning things and lifting myself. It means membership in the international democracy of culture ... to tell the good from the bad ... good music, good books."

At the time these films were released, less than one-tenth of Americans between the ages of eighteen and twenty-four was enrolled in an institution of higher learning. Today that ratio is more than one in every three. Even when few Americans were attending college, movie audiences enjoyed watching young people romance, score touchdowns, and occasionally go to class. Because the Hollywood dream factory exists to make money, and profits depend on entertaining the public, it isn't surprising that movies about college life dwell on the fun students have rather than the coursework they do. After this formula proved successful in the 1910s and 1920s, studios recycled the same storylines and stock characters for years. The cookie-cutter nature of these movies makes them "better indexes of public concerns, shared myths, and mores than are individually conceived, intentionally artistic films."[1]

Movies and Social Reality

Over the years, college movies have influenced the way people perceive the undergraduate experience by both distorting it and accurately mirroring it. One reason for the distortion is suggested by a studio executive in *She Loves Me Not* (1934); he remarks about a movie his company is making: "It's a college story, and none of my writers has ever been to college."

The allure of college for Kay (Janet Gaynor) in *Small Town Girl* (1936, Metro-Goldwyn-Mayer) is a life more promising and fun-filled than the one she leads in her humdrum hometown. Here she is pulled away from her work in a grocery store by a group of exuberant Harvard students on their way to a football game with arch-rival Yale.

If the movies sometimes present an inaccurate or incomplete picture of campus life, at times they also reflect the reality of that world. Movies from the 1930s in which a football hero wins the game and the girl of his dreams as time expires, and in which students never seem to open a book or go to class, are less a distortion of reality than they might seem, for historians have documented that campus life at the time was often centered around intense football rivalries and getting by with a "gentleman's C."[2] If football and romance offered audiences an escape from the harsh realities of the Great Depression, other movies of that era examined the impact of social inequality and unemployment on students. College movies often mimic reality, but because there are many "realities" of campus life, small liberal arts colleges being quite different from large state universities, no single film can present the undergraduate experience in all its complexity.

Demonstrating that films affect social reality is difficult, but the many football-and-romance movies of the 1930s probably shaped popular views of college life, and the raucous partying and rampant sexual activity common in movies since the late 1970s have likely had an impact on public attitudes toward college students. *National Lampoon's Animal House* (1978), the best known of all college movies, might have altered the behavior of first-year students by changing their expectations of campus life, and it could have strengthened administrators' hostility toward Greek-letter organizations. More recent movies such as *Coming Soon* (1999) and *The Perfect Score* (2004) might have reinforced anxiety about getting into brand-name schools among high school students and their parents. At the very least, nearly a century's worth of college films has not fostered an image of the campus as a place dominated by hard-working students intent on getting the best possible education. Whatever effects the movies have had on perceptions of campus life have probably diminished over time as increasing numbers of Americans have attended college and had experiences there that let them evaluate more critically what they see on the screen.

The tagline on this lobby card for *National Lampoon's Animal House* (1978, Universal) reads: "It was the Deltas against the rules ... the rules lost!" Has the behavior of John "Bluto" Blutarsky (John Belushi) and his fraternity brothers in this film influenced the attitudes and actions of generations of college students?

Movies about undergraduate life have a cumulative impact on the culture. Even films that no longer exist or are rarely seen today have influenced current ideas about campus life because they have seeped into the culture and affected the content of subsequent films. As early as 1925, Harold Lloyd in *The Freshman* prepares for his first day of college by emulating the character in a movie poster of *The College Hero* that hangs on his bedroom door. In *That's My Boy* (1951) the football coach mockingly denies a plea by the inept Jerry Lewis for a shot at trying for an extra point: "Son, you've been seeing too many college movies where the hero goes in at the last minute and wins the game." Another player misses the extra point, but Lewis eventually kicks a winning field goal and is carried off the field on his teammates' shoulders. Self-reflexive movies of this sort recycle time-worn motifs for new generations and in the process reproduce perceptions of campus life.

The College Years

For much of the twentieth century, most college students were in their late teens and early twenties, but today one of every seven is older than twenty-four. Nonetheless, college movies continue to feature students who are in late adolescence. Adolescence encompasses the years from twelve to twenty-one, but a case can be made that today it begins before twelve and often extends beyond twenty-one. Adolescence emerged as a separate stage in the life cycle between childhood and adulthood during the Industrial Revolution, when young people for the first time were exempted from full-time labor so they could learn the skills required for work in an economy based on complex technology. Schools provided an opportunity for young people to interact free of parental supervision for a good part of each day, giving rise to distinctive adolescent values, attitudes, and behavior patterns.

Most college students who are in late adolescence do not consider themselves adults.[3] For them, the college years are a rite of passage from childhood to independent adulthood, a time when they achieve competence, learn to manage emotions, become responsible, form mature relationships, forge identities, and clarify goals and values.[4] Rather than form a monolithic subculture, they identify to varying degrees with several different subcultures, each defined by its relationship to college life and the years that lie ahead. A present-oriented *collegiate subculture* emphasizes having a good time rather than preparing for a career. On most campuses from the 1920s until the 1960s, collegians did enough coursework to stay in school and graduate, but their true interests were their extracurricular activities, sports teams, fraternities and sororities, and social life. Also present on campuses during this period was an *outsider subculture* of men who were studying for the ministry and immigrants' sons and daughters who were working for the credentials needed to get good jobs.

The title *Life Begins in College* (1937, Twentieth Century–Fox) implies that adulthood starts in college, even though most of today's students and their parents would disagree. Ironically, the Ritz Brothers were all in their thirties when the movie was made. The tagline at the top of the card refers to *Pigskin Parade*, a popular college musical released a year earlier.

These "grinds" were disparaged by the collegians for their bookishness and lack of interest in having a good time. In the 1960s, on many campuses a *rebel subculture* challenged the authority of the college and sought to reform the world outside the ivory tower. Only during the 1930s had American campuses seen such political activism. In her history of campus life, Helen Lefkowitz Horowitz added to her analysis of these three subcultures by characterizing colleges in the late 1980s as dominated by a *new outsider subculture* of privileged students whose "grim professionalism" was aimed at guaranteeing for themselves the economic and social advantages enjoyed by their parents. These students began early in high school to prepare for admission to the most prestigious college possible in order to gain a competitive edge in the quest for a rewarding career.[5]

Movies from all eras emphasize the activities of the collegiate subculture (romance, football, and parties) rather than those of the outsider or new outsider subculture (attending class, studying, and writing papers). Except for a few years around 1970, the political activism of the rebel subculture has been largely absent from the screen. These emphases are the result of the need to entertain: Social life and athletic contests have more audience appeal than writing a ten-page paper or taking a two-hour exam. In addition, the daily lives of college students involve much more than coursework. Full-time undergraduates are rarely on campus more than thirty-five weeks a year; and even when school is in session, few of them spend more than forty hours a week attending classes and doing assignments.

The College Movie

Some aspects of undergraduate life show up in movies from all eras: getting admitted to college; paying for an education; adjusting to campus life; doing coursework; interacting with professors; pursuing romance and sex; and participating in fraternities and sororities, sports, and other extracurricular activities. These themes are emphasized to varying degrees in movies from different periods, reflecting both changes in college life over time and trends in the entertainment industry. For instance, the idea that a high school graduate could simply show up on campus in the fall is implicit in many films made before the mid–1980s, but since then the movies have reflected the growing competition among students to get into the most highly selective institutions.

The films examined in this book deal with students who are applying for admission to or are enrolled in post-secondary, undergraduate institutions. "College" is used to refer to four-year schools (colleges), institutions that offer both undergraduate degrees and graduate degrees in fields such as law and medicine (universities), and schools that offer two-year degrees (junior or community colleges). Military academies are excluded because of their atypical admissions processes, their distinctive student life, and their pre-professional focus. Films about graduate students are not included because their professional training requires behavior quite different from that expected of undergraduates, and because graduate school is a less sharply defined stage in the life cycle than the undergraduate years. Also omitted are movies in which a professor is the main character and students appear briefly just to establish the professor's academic credentials, but films in which students interact with professors are included.

Themes of college life are explored in U.S.–made, live-action (rather than animated), theatrically released (rather than made for television), feature-length films set in the United States and released between 1915 and 2006. To identify these movies, I began with the American Film Institute's multi-volume *Catalog of Motion Pictures Produced in the United States*, which provides detailed information on all theatrically released films made in the United States between

1893 and 1970. I searched the catalog's indexes for keywords such as college, university, campus, and student. Some movies were dropped from consideration because the AFI's plot summary or my own viewing indicated that college life played virtually no role in them. I added to the list by doing keyword searches of the Internet Movie Database (imdb.com), again eliminating movies which had little to do with college life. What to include and exclude was a judgment call, but I erred on the side of over-inclusion, because some films that deal very briefly with college life are worthy of comment. For example, *The Fountainhead* (1949) begins with a fifteen-second scene in which a dean tells an architecture student that he is being expelled for being too creative, and *Edge of Seventeen* (2000) includes a short segment set in the "gay wing" of an Ohio State University dormitory. I made every effort to include all movies with a significant college theme so as to avoid generalizing from a selective and possibly biased sample. I was able to watch 589 of the 681 movies on my list, which appears in the filmography at the end of the book.[6]

A Brief History of College Movies

Harvard Crew (1897), a short documentary, was the first American film to depict college life. The first fictional one, also a short film, was *The Professor of Drama* (1903). *The College Widow*, the first feature-length college movie, was released in May 1915; three other films about undergraduate life appeared later that year. The number of movies with a college theme grew rapidly from 1915 through the end of World War II, diminished over the next two decades, and has increased steadily ever since. This kind of movie is now at its peak of popularity; nearly one-fourth of all college movies were released between 1995 and 2006. This extraordinary output is the result of the historically high number of Americans with a college education, or an aspiration to get one, and the large amount of money that high school and college students spend on entertainment.

The introduction of sound to the movies made possible the college musical. *Howdy Broadway* and *Words and Music* were the first in 1929, followed by *Sunny Skies* and *Good News* the next year. The latter was remade in 1947 during the decade of the college musical's greatest popularity. Only a few of these films were released in the 1950s, one of the best being *The Affairs of Dobie Gillis* (1953). College musicals disappeared after the 1960s, a decade that saw a handful of movies that tacked the equivalent of live music videos onto weak stories about students who were spending their breaks from classes at the beach or in the mountains.

Nearly half of all college films include a varsity team or informal athletic activity. Football is by far the most popular collegiate sport in the movies, reflecting its dominance on American campuses since the late 1800s. All but a handful of the nearly two hundred movies about football were released prior

The college musical *Sweetheart of the Campus* (Columbia) was released in 1941 at the height of the genre's popularity. The film starred the popular Ruby Keeler and Ozzie Nelson and his wife Harriet Hilliard.

to 1954, their appeal diminishing once mass ownership of television provided the public with direct access to real games rather than their truncated and artificial cinematic versions. This decline was also caused by a growth in the popularity of professional football following the exciting 1958 National Football League championship game. During their heyday in the 1930s and 1940s, college football movies contributed to the enormous popularity of the sport by educating the public about the nuances of the game through the use of announcers who described the play-by-play action to fans in the stadium and radio audiences at home, a device that was used to prevent long no-dialogue stretches on the screen.

Most college movies with a sports theme include a romantic relationship; indeed, romance is the most common of all themes in movies about undergraduates. This theme has been present in college movies since their inception, but Hollywood's Production Code, adopted in March 1930 but not strictly enforced until July 1934, prohibited explicit portrayal of or reference to sexual activity so as to avoid governmental censorship of the industry. The Pro-

This title card from *The College Hero* (1927, Columbia) nicely captures the dual themes of sports and romance common to many films from that era. Football players and roommates Happy (Robert Agnew, left) and Jim (Rex Lease) compete for the affection of Vivian (Pauline Garon), and Happy walks off with her after scoring a winning touchdown and extra point.

duction Code was relaxed in the late 1950s and early 1960s, abandoned altogether in 1967, and replaced with a version of the current movie-rating system, which relies on local theater owners rather than the film industry for enforcement. A few pre–Code movies deal implicitly with the sex lives of undergraduates, most notably *Confessions of a Co-ed* (1931), in which a student has to withdraw from college when she gets pregnant; but the first movie to deal openly with sex is *College Confidential* (1960), a film about a sociology professor who is doing a survey that includes questions about students' sex lives. Promoted as "a Kinsey Report on the campus," this movie was a direct response to that groundbreaking study, which profoundly changed American culture by stimulating public discussion of sexual behavior and by giving filmmakers greater latitude in what they could show on the screen. The gay rights movement, which began in the late 1960s, has so far had a limited impact on the portrayal of romance and sex in college movies; most of the few gay-themed college films are independent productions that have attracted small audiences.

Marriage was a common theme in college movies released between the end of World War II and the emergence of the modern feminist movement in the mid–1960s. Female students in films from this era were often portrayed as husband-hunters who had to entice their reluctant prey into marriage. This was explicit in the title of a non-college film released in 1948, *Every Girl Should Be Married*, and reached its zenith in a college movie in *Tall Story* (1960), in which the soon-to-be feminist Jane Fonda plays a student who transfers to a college to pursue its star basketball player.

In response to the escalation of campus protests between 1964 and 1970, Hollywood studios made several films dealing with student activism, a theme virtually absent from earlier college movies, and one that rarely appeared after 1970, a year that saw the release of six films about campus demonstrators. This decline in the number of movies about student activism paralleled an actual decrease in campus protests following the May 1970 killing of four Kent State University demonstrators by members of the Ohio National Guard.

College movies made after the end of American involvement in the Vietnam War in 1973 reverted to the escapist fare of the past, but with some important differences. The abandonment of the Production Code and a more eroticized culture shifted the emphasis from the pursuit of romance to the pursuit of sex. Attitudes fostered by the antiwar movement encouraged students to challenge the authority of college administrators. These changes were apparent in *Animal House* (1978), a movie that appealed to the increasingly lucrative youth market by highlighting behavior still common in today's college movies: binge drinking, gluttony, the aggressive pursuit of sex, and antagonism toward administrators.

Another type of movie that emerged around this time is the horror-suspense film in which an evil, insane, or monstrous killer stalks and murders adolescent victims. Most of the slasher movies that featured college students were released in the 1980s, but several have appeared since then. Because nudity is a surefire way for these movies to get an "R" rating, and because a "G," "PG" or "PG-13" rating will drive away the intended audience, these films typically include scenes of young women in a state of undress. Nudity risks violating the federal law against child pornography if the females are under the age of eighteen, so college campuses are ideal settings for these movies; the women there are legally adults but young enough for audiences to identify with. The killer's stalking is scariest if his intended victims are alone, so filmmakers can make this type of movie on a limited budget with a small cast.

College movies have changed since 1915, with last-minute football heroics giving way to binge drinking, and a yearning for romance being replaced by the pursuit of sex. Other themes, such as students' interest in having fun and their concern with being popular, remain much the same. Unchanged is the minimal amount of attention paid by most of these movies to academic matters.

1

Getting In

Three questions must be answered before a high school graduate enrolls in college: Why should I go? How do I get in? How will I pay for it? By showing how fictional characters answer these questions, college movies influence the way that real students and their parents think about them.

Why Go to College?

In rejecting his son's suggestion that he take a job rather than go to college after he's turned down by all the schools that he's applied to, a man in *Accepted* (2006) advises: "Society has rules. And the first rule is ... you go to college. You want to have a happy and successful life, you go to college. You want to be somebody, you go to college. If you want to fit in, you go to college." A high school senior in *Orange County* (2002) offers a more succinct answer to his mother's question about why he has to go to college: "Because that's what you do after high school."

Today most seniors would agree, but this hasn't always been the case. Movies made during World War II, such as *Youth on Parade* (1942) and *You Can't Ration Love* (1944), show young men torn between going to college and enlisting in the armed forces. In *Class of '44* (1973), which takes place during that war but was made during the Vietnam War, three high school graduates discuss their plans: One is heading to college, another is going to college but thinks he should be joining the army, and the third has enlisted in the Marines.

Since 1966, UCLA's Higher Education Research Institute has been asking samples of first-year students why they decided to go to college. Many of them give multiple reasons, but in recent surveys their answers are of four main types. The most common one is *to become a more educated person*. Students say they want to learn more about the things that interest them, gain a general education and appreciation of ideas, and become more cultured. Many freshmen also mention the *pragmatic value* of a college education, saying they enrolled to get a better job, make more money, get training for a career, or prepare for graduate or professional school. Fewer students cite the *influence of a parent, mentor, or role model* as an important factor in their decision to go to college. The least frequently cited reason is that college was the *best option available*, better than living at home, being unemployed, or having nothing to do.[1]

The pragmatic value of a college diploma is well established. The lifetime earnings of the average college graduate are now more than a million dollars greater than those of the average high school graduate, and the gap has grown substantially since the 1970s.[2] Reflecting this change, the percentage of freshmen in the HERI survey who cited making more money as a very important reason increased from 45 in 1971 to 69 in 2006.

College movies emphasize the pragmatic value of a degree. Rather than look at the impact of higher education on intellect, skills, and values, they present college as a way to land a rewarding job, move up the social ladder, collect an inheritance, pursue a love interest, become an admired athlete, break free from parents, or escape from an uncomfortable predicament.

Students who go to college to learn appear in the movies infrequently. One exception is "Slapsie" Maxie Rosenbloom in *Harvard, Here I Come* (1941). The boxer-actor-nightclub owner decides to go to Harvard to get "smarted up" after receiving an award from the *Harvard Lampoon* humor magazine for his "extreme pediculousness," which he thinks means dumbness. Another exception is also an older student, a successful middle-aged businessman in *High Time* (1960) who enrolls as a freshman and takes his coursework seriously, but still finds time to make young friends, join a fraternity, and get romantically involved with a professor.

Several movies feature young women who are intent on getting a college education, consistent with recent evidence that females, who are now 58 percent of all undergraduates, do better academically than their male classmates.[3] A dancehall instructor in *Here Come the Coeds* (1945) earns high grades after being awarded a full scholarship by a dean who sees her in a magazine photograph in front of the college gate, declaring, "I'm saving my money to go to Bixby, the college of my dreams." A desire to learn also motivates a well-to-do young woman in *Baby, It's You* (1983). When her working-class high school boyfriend, who hopes to become a lounge singer, asks why she wants to endure four more years of school, she says that in college she'll get to study what she wants and delve into things more deeply. In the film *In Good Company* (2004), a student transfers from a state college to New York University because of its excellent writing program. NYU's higher cost forces her parents to take out a second mortgage on their house, but her father says it's worth the sacrifice because she's smart and her education means everything. More than half a century earlier, another woman went to college to hone her writing skills in *She's Working Her Way Through College* (1952). Burlesque performer "Hot Garters Gertie" (Virginia Mayo) runs into her former high school teacher

"Slapsie" Maxie Rosenbloom, playing a character with the same name in *Harvard, Here I Come* (1941, Columbia), enrolls at Harvard to get educated but becomes distracted by romance. Researchers at the university declare him the nation's number one moron, and he uses the title to sign a lucrative contract to pitch products to the other twenty-three million morons in the country.

(Ronald Reagan) after a show and tells him that she's been writing a play but that it's been rejected. She says she went into burlesque to earn the money for college, he tells her a "college education is the inalienable right of every American," and she enrolls at the university where he teaches playwriting.

Several movies briefly acknowledge that college is about education before getting to the real message of the film: College is for fun. This emphasis is not that different from the way some institutions market themselves. During one student-guided campus tour conducted under the auspices of the admissions office,

> prospective students and their parents learned about festive occasions, but not who teaches undergraduate classes. They visited the student union and the dorms, not the library. The winning football record was discussed, but no mention was made of academic honors. Visitors heard about "keg parties," not about concerts and lectures. One had the distinct impression that the campus was a place with abundant social life. Education was ignored.[4]

In similar fashion, *Girl o' My Dreams* (1934) begins with shots of an idyllic campus, zooms in on a dictionary's definition of college as "an institution of learning devoted to the pursuit of the higher arts," and then moves on to a series of scenes from a track meet, a football game, a baseball game, and a crew race. *Senior Prom* (1958) starts with a voice-over describing the "typical American university" where the film is set as a place where the future leaders of the world come to learn from great minds and from vaults filled with the wisdom of the ages. The students are described as serious-minded but involved in other things when they're not studying, and the camera zooms in on two students who are kissing. The rest of the movie pays virtually no attention to the academic side of college life. *Wild, Wild Winter* (1966) opens with a scene of a university from which 600 students dropped out the previous year because of a difficult science curriculum, shifts to a second campus where 950 students dropped out because of a difficult mathematics curriculum, and then settles at "Alpine College," where 1,200 students "dropped in" the year before because of the school's extracurricular activities: skiing and the pursuit of romance.

College movies often downplay the importance of academic success by emphasizing the feats of athletes, even implying that career advancement is easiest for those who excel at sports, especially if they are disadvantaged by race, ethnicity, or social class.[5] In *Braveheart* (1925), an American Indian football player has part of his educational expenses paid by his tribe so he can become a lawyer and help his people win back their fishing rights from white people. *The Band Plays On* (1934) begins with four destitute boys being apprehended for stealing a car. The judge turns them over to the local college's football coach, who spends his off-seasons teaching them to play the game. Later they enroll at his school and become the devastating "Four Bombers" backfield. Two of them plan to become lawyers, one wants to be an engineer, and the fourth hopes to go to medical school. In *Hold That Line* (1952), two "Ivy University" alumni, "bluebloods through and through," make a wager, the loser to pay for an addition to the school's chemistry building. One claims that any boy from any background can make the grade at Ivy, the other disagrees, and a group of working-class boys are recruited to resolve the difference of opinion. One of the boys, a reputed chemistry whiz, mixes a random concoction that gives him extraordinary strength and makes him a track and football star. On- and off-the-field antics dominate the rest of the movie, and little more is heard about the impact of an Ivy education on the disadvantaged.

Several biographical films also suggest that athletics is the way for students from modest backgrounds to find rewarding careers. In *The Pride of the Yankees* (1942), the mother of Lou Gehrig (Gary Cooper) yearns for him to become an engineer like his German immigrant uncle. Lou attends Columbia University, where he is scorned by members of the fraternity for which his mother cooks and he waits on tables. When he tells her he's signed a contract with the New York Yankees and has been assigned to their Hartford farm team,

"Sach" Jones (Huntz Hall) and his friends are sent to "Ivy University" in *Hold That Line* (1952, Monogram) to settle a wager between two alumni who have different views about the ability of their alma mater to educate boys from any background. Here Professor Wintz (Ted Stanhope) reacts to one of Sach's chemical concoctions.

she thinks he's said Harvard and is thrilled that he'll be going to a school with such a good engineering program. In *Jim Thorpe—All American* (1951), the American Indian track and football star, played by Burt Lancaster, attends Pennsylvania's Carlisle Indian School, a college established to help members of all tribes enter "respectable" careers and assimilate into the mainstream. One of Jim's roommates wants to be a lawyer, and another hopes to be a cattle farmer.

Working-class high school students use their athletic prowess to get into college in several movies. In *All the Right Moves* (1983), Tom Cruise is a senior in a Pennsylvania steel town who hopes that his modest football skills will win him a scholarship from a college where he can study to be an engineer. His girlfriend (Lea Thompson) complains that football players have a way out of town, while she'll end up stuck there as a grocery clerk, because there aren't any scholarships for students like her who want to study music. In *School Ties*

(1983), which takes place in the 1950s, Brendan Fraser, who also plays a working-class student from Pennsylvania, is recruited by an exclusive Massachusetts prep school to play quarterback for just his senior year in order to satisfy the alumni's demand for a victory over an arch-rival. At the end, he tells the headmaster, "You used me for football. I'll use you to get into Harvard." A classmate (Matt Damon) expresses doubt about the wisdom of this course of action: "Good grades, the right schools, the right colleges, the right connections. Those are the keys to the kingdom. None of us ever goes off and lives by his wits. You do the thing they tell us to do, and then they give us the good life. Goddamned hope we like it when we get it." Yet another high school student with a plan to use football to get ahead is Mox (James van der Beek) in *Varsity Blues* (1999). Anxious to leave his small Texas town, he gets admitted to Brown University and is offered the financial aid he needs, but his plan is jeopardized when his coach threatens to alter his transcript and "get this whole deal blown" unless Mox follows his instructions in a big game. In a voice-over at the end, Mox says he never played football again after that game, but he took the scholarship and will soon graduate from Brown.

In addition to showing that college offers an opportunity for disadvantaged students to improve their prospects, the movies have portrayed higher education as instrumental in opening up to women careers historically dominated by men. Upper-class sponsorship is the means by which a poor orphan girl gets a college education in the three versions of *Daddy Long Legs* (1919, 1931, 1955). In the 1931 film, a well-to-do trustee of the girl's orphanage is scolded for being reluctant to pay for her to attend college, even though he's paid for a boy to go to Notre Dame, an early acknowledgment of gender inequality in access to higher education. The trustee relents and the girl blossoms in college. The biographical film *The Girl in White* (1952) follows Emily Dunning (June Allyson) through a rigorous undergraduate and medical school program at Cornell University early in the twentieth century, showing her battling gender discrimination to become one of the nation's first female physicians. A woman also has to overcome gender bias to get a college education in *My Big Fat Greek Wedding* (2002), in which the mother of Toula (Nia Vardalos) has to convince her traditionalist Greek-American husband to let their daughter take computer science courses at a local college to acquire the skills she needs to make her aunt's travel agency more profitable.

A far-fetched storyline used in several movies requires a student to enroll in college to collect an award or an inheritance, a contrivance that conveys the financial benefit of higher education without having to follow the character into a rewarding career. In *Mr. Belvedere Goes to College* (1949), a middle-aged man (Clifton Webb) registers as a freshman in order to collect a $10,000 prize he has won for his novel, the award oddly being contingent on having a college degree. In *Cinderella Jones* (1946), a band singer and radio show hostess (Joan Leslie) can inherit $10 million from her uncle's estate only if she mar-

In *Mr. Belvedere Goes to College* (1949, Twentieth Century–Fox), "non-traditional learner" Lynn Belvedere (Clifton Webb) enrolls in college to qualify for a literary prize. The middle-aged man earns his diploma in a year, but not before encountering his match in Ellen Baker (Shirley Temple), a non-traditional student who is a widowed mother.

ries someone with an IQ of at least 150 before a specified date. Convinced that she will find such a bright person only on a college campus, she talks her way into an all-male engineering school by hinting that she'll pay for a new chemistry laboratory. At the end, she marries her radio show's bandleader, who has an IQ in the 200s, graduated from law school with honors, and yearns for domesticity, the implicit message being that a woman doesn't have to go to college to find a smart husband. A college senior in *Preppies* (1982) can collect an inheritance only if he graduates; to do so, he must pass an economics exam. His cousin, who will claim the money otherwise, hires three women to distract him from his studies. After being expelled from several universities for sexual misconduct, a young man in *Hamburger—The Motion Picture* (1986) enrolls in a twelve-week management training course disguised as "Busterburger University" to earn the college degree his grandfather's will requires before he can collect his $250,000 inheritance.

The movies certainly exaggerate the importance of collecting an inheritance as a reason for going to college, but they're on the right track in drawing attention to the efforts of family members to influence the decision to go to college and the choice of a school. Parents in the movies frequently push their sons and daughters to attend their alma maters. A father wants his son to go to the school he graduated from in *One Minute to Play* (1926), but the boy insists on attending a college with a better football team. A man in *Mr. Doodle Kicks Off* (1938) uses his wealth to get his son admitted to his alma mater. In *That's My Boy* (1951), a man whose den is full of trophies and photographs from his glory days as a campus football hero insists that his athletically inept son (Jerry Lewis) enroll at his alma mater. Junior meekly expresses a preference for an experimental college where he can study to become a veterinarian, but he accedes to his father's wish. When his well-to-do father urges Bud (Warren Beatty) to attend Yale, his alma mater, in *Splendor in the Grass* (1961), Bud says he wants to marry his girlfriend and study for a couple of years at a good agricultural school instead. He tells his father he isn't a very good student and doesn't want to go to Yale, but his father persuades him to enroll. *How I Got Into College* (1989), *She's All That* (1999), and *10 Things I Hate About You* (1999) are three more comparatively recent films in which parents pressure their children to attend their alma maters, but in these movies the children are more likely than those in the earlier ones to do what they want.

In movies made since the mid–1980s, parents often want their children to go to the best possible college, even if it isn't their alma mater. Al Franken in *Harvard Man* (2001) responds to his daughter's argument that Duke would be a lot more fun than Harvard by advising her that a degree from Harvard is "a great calling card. Doors just open up." In several films, immigrants urge their children to attend the most prestigious college they can so as to ensure a financially rewarding career. In *Freshmen* (1999), the mother of a Chinese-American student who goes to a school much like UCLA encourages him to transfer to Berkeley, which she describes as number four in the country, or Stanford, which she says is number three. She wants him to become a doctor, saying that's why she moved from China to the United States, but he plans to major in English instead. Similar intergenerational conflicts appear in two movies about Indian-American students, *American Chai* (2001) and *American Desi* (2001), and one about a Filipino-American, *The Debut* (2000). In the latter, a high school senior sells his comic book collection, draws his savings from the bank, and takes out a loan to pay for art school, because his father refuses to support his "hobby" of drawing "cartoons," though he is willing to spend $25,000 a year to send him to UCLA to study pre-med.

In contrast to these movies, in which parents eventually accept their children's educational plans, other films feature parents who don't reach an accommodation with their rebellious offspring. In *'68* (1988), an immigrant from Hungary wants his son to become a famous lawyer, but the boy is expelled from Berkeley and tells his father he won't be returning to school. A black student in *Drumline* (2002) tells his father that he has graduated from high school without his help, hasn't been arrested or fathered any children, and is going to do something with his life, go to college on a full scholarship and play drums in the school band. In *The Human Stain* (2003), a student decides to attend the University of Pittsburgh on a boxing scholarship instead of fulfilling his father's wish that he enroll at Howard University. Another rebellious student thwarts his father's plans for him in *A Cinderella Story* (2004), deciding to go to Princeton to become a writer and be close to his girlfriend rather than play football at the University of Southern California.

In recent college movies, girls are as likely as boys to reject their parents' plans for them. A high school senior in *American Pie* (1999) goes to the University of Michigan rather than her parents' choice, Northwestern, claiming the essays on Northwestern's application were too hard. After opening an envelope, Julia Stiles's character in *10 Things I Hate About You* (1999) excitedly screams, "I got in." Her father says, "Honey, that's great, but isn't Sarah Lawrence on the other side of the country?" She replies, "Thus the basis of its appeal." He says, "I thought we decided you were going to stay here and go to school, U-Dub [University of Washington], like me, be a Huskie." She responds, "No, you decided." Later he acknowledges she needs her independence and sadly realizes he's going to play a smaller role in her future. A similar scene appears in *Ice Princess* (2005). After Casey (Michelle Trachtenberg) walks out of a Harvard admissions interview to pursue a career in ice skating, her mother says, "You can't do this, Case. You're giving up your dream." Casey replies, "No, Mom. I'm giving up your dream. I'm going after mine." A mother in *The Upside of Anger* (2005) tells her three daughters they have to go to college, but one of them takes a job with a radio station instead. The mother tells another daughter she wants her to go to Michigan (rather than to some New Age art school to study dance), but she relents when they go to the ballet and she sees how much dance means to the daughter.

When parents in older movies sent their daughters to college, often it was to temper their wild behavior or find them a suitable husband, rather than to make sure they got a good education or prepared for a career. Wealthy parents in *The Girl Who Couldn't Grow Up* (1917) ship their unruly daughter off to college after she sneaks aboard a yacht and meets a nobleman, but she encounters him again at school and they elope. In *The Campus Flirt* (1926), a spoiled socialite is sent to college by her father to expose her to the less fortunate and cure her snooty ways. Parents in *This Reckless Age* (1932) are distraught when their son informs them he's dropping out of college to get married, because they see it as the end of the career they had planned for him, but they're delighted when their daughter quits college to marry her well-to-do godfather, even though he's two decades older. This attitude toward the function of college in a young woman's life persists in *Take Her, She's Mine* (1963), in which a father expresses concern about his daughter's future. What he really means is that he wants her to marry well; her women's college is described as being near the best Ivy League schools where she can meet the most suitable boys. In *Superdad* (1974), after a business associate points out that a young woman is getting toward the marrying age and describes "Huntington College" as a place for her to find "the right kind of husband," her father pretends that she's won a scholarship to attend the school, which is far from the local college her disreputable surfer friends will be attending.

Young people in the movies sometimes choose to attend a college to be near someone with whom they are romantically involved. In *False Women* (1921), a man abandons his studies at a Catholic mission to enroll at a school where the woman he's fallen in love with goes. In *College* (1927), the "most brilliant scholar" (Buster Keaton) gives a high school graduation speech about the "curse of athletics," describing it as a waste of time for the ignorant. After the girl he loves tells him, "When you change your mind about athletics, then I'll change my mind about you," he follows her to college and tries out for various teams in an effort to win her heart. Lucille Ball's character in *Too Many Girls* (1940) enrolls at her father's alma mater to be close to a playwright she fell in love with while traveling in Europe. In *Bathing Beauty* (1944), a man follows his fiancée to an all-women's college and is admitted as a student after he learns that the school's charter requires it to accept men. *Love Laughs at Andy Hardy* (1947) finds Mickey Rooney's series character returning home from the military and announcing he's going back to college to complete his degree and then on to law school. His enthusiasm is actually the result of his love for another student, to whom he plans to propose immediately. When he learns she's going to marry her guardian, he drops out of school. Eventually his father convinces him to return.

Occasionally romance is a reason not to leave home for college. The difficulty of ending a high school romance is nicely captured in *American Graffiti* (1973), director George Lucas's quasi-autobiographical film set in 1962. Curt (Richard Dreyfuss) is able to leave his California hometown for a college in the East because he doesn't have a girlfriend to keep him there, but his pal Steve (Ron Howard) is persuaded by his girlfriend to stay near her and go to the local junior college rather than the school in the East he planned to attend. He tells Curt he'll follow him east after a year, but the film's coda indicates that he never does. A similar decision is made by Shaun (Colin Hanks) in *Orange County* (2002); he abandons his dream of studying at Stanford with a novelist he admires and decides instead to attend the local university to be near the girlfriend and family members who inspire his writing.

If some movies treat college as the path to romance or a good job, others give the impression it's primarily a place to play sports. In *Rudy* (1993), a film based on the life of Daniel E. Ruettiger (Sean Astin), a working-class high school graduate of modest academic and athletic abilities works for four years in a steel mill to earn money to pay for the Notre Dame experience he covets. Unable to get in, he matriculates at Holy Cross Junior College, an Indiana school that occasionally sends a student to Notre Dame. He's told his grades are mediocre and not everyone is meant to go to college, but he persists, not because he cares about getting an education or even because a degree will get him a good job, but because he craves the glory of playing football for Notre Dame. He wears a Notre Dame jacket, is tutored by an honors student from the school, works as a groundskeeper at the football stadium, and tries to sign up for the booster club but is denied membership because he isn't enrolled at the school. His perseverance pays off and he's admitted on his third attempt. Against all odds, he makes the football team and actually gets to play briefly at the end of the final game of his senior year. What sets this film apart from other movies about collegiate sports is less Rudy's love of the game than the years he devotes to getting on the field for just a few plays in a game whose outcome has already been determined.

In other movies, college is used as a refuge. A popular radio singer in *Campus Rhythm* (1943) wants to quit her job and live on a campus that has sororities and proms; coursework is apparently not part of the life she envisions there. When she learns that her guardian has extended her contract, she runs away and enrolls under an assumed name. A college campus is also a sanctuary in *She Loves Me Not* (1934) and its remake *How to Be Very, Very Popular* (1955). In the first movie, a young woman witnesses a murder in the honky-tonk where she sings and dances. Fearing the killer wants to silence her, she spends all her money on a bus ticket that gets her as far as Princeton University. There two students make her over to look like a boy and pass her off as a visitor who is considering enrolling at the then all-male school. They hide her from both the gangsters who are pursuing her and the college administrators who would expel them if they found her in their rooms. A playboy is forced to transfer colleges to escape the consequences of his actions in *Girl Crazy* (1943) and its remake *When the Boys Meet the Girls* (1965). In the earlier film, a Yale student, described as having won no academic honors, is confronted by his father with newspaper headlines about his carousing in New York nightclubs. The man tells his son he can't return to Yale and sends him out west to "Cody College of Mines and Agriculture." In the remake, a student at a fictional college is exiled to "Cody College" by his guardian after being discovered in a dormitory with a group of chorus girls, one of whom has filed a breach of promise suit against him.

How well do the movies reflect the reasons today's students give for going to college? Few feature students who say that becoming a better-educated or more cultured person is their main reason for attending college. Many deal with parents trying to influence their children's decisions about college. In recent movies, young people frequently rebel against their parents' plans for them, and their parents typically accede to their wishes rather than refuse to

When playboy Harve Presnell is caught with a dormitory room full of chorus girls, there's only one way out — the window!

M-G-M presents "WHEN THE BOYS MEET THE GIRLS" Panavision Metrocolor

The caption on this lobby card from *When the Boys Meet the Girls* (1965, Metro-Goldwyn-Mayer) reads: "When playboy Harve Presnell is caught with a dormitory room full of chorus girls, there's only one way out—the window!" His guardian responds to this scandalous behavior by shipping him out west to "Cody College."

pay for college. Rarely do the movies suggest that students go to college because there's nothing better to do, but many films suggest that students attend college for reasons not included in the annual HERI freshman survey: to have fun, pursue romance, or play a sport.

College movies reflect the importance that students attach to the pragmatic value of higher education. Rather than emphasize the way that college leads to careers with rewards that lie in the distant future, which cannot easily be shown on the screen, the movies present disadvantaged students striving for middle-class respectability by working for a diploma. This was a common theme during the Great Depression, but it persists today in movies about immigrants who moved to the United States to find a better way of life for their children.

Getting Into College

Few movies made before the mid–1980s brought up the need to apply for admission to college; none showed high school students strategically planning where to apply and agonizing over their choice of a school. The increased emphasis on college admissions in movies released after the mid–1980s reflected the growing belief that good jobs were getting scarce and a degree from the "right school" would enhance the chances of finding one. Income inequality grew after the late 1970s, and so did the gap between the lifetime earnings of the college-educated and those of the rest of the population. The admissions frenzy of recent years has also been fueled by an increase in the number of high school graduates who go to college. Because the most selective institutions in the country did not significantly expand their enrollments to accommodate the growing demand for a college education, competition to get into them intensified and acceptance became a source of prestige. Well-to-do parents began to hire private counselors, sometimes for as much as $30,000, to help their children with the application process; some counselors made "contributions" to their clients' application essays and lobbied admissions officers on their behalf. Anxiety over college admissions was largely confined to the Northeast and the West Coast until recently, but concern about the "bumper-sticker value" of schools has begun to spread to the rest of the country.[6]

Attention to the prestige of colleges increased markedly after *U.S. News and World Report* began to rank the nation's educational institutions in 1983. The magazine's rankings, which are now published every year in time for consideration by students who are applying to college, are based on the following variables:

- peer assessment, based on a survey of college administrators (25 percent)
- faculty resources, as measured by percentage of full-time faculty, student/faculty ratio, and class size (20 percent)
- graduation and retention rates (20 percent)
- student selectivity, as measured by applicant acceptance rate, high school class standing, and SAT (Scholastic Aptitude Test) and ACT (American College Testing Program) scores (15 percent)
- financial resources (10 percent)
- graduation rate performance (5 percent)
- alumni giving (5 percent)

College administrators frequently criticize the rankings, invariably believing their institution should be prized more highly, but they also adjust their school's policies to enhance its ranking, which many think affects "the number of students who apply to a school, donations from alumni, pride and satisfaction among students and faculty members, and even the terms on which colleges can borrow money in the financial markets."[7] A dean alludes to the rankings in *Accepted* (2006) when he asks, "Do you know what makes Harmon a great college? Rejection. The exclusivity of any university is judged primarily by the amount of students it rejects."

Many students now worry that the academic and extracurricular choices they make in high school will determine whether they get into the college of their choice. Some do volunteer work or join sports teams, *a cappella* groups, or debate clubs to embellish their résumés, rather than because they enjoy the activities. Others take so many Advanced Placement courses, they have completed a semester or more of college work before they even set foot on campus. Still others fill their summers with courses, community service, and activities that will set them apart from other applicants, rather than using summertime for the leisurely pursuits common to earlier generations. A high school student in *Welcome to the Dollhouse* (1995) convinces a popular classmate to join his new band, hoping it will lead to some good gigs. He tells his family, "This is exactly what I needed for my college résumé. With this kind of substantial extracurricular activity, I'm gonna have it made. Maybe not the Big Three, but an Ivy at least." His mother responds, "Well, we'll have to see about those SATs." Later, his sister asks, "Do you think about girls?" He replies, "What, are you kidding? I want to get into a good school. My future's, like, important. And besides, none of the girls at the school are that pretty anyway." When she later says she doesn't want to go to Disneyworld on a school concert tour, he advises, "Don't be stupid. If nothing else, it'll look good on your college résumé." In a similar vein, a high school student in *Better Luck Tomorrow* (2002) recognizes that "you can't count on good grades to get into a decent school anymore" so he learns a new word every day in order to raise his verbal SAT score sixty points so he'll have a perfect score. He plans to mention his fast-food restaurant experience on his college "apps" and plays on the junior varsity basketball team because it will look good to colleges. He explains that he steals from stores because he likes doing something he can't put on his applications.

Coming Soon (1999) satirizes the experience of applying to college at a Manhattan private school whose students are described as obsessed with sex and to a lesser degree with getting into the right school. Spalding Gray plays a guidance counselor who greets his students by asking what they've done to get into college today. He tells them, "College admission committees are trained to sniff out bullshit. Not that we couldn't blow a little smoke in that direction. That's what I'm here for." He has them read his book, *Getting In: How to Market Your Way Into the Ivy League,* and brags that the previous year he got 40 percent of his seniors into Harvard, Yale, or Princeton, and 70 percent of them into Ivy League schools. When he tells one girl that her grades and SAT scores won't get her into Brown, she replies, "It's okay. My father bought me a learning disability," and shows him a letter from a respected medical authority claiming her grades and SAT scores are the result of an attention-deficit disorder rather than a limited intelligence. She gets into Brown after her father makes a large donation to the school.

The fairness of Harvard's admissions procedure is challenged in *The Freshman* (1990). When an NYU student expresses surprise after a young woman tells him she plans to transfer to Harvard following her sophomore year at "The College of the Sacred Virgin," where she has a B- average, she explains that her father simply told the people at Harvard she wanted to go there, and they said, "Oh, sure." Her father is an organized crime boss, and she explains that Harvard wanted to avoid strikes by its janitors and make sure its laundry and gardening got done. Tactics for getting into Harvard are also discussed in *Harvard Man* (2001), in which an alumnus tells his daughter that getting admitted there has become so difficult he might not even be able to get in today. He says that being a legacy gives her an advantage over other applicants and advises her to use her letter from Hillary.[8]

Memorable interviews with admissions officers appear in several movies, one of the earliest being *Risky Business* (1983). When the parents of Joel (Tom Cruise) leave town, he and a prostitute throw a party in his home so her co-workers can meet his well-to-do friends and he can use his cut of their transactions to repair the damage he's done to his father's Porsche. Princeton admissions officer Bill Rutherford (Richard Masur) arrives during the party to do an interview scheduled by Joel's father. Reviewing Joel's SAT scores, grade point average, class rank, and extracurricular activities, Rutherford says it's a respectable record, but "it isn't quite Ivy League, is it?" He then joins the party and spends the night with the prostitutes, telling Joel as he leaves the next morning that he'll see what he can do about getting him admitted. Joel's father later reports that Rutherford has told him, "Princeton can use a guy like Joel" and that Joel is as good as in and he's proud of him, unaware that it was his son's procuring of prostitutes for the admissions officer that got him admitted. In *How I Got Into College* (1989), Jessica (Lara Flynn Boyle) is assigned to an admissions officer described as a reject who interviews only "dime-a-dozen" applicants, who are described as students with qualifications like Jessica's. Her interview goes poorly, and in a panic she bares her breasts to the inattentive interviewer and dashes from his office. After Shaun is rejected by Stanford in *Orange County* (2002), he, his girlfriend, and his brother show up unannounced at the home of the dean of admissions. The dean is impressed by Shaun's high school transcript but says he needed it sooner. He warms up after Shaun's girlfriend slips him a hallucinogenic drug, and they go to the admissions office to add Shaun's name to the roster of accepted students, but his brother and an office worker, both stoned, have set the building on fire. Shaun seems to be out of luck until his father buys his way into the school with a donation to put up a new building to house the admissions office.

Performance on a standardized test such as the SAT or the ACT is usually more important than an interview in winning admission to a selective college. However, recent movies have exaggerated the role of test scores in the admissions process by focusing almost exclusively on students who are intent on getting into the most highly competitive schools, usually ones in the Ivy League. In reality, test scores are less critical for most applicants, because admissions officers find that difficulty of high school curriculum and class rank are better predictors of academic performance in college. Moreover, the nation's four-year colleges together accept about 70 percent of all applicants, and some take virtually anyone who applies.

When highly selective institutions that used to admit students on the basis of family background, graduation from a well-regarded preparatory school, athletic skill, and "character" began to diversify in the 1960s in response to the civil rights and feminist movements, the SAT became more widely used to assess the aptitude for college work of applicants from a broader range of backgrounds.[9] Rather than use test scores in a rigid way, admissions officers now consider them in light of an applicant's secondary school, extracurricular activities, letters of recommendation, race and ethnicity, social class, and parents' educational attainment and fluency in English. Standardized test scores are given less weight if an applicant has graduated from an academically weak high school or will be the first in his or her family to attend college. Applicants who went to strong secondary schools and whose parents are well-to-do, college-educated, and English-speaking are expected to score higher.[10] Because test scores can be raised by coaching, a lucrative test-preparation industry has developed. Programs such as Kaplan and Princeton Review are expensive and thus reinforce the advantage that well-to-do students already have.

Because the SAT has long been used by the nation's most selective institutions, the ones invariably aspired to by students in the movies, the ACT, which is taken by nearly as many students, has been virtually ignored by filmmakers, while obsession with SAT scores has become a staple of the modern college movie. In *Risky Business* (1983), the first movie to refer to SAT scores, a student whose 1545 has won him admission to Harvard is the envy of his friends, who are sure a degree from there will guarantee him a high-paying job. When the mother of another student asks how he did on the exam, and he answers 597 in math and 560 in verbal, she suggests he might want to take the test again. *How I Got Into College* (1989), in which a student says her SAT scores won't get her in anywhere that she'd want to go, features a test-prep course filled with students who plan to retake the test. The instructors claim that getting into college is more about selling yourself than about how smart you are, but a student says they're only interested in raking in the money and his scores didn't improve much after taking their course. The instructors reply that for $1,000 they can make anyone's life seem interesting to admissions officers, and they convince the student to buy their book of application essays that have gotten their authors into desirable schools. An SAT tutor in

Coming Soon (1999) tells a high school student to remember he's smarter than the people who make up the exam and advises him never to chose "E" on multiple-choice questions. The boy tells a girl that the tutor is worth his $1,000-an-hour fee because his brother's scores improved 200 points after coaching.

Obsession with SAT scores reached a new peak in *The Perfect Score* (2004). Anna (Erika Christensen) is so intent on getting into Brown that she randomly calls students at the school late at night to ask the lowest scores they know of among their classmates. Her friend Kyle (Chris Evans) claims a 500 will get you a bus ride to the local community college, but a 1600 will get you to the Ivy League and let you drive a Porsche. He's an average student who sees the test as an obstacle to achieving his goals and firmly believes "the SAT is about who you'll be." He has scored a 1020 on the SAT but tells his guidance counselor he needs a 1430 because he wants to go to Cornell, which has the finest architecture school in the country. He and five others break into the Educational Testing Service office in Princeton, New Jersey, to steal the answers to the upcoming test, but they can't find them. They do find the test itself and work on it together to get the correct answers. Eventually Kyle decides to retake the test without relying on their answers. He improves his score and ends up at Syracuse University.

For many years, applicants had to wait until April to learn if they had been accepted, wait-listed, or rejected. Since the introduction of early decision, early action, and rolling admissions, many learn their fate much sooner. Applicants are seen opening letters of acceptance or rejection in just two movies from before 1988 but in seventeen released since then, an indication of the growing anxiety spawned by an increasingly competitive admissions process.

Failure to get into the college of one's choice sometimes has devastating consequences, an overworked theme in the movies in light of evidence that most applicants get into the school that is their first or second choice.[11] A prep school senior in *School Ties* (1992) comments, "When the guy from Princeton says they might be willing to accept a C in French, and you're flunking French, life is pretty much over, don't you agree?" A classmate replies, "Princeton isn't the only school in the Ivy League," and the student says he has to go there because five generations of his family have, and he can't let them down. He later attempts suicide after doing poorly in French class, and though he survives, he leaves school. Another student remarks that during his sophomore year, a senior who didn't get into Harvard hanged himself.

Because the admissions process used to be much less competitive, older movies cannot be criticized as unrealistic for implying that students could go to college wherever they wished. Only four films prior to 1983 show a student being rejected by a college that is his or her first choice; three of these students eventually get in. A handful of movies released between 1939 and 1949 show students taking a school's entrance exam to prove they can do the coursework, but no movie released before 1983 suggests that a competent student has to compete with other applicants for a limited number of spots in the freshman class. In contrast, since the mid–1980s, college movies have depicted the admissions process as one in which high school students build their résumés, obsess about their SAT scores, visit and apply to many colleges, and worry about getting into the "right school." These films distort reality with their near-exclusive attention to the small number of students who are fiercely competing for admission to schools at the very top of the prestige hierarchy.

Paying for College

Before their arrival on campus, students get a bill for tuition, room, and board. They also have to pay for room furnishings, textbooks, and supplies. The cost of college has increased so much in recent years that the federal government has considered ways to force institutions to keep their tuition down.[12] One-fifth of freshmen who enroll in their second-choice school say they couldn't afford to go to their first choice.[13]

In the movies, undergraduates and their parents complain less about the cost of tuition, room, and board than about the price of textbooks, perhaps because they became accustomed to free textbooks in public school and because college textbooks are more expensive than other books. In *The Affairs of Dobie Gillis* (1953), three friends try to raise money for a trip by selling something they say they don't use much, their books. They're outraged to learn that the bookstore will pay only $2.50 for a book that cost $4.25, so they go into the book business themselves. When their English professor publishes a second edition of his textbook, they're stuck with 300 obsolete copies of the first edition. Wes (Gary Busey), a naïve freshman in *Foolin' Around* (1980), is convinced by Bronski (William H. Macy) to buy used books from him rather than expensive new ones from the campus store. When Wes learns that he's wasted his money on out-of-date books, he wants his money back. Bronski refuses, so Wes and his friends hoist Bronski's sports car into a tree and threaten to vandalize it. Bronski returns Wes's money. A film studies professor in *The Freshman* (1990) tells a student he can't function in his class without buying the two books he's written and several other required texts, all of which cost more than $700, well beyond the student's means. When a freshman in *House Party 2* (1991) complains to a bookstore clerk about having to pay $123 for his books, she replies that she spent so much on hers that she can't afford to go home for vacation.

Borrowing money is one way to pay for books and other educational expenses, but taking out a loan has little entertainment value, so it's rarely mentioned in the movies. Since the early 1990s, the average debt burden for graduating students has increased significantly. Today two-thirds of students use educational loans to pay for college, and many have additional loans from private parties and credit-card debts. Moreover, many of the students' parents have incurred debts of their own to pay for their children's education.[14]

College movies occasionally show parents straining to pay for their children's education. In *Spencer's Mountain* (1963), Clayboy (James MacArthur) is the first from his large Wyoming ranching family to graduate from high school. His teacher says he has an inquiring mind and could be a leader rather than work in the local quarry, but his parents lack the money to pay for college and he doesn't get a much-needed scholarship. His father (Henry Fonda) then sells some of his precious land to pay for college, hoping his children will "turn out to be doctors and nurses and lawyers, even presidents." Parental sacrifice is mentioned by a student in *Carnal Knowledge* (1971) in response to a question about whether he likes Amherst: "Sure, why shouldn't I? My parents work very hard to send me ... I better like it." A family member also helps to pay for college in *Stealing Harvard* (2002), though in a less conventional manner. Noreen (Tammy Blanchard) and her mother invite Noreen's Uncle John (Jason Lee) to watch a family film that shows a much younger Noreen crying after she loses a spelling bee on an easy word. To cheer her up, John promised to pay for college for her, assuming she'd never get in. Noreen has been admitted to Harvard and tells him she needs $29,879 to make up the difference between the total cost and the financial aid she's been offered. John is unable to raise the money until a friend gives him $1,000 and he places a winning bet on a horse race.

In the movies, college expenses are sometimes met by students winning a scholarship. An oarsman in *All-American Sweetheart* (1937) turns down an athletic scholarship in favor of working his way through school, but he's forced to accept the scholarship when a female admirer, who wants him to row, gets him fired from his job. An attempt to win a much-needed scholarship goes awry in *The Girl Next Door* (2004) when a high school senior loses a competition by delivering his speech while on Ecstasy. A young woman in *New York Minute* (2004) has better luck, winning a four-year scholarship despite being unable to give her speech at a similar competition.

College movies since *Plain Jane* (1916) have shown students working their way through school, reflecting the reality that three-fourths of undergraduates help to pay their educational expenses with money they earn from a part-time or full-time job.[15] After a young man in *The Sophomore* (1929) gambles away the tuition money his widowed mother has given him, he takes a job at a soda fountain, a frequent source of income in movies from the 1920s through the 1940s. Students in *Good News* (1947) and *Killer Me* (2001) pay their way through school by working in a library. The middle-aged title character in *Mr. Belvedere Goes to College* (1949) takes a menial job in a sorority house as a "hasher," a waiter who helps with food preparation. A young man in *First Love* (1977) supplements his scholarship with a job in the school cafeteria, and two students in *The Prince and Me* (2004) work in the pub in the campus center.

Elgin (William Katt) meets Caroline (Susan Dey) by offering to get her a cup of tea while he is working in the school cafeteria in *First Love* (1977, Paramount). He impresses her by recommending a better translation of Gustave Flaubert's *Madame Bovary* than the one she is reading.

An undergraduate who works in an audiovisual center in *The Land of College Prophets* (2005) thinks he's indispensable because no one else knows where to find the equipment, but he's fired and expelled from school by the dean after he abuses a professor who urgently needs a VCR and television monitor for class.

Female students in several movies work in burlesque houses or nightclubs to earn money to pay for college. A club singer in *Murder on the Campus* (1933) fears her reputation will suffer if her classmates learn where she works, so she refuses to be interviewed by a journalist who is doing a story on how women pay for college. A well-to-do student in *Eadie Was a Lady* (1945) works in a burlesque house, but her secret is discovered by the dean. Her academic career is saved when her boyfriend convinces the trustees that she was doing research there for the college's Greek Festival.

After the mid–1960s, abandonment of Hollywood's Production Code and the increased eroticization of American culture made it possible for filmmakers to show students paying for college in some highly unusual ways. The four title characters in *The Seniors* (1978) convince a friend to get his professor to sign a grant application so they can conduct a study they call "Sex and the Liberated College Girl." Their proposal is funded and they hire female students to participate in their "study," which is actually just a way for the four seniors to have sex. When their grant money begins to run out, they rent a motel and recruit men to pay "tax-deductible donations" to have sex with the students, who are paid $20 a session while the student-pimps net $72,000 a week. Because she doesn't qualify for a scholarship, Dora (Mena Suvari) in *Loser* (2000) waits on tables in a club to pay for college. When she complains to a financial aid officer that student jobs don't pay enough to get by on, she's told that not everyone can afford college and is advised to get emancipated from her parents, but she can't afford to pay a lawyer to do that. When she's fired for refusing to use the club's recommended techniques for getting customers to spend more money, she decides to have her eggs harvested for use by infertile couples, even though a friend warns her of the risks associated with taking the fertility drugs required for the procedure. In the end, she gets financial aid and doesn't have to sell her eggs. Two other creative ways that students pay for college are the "Topless Tutors" business organized by the title character in *Van Wilder* (2002) and the marketing of a sex-education video in *The Girl Next Door* (2004).

Many of the films released since 1990 that recognize that students often have trouble paying for college feature black or Latino students, an appropriate emphasis because minority and low-income students are less likely than more advantaged ones to enroll in college and to complete a degree if they do.[16] In *House Party 2* (1991), Kid (Christopher Reid) leaves his scholarship check in the car of his best friend Play (Christopher Martin), who cashes it and uses the money to get himself a recording contract. A white dean threatens Kid with expulsion if he doesn't pay his term bill by the end of the week. When Kid tells Professor Sinclair (Georg Stanford Brown) that he has to leave school because of money problems, Sinclair says that Kid has earned a place at the school and offers him a job as his assistant. Kid replies that even that wouldn't provide enough money to stay in school, so he's going to get a full-time job and come back to college later. Sinclair says he's heard that from other black students who have never returned, and he tells Kid to make sure he does. Play then sells his car to pay Kid's term bill, which the movie portrays as an act of friendship, though it's really repayment for Play's theft and forgery of Kid's scholarship check. Professor Phipps (Laurence Fishburne) in *Higher Learning* (1995) asks a student in his political science course to read the asterisked names from a class list, and then he tells those whose names have been called to leave the room and not return until they've paid their term bills. Clearly breaching the students' right to confidentiality, Phipps sternly advises them there are no handouts in the real world. In *Senseless* (1998), the financially strapped Darryl (Marlon Wayans), a black student who is supporting his mother and three siblings, supplements his meager financial aid by working in the cafeteria and delivering mail on campus. When he still can't pay his tuition bill, he tries to raise money by selling his blood, his sperm, and his hair. Another African-American student who has trouble paying for college is Tonisha (N. D. Brown) in *Freshmen* (1999). Taxed by her coursework and her job in a grocery store, she tells her mother she's not sure she can get through school. Her mother tells her to remember why she wanted to become a doctor in the first place. When Tonisha tells a white student she's thinking of dropping out of school to work full-time, he says she's the smartest one in the class and he's sick of her feeling sorry for herself. She stays in school. In *Outta Time* (2002), David (Mario Lopez) loses his soccer scholarship when he's cut from the team after injuring his knee. He travels from Los Angeles to Mexico to visit his mother, who has two jobs to keep him in school, and who had held three jobs before he got the scholarship. He feels he can't ask any more of her and vows to get money on his own so he can become the first in his family to earn a college degree. He accepts a large amount of cash and has his tuition paid in exchange for smuggling a package into Mexico.

In the movies, college is usually paid for with income from student employment or with a scholarship, which is often awarded for athletic ability rather than financial need. Parents' contributions are referred to only half as often as students' jobs, an unrealistic picture of how most educations are paid for, but one that is understandable because college movies are aimed at a young audience and therefore focus on students rather than their parents. Perhaps the payment of term bills by parents is so commonplace it is simply assumed rather than shown, but the movies convey the incorrect impression that educational expenses are typically covered by students rather than their parents.

Only after students have decided to go to college, been accepted by a school they are willing to attend, and figured out how to pay for their education can they begin their freshman year, a rite of passage that uproots them from family and friends but promises a new and exciting future.

2

FRESHMAN YEAR

Leaving home for college evokes a nostalgic look back at high school days and an anxious anticipation of a future filled with new friends and experiences. Students who will live on campus realize their attachments to family, friends, and romantic partners will weaken. They worry about how they'll adjust to living with a stranger as a roommate. They welcome independence from their parents but aren't sure how they'll get their laundry done.

Leaving Home

The anxiety of going off to college is lampooned in *The Freshman* (1925). Imagining what campus life will be like before he leaves home, Harold (Harold Lloyd) dons a beanie and letter sweater and practices college cheers. Looking through the school yearbook, he admires the most popular man on campus, the captain of the football team, and he's inspired to study a football instructional manual. He reads about the kind of clothes he should wear and imitates a handshake and a jig he saw in a college movie.

The difficulty first-year students have in separating from their parents is captured nicely in *Andy Hardy's Double Life* (1942). Judge Hardy (Lewis Stone) plans to take his son Andy (Mickey Rooney) to "Wainwright College," his alma mater, and he's looking forward to reminiscing about his glory days there. When Andy learns that being accompanied by his dad will get him labeled a "pantywaist" and make his fellow students think the good grades he plans to get are the result of favoritism, he convinces his father to let him take a train to college by himself. In the opening scene of the next film in the series, *Andy Hardy's Blonde Trouble* (1944), the judge speaks in voice-over as Andy travels by train to Wainwright, telling him he's been spoiled at home and will have to conform to "a group pattern of living" on campus. Andy meets Kay (Bonita Granville) on the train and is delighted to learn she'll also be attending Wainwright, which has just admitted its first women. Andy is unaware his father has arranged with a dean and professor, a former classmate, to be Andy's academic adviser and oversee his adjustment to college life, so Andy won't escape his father's attention even while away from home. In contrast to Andy's supportive but intrusive adviser is *The Freshman*'s (1990) Professor Fleeber (Paul Benedict), who tells an NYU freshman who has just been robbed of all his money and possessions, "I'm your academic adviser, not your case worker. I'm only interested in your academic career. And may I say, quite candidly, that you're off to an extraordinarily unimpressive start."

This Side of Heaven (1934) features an unusual departure for college. When her mother won't allow Peggy (Mary Carlisle) to drive with her boyfriend to Smith College to start her freshman year, Peggy gets off the train and meets him anyway. She tells him she wants to spend the night with him. When Peggy's boyfriend gets carried away while kissing her, she suggests they get engaged. He counters that they should get married, and they go to a justice of the peace. At the last minute she finds a note hinting at trouble at home in a going-away gift her father has sent with her, so she calls off the wedding and returns to her family.

In an early example of parents concerned about sending their children to college, a man in *Brown of Harvard* (1926) jokingly tells his wife not to cry about their son's impending departure, because he's going to Harvard, not Yale, but both of them are saddened when he goes to a party his friends are throwing for him rather than spend his last evening at home with them. The father in *Superdad* (1974) worries so much about his daughter that he drives to campus, where he's upset to find her living in a coed dorm. When he can't get in because visiting hours are over, he climbs a ladder to enter through a window, but he gets the wrong room and frightens its occupant, leading to his arrest. The parents of Rebecca (Carla Gugino) in *Son in Law* (1993) drive her from their North Dakota home to her college in Los Angeles. Their worries about the lifestyle awaiting her in the big city are confirmed when they encounter a naked male in her coed dorm, watch her lesbian roommate kiss a girlfriend goodbye, and meet her unconventional resident adviser Crawl (Pauly Shore). To open the heavy trunk he has hauled into Rebecca's room, her father asks Crawl for a screwdriver. The RA replies, "I'm sorry. I'm all out of vodka." In *First Daughter* (2004), the president of the United States tells his daughter Samantha (Katie Holmes), who objects to being accompanied by four Secret Service agents on her trip to college in California, that she isn't like every other freshman and can't expect to drive there on her own. Samantha is embarrassed when she leaves Washington with a big send-off and is greeted by another crowd when she arrives on campus.

Other parents accept the beginning of their children's college years with equanimity. In *Take Care of My Little Girl* (1951), the father of Liz (Jeanne Crain) helps her pack to go off to the same school he and his wife attended. On campus, Liz tells a classmate she came to college because her mother said she was too young to marry and too old to hang around the house. When a freshman and his mother arrive at Harvard in *A Small Circle of Friends* (1980), they calmly discuss his plan to become a physician like his deceased father.

Freshmen are sometimes embarrassed by the mere presence of their parents, who are visible reminders of their dependence. Twins are mortified in *Only 38* (1923) when their mother takes a job at their college, starts to dress more fashionably, and has a good time with a man at a school dance. In *Most Precious Thing in Life* (1934), a woman who turned over her son to her ex-husband to raise many years before realizes that as a freshman he would be ashamed to learn that his dorm maid is his mother, so she keeps her identity secret. First-year students show discomfort when their parents help them move into their dorms in *Son in Law* (1993) and *Dead Man on Campus* (1998), but the most embarrassed freshmen are two students in *American Pie 2* (2001) whose love-making is interrupted when their parents barge into a dorm room.

Parents sometimes irritate freshmen by offering unwanted advice before leaving campus. A father who helps his daughter move into her dorm at Sarah

It is difficult to tell who is more surprised in this scene from *American Pie 2* (2001, Universal), Jim (Jason Biggs) and Natalie (Joelle Carter), who have been interrupted while making love, or their four parents, who have burst into his dormitory room unannounced.

Lawrence College in *Baby, It's You* (1983) reminisces about his college days. A nerdy father who drives his equally nerdy son to college in *Revenge of the Nerds* (1984) says all that college guys care about is sex and advises him not to break too many hearts. In *Little Sister* (1992), a father suggests that his son use poetry to impress the girls and tells him to join a fraternity. Mrs. Wurtzel (Jessica Lange) in *Prozac Nation* (2001) tells her daughter on their arrival at Harvard that the first days of college are when you make all your friends, creating additional stress for the girl, who didn't fit in with her classmates in high school.

Mrs. Wurtzel is a "helicopter parent," a meddler who regularly intervenes to micro-manage her child's life. Parents of this sort intend to help their children make a smooth transition to life on campus, but administrators believe this is best done by allowing students to make their own decisions and solve their own problems. Until the late 1960s, institutions of higher learning acted *in loco parentis*, supervising and protecting students as their parents would. This began to change when the courts decided that colleges lacked the legal power to control their students' off-campus behavior. The Family Educational Rights and Privacy Act of 1974, often called the Buckley Amendment, prohibited colleges from informing parents about a student's academic performance or social conduct without the student's permission. Privacy protection was later extended to information about the student's mental and physical health.

While the law has increased students' independence from their parents, changes in technology have made it possible for parents to communicate more easily with their children and intervene more actively in their daily lives. One survey found that three-fourths of college students' parents communicate at least twice a week with them, and one-third of the parents are in touch at least once a day. Cell phones are used by 90 percent of these parents and e-mail by 58 percent, and 75 percent of them visit campus at least once a semester.[1] Parents are more likely now than in the past to make demands of administrators and to contact professors about grades. Some have even pressured legislators to pass laws requiring colleges to change their policies. Today, many parents believe that because they are paying for college, they have the right to intervene and change the educational process to serve their needs and those of their children.[2]

Arriving on Campus

In *The Drop Kick* (1927), the emotional impact of the start of the school year is described by an intertitle: "Once more, the flood of youth swept over old Shoreham College—a new fall term—excitement—anticipation—the warm handclasp of friends, old and new." Other films treat the arrival of students in less sanguine terms. Harold in *The Freshman* (1925) has his clothes and

In *The Fair Co-ed* (1927, Metro-Goldwyn-Mayer), Marion (Marion Davies, center) is at first reluctant to go to college, but she changes her mind to follow an attractive basketball coach to "Bingham College," where she joins the team and becomes a star. Here she gets a "hot reception" when she first arrives on campus.

behavior mocked by other students as soon as he gets off the train. A freshman arrives by trolley in *Brown of Harvard* (1926) and asks an upperclassman for directions to his dormitory, and he's deliberately misdirected to an honorary society house from which he is forcibly ejected. A cab driver tells a freshman in *Andy Hardy's Blonde Trouble* (1944) that he'll charge him an extra quarter for the ride from the train station to the campus if he has to listen to him cry.

One of the first-year student's earliest encounters with college life is the orientation program run by the school just before classes start. In recent years, some institutions have added pre-orientation programs for freshmen—and sometimes their parents—earlier in the summer, before school begins. Pre-orientation programs introduce incoming students to campus life and to some of their classmates and can be an opportunity to express a preference for a roommate. Orientation programs are often cautionary in nature; in the past they have threatened expulsion for bad grades or misconduct, and today they warn stu-

The struggles of Gilbert (Anthony Edwards, left) and Louis (Robert Carradine) are just beginning as they lug their belongings across campus on their first day at "Adams College" in *Revenge of the Nerds* (1984, Twentieth Century–Fox).

dents about alcohol abuse and acquaintance rape and advise them not to reveal too much personal information on Facebook or MySpace.

Freshman pre-orientation and orientation programs are virtually absent from college movies, which more often show new students being disillusioned by the upperclassmen they encounter. In *Maker of Men* (1931), a tour guide points out the campus library to freshmen but says they probably won't have much use for it. An upperclassman in *PCU* (1994) tells freshmen they shouldn't take any classes before eleven o'clock but should drink a lot of beer and stay away from women. When he arrives on campus, the middle-aged title character in *Mr. Belvedere Goes to College* (1949) is disgusted that he has to translate a Latin inscription on a statue for two students who lack his self-proclaimed genius.

Sometimes an administrator is the source of a freshman's first impression of campus life. A young woman in *Confessions of a Co-ed* (1931) hears the president tell the new students to be honest with their bodies, foreshadowing her dropping out of school when she gets pregnant. At a "homesick breakfast" for freshmen in *Andy Hardy's Blonde Trouble* (1944), the dean tells the students they will find campus life new and confusing but will have to adjust to the college family, which differs from their more tolerant families at home. More ominous is a dean's message in *High Time* (1960): Freshmen flunk out at a high rate, and there are equally qualified students ready to take their place if they do.

Soon after they get to campus, freshmen must register for courses. As a public-address announcer in *Son in Law* (1993) warns, "If you don't register, you don't exist." At registration in *Mr. Doodle Kicks Off* (1938), a professor offers a set of dishes to anyone who'll sign up for his course. When the title character in *The Affairs of Dobie Gillis* (1953) tells a registration worker he'd rather have fun than take courses he has to work at, he's told that the university requires him to sign up for something. Leo (Brad Davis) in *A Small Circle of Friends* (1980) shows up at registration with a cane and dark glasses, pushes his way to the head of a long line, and announces what courses he wants to take. One is creative photography, prompting a worker to ask why a blind student would sign up for such a course. Leo is faking blindness, and his bold

This scene from *Secrets of a Sorority Girl* (1945, PRC) suggests that registration is as much for meeting other students as for signing up for courses.

attempt to jump the line brings him notoriety on campus. Thornton Melon (Rodney Dangerfield) in *Back to School* (1986) has his chauffeur divert students from registration by holding up a Bruce Springsteen sign near his limousine so that he, his son, and his son's friends can sign up for courses without having to wait in long lines. In *Little Sister* (1992), a freshman annoys a registration worker when he can't get into a course he wants and is handed the last card for a sociology course; he soon discovers he's the only male in the class, which is about the importance of women in history.

Even as they try to cope with their coursework, freshmen experience homesickness and other problems of adjustment to college life. A first-year student in *The Sterile Cuckoo* (1969) has two roommates move out on her and is unable to find another one, gets drunk and behaves foolishly at a party, aggressively pursues a boy to the point of stalking, and eventually drops out of school. Three maladjusted freshmen are berated by a dean in *Preppies* (1982) for failing every subject, disrupting their classrooms, turning their rooms into nests of bacchanalia, and making a mockery of the venerable institution. A young woman praises her college's diverse and interesting student body in a letter to her parents in *Baby, It's You* (1983), but she's really miserable because no one likes her and she misses her high school boyfriend. Even after she seems to settle in by getting a new hairstyle, dressing more acceptably, and smoking marijuana, she says she's still trying to become someone but is so far a complete washout. When freshman Rebecca in *Son in Law* (1993) announces to her resident adviser Crawl that she's going to quit school, he says she hasn't given it a chance yet. He encourages her to mingle with the other students and takes her to get new clothes, a more attractive hairstyle, and a tattoo, after which he and Becca, as she's now called, fall in love.

First-year students have had to adapt to informal campus dress codes for years. In 1931's *The Spirit of Notre Dame*, a freshman is told by an upperclassman not to wear his high school letter sweater, because what is important is who you are now, not what you were in the past. The need to dress appropriately is implicit in *Young Ideas* (1943). After a mother persuades her son and daughter to register at the college where their new stepfather teaches, the two emerge from the administration building in beanies, the boy wearing a striped blazer and slacks and the girl dressed in a sweater, skirt, and saddle shoes. The daughter of a middle-aged student in *Mother Is a Freshman* (1949) tells her that she needs to change her wardrobe. After she does this, she draws wolf whistles and compliments as she crosses campus, attention that she responds to favorably. More recently, a new student in *My Big Fat Greek Wedding* (2002) is socially accepted by her classmates only after she pays more attention to her appearance.

First-year students make other changes to fit in and be popular. Harold in *The Freshman* (1925) hopes to win friends by hosting the school's Fall Frolic at the local hotel. There he rescues a female admirer from the amorous attentions of the "college cad," who tells him, "You think you're a regular fellow—why, you're nothing but the college boob." Harold is hurt that the other students see him as a loser, but the young woman tells him to be true to himself and not pretend to be what others want him to be. The title character in *Andy Hardy's Double Life* (1942) tries to create a good impression on campus by asking two girls from his hometown to write him letters, maybe three a day, to build his reputation as a ladies' man. Freshmen are usually most concerned about how they are regarded by other college students, but in *American Pie 2* (2001) one of them asks a group of high school students if they think he and his friends are cool because they're in college now or if they think they're weird because they still hang out with high school kids.

Freshman Hazing

Arriving on campus with an intense desire to fit in, first-year students of the past were greeted by upper-class students who made it clear they were not yet part of the college community. Freshman hazing took the form of ritualized and sometimes violent confrontations between college classes, usually freshmen and sophomores. Similar to the indoctrination of recruits in the armed forces and the intimidation of first-year students at military academies, this hazing was supposed to assert the prerogatives of experienced students and instill loyalty to the freshman class and the college. Freshman hazing became less common after 1930 because of student opposition.[3]

For many years, freshmen wore beanies or "dinks" to identify them as new students and make them look "fruity," according to a student in *Animal House* (1978). No one looks sillier in a beanie than the pompous Lynn Belvedere (Clifton Webb) in *Mr. Belvedere Goes to College* (1949). This middle-aged freshman's sophomore roommate requires him to light his cigarettes, make his bed, and grow a beard. When Belvedere shaves off his beard without permission, the sophomore council makes him wear an absurd costume beard. In *Old Man Rhythm* (1935), another middle-aged student is required to wear a beanie and plaid jacket and push a peanut on the sidewalk with his nose; he's also paddled for walking on a path reserved for seniors. Freshmen have to carry cigarettes and matches for upperclassmen and wear dinks at all times in *Saturday's Hero* (1951), though student-athletes are apparently exempted from these demeaning rituals.

Hazing was sometimes used to reinforce gender differences and the privileges of the dominant males on campus. In *Freshman Year* (1938), boys but not girls have to wear beanies, giving upperclassmen an edge in the competition for first-year girls by making their male classmates look ridiculous. Only the freshmen boys participate in the physically grueling freshman-sophomore brawl, flag rush, mud battle, and tug of war; their female classmates simply

In *Freshman Year* (1938, Universal), only first-year men are required to wear beanies or dinks, a practice that reinforces the privileges of upperclassmen by making first-year men appear ridiculous to their female classmates.

watch and cheer them on. First-year boys in other movies are required to dress in women's clothing, a symbolic demotion in status. Two cross-dressed freshmen in *The Plastic Age* (1925) have to enter a woman's dormitory, sing, and perform a Salome-like dance, after which one has the rug pulled from under him. In *Life Begins in College* (1937), a freshman is blindfolded and told that he's being taken for a physical exam, but instead he's dressed in a woman's nightgown and pushed into a classroom with a WOMAN STUDENTS ONLY sign on the door. An upperclassman explains he was just being given the old "Lombardy College" welcome.

Freshman hazing involved the assignment of unpleasant tasks, which upper-class students made it difficult to complete. Two beanied frosh in *So This Is College* (1929) are told to carry a large trunk to the second floor, but whenever they start up the stairs an upperclassman walks down and they have to retreat and begin all over again. They're paddled, forced to clean the floor, and made to kiss the "royal shoe" that kicked a winning field goal. In *College Humor* (1933), an upperclassman makes a first-year student light his cigarette, instructs him to try out for the freshman football team, borrows $10 from him, and tells him to buy larger shirts so he can wear them.

Pranks against freshmen abound in films from the 1920s and 1930s. In *Sunny Skies* (1930), two older students play keep-away with the luggage and clothing of arriving freshmen. A new student in *Over the Goal* (1937) rigs a bucket of water to douse his classmates when they enter his room, but he inadvertently soaks the football coach and the college president. In *Campus Confessions* (1938), freshmen and sophomores engage in a hose fight, and upperclassmen make a first-year student pick up a small stick as if it were a heavy log, then kick him in the seat of his pants. One freshman singled out for particular abuse is the stuffy Wayne (William Henry), who arrives in a limousine, announces that the purpose of a university is the disciplined training of the mind, and proclaims that his private tutoring has given him an edge over the other students. Sophomores respond by sitting him on the hood of a car and driving off, slowing down and speeding up to frighten him. When his

Sophomore men place stuffy freshman Wayne Atterbury, Jr. (William Henry), on the hood of a car in preparation for a frightening ride in *Campus Confessions* (1938, Paramount). The hazing is watched by campus newspaper reporter Joyce Gilmore (Betty Grable, in front of the car).

wealthy father threatens to pull him out of school and stop making donations, Wayne says it was his fault for insulting his tormentors, apparently preferring hazing, which promises acceptance into the college community, to being ignored.

Freshmen have been seriously injured and even died from hazing, and a few movies reflect the dangerousness of this practice. In a life-threatening prank in *The College Hero* (1927), a young man detaches parts of a classmate's car. When the boy drives away with a girl, the steering wheel and other parts fall off and the car crashes into a rock. Neither student is seriously injured. In *The League of Frightened Men* (1937), men who crippled a freshman during a hazing incident begin to get threatening letters years later, and two of them are murdered.

The hazing of first-year students at non-military institutions rarely appears in films after the 1940s, but the hazing of fraternity and sorority pledges, long a staple of college movies, and typically crueler than the hazing of freshmen, has continued unabated. Hazing in Greek-letter organizations is examined in Chapter 6.

Living on Campus

Because most first-year students leave home for college, their earliest undergraduate experiences are of life in a residence hall.[4] Sharing a room with a stranger, often in cramped quarters, frequently leads to problems, despite the best efforts of the housing office to ensure compatibility.

Few first-year students are as traumatized by a new roommate as Jones (Elijah Wood) in *All I Want* (2002). When his roommate says Jones looks too young to be in college, announces he only listens to ska music, and stakes a claim to the bottom bunk on which Jones is lying, the distraught freshman hauls his large trunk out of the dorm and is nearly run down by two students driving recklessly across campus. He rents a room off campus and drops out of school on his very first day to pursue his dream of becoming a writer, saying he had enrolled only to please his grandfather. Another unsettling introduction to dorm life appears in a film made seventy-five years earlier, *The College Hero* (1927). After Jim (Rex Lease) tells his newly assigned roommate Happy (Robert Agnew) to remove his things from the room and then starts to throw them out himself, Happy beats him up. Happy then apologizes and concedes that the room does belong to Jim, and he's accepted by Jim and his friends as one of their crowd. Conflict among roommates is present from the outset in *Dead Man on Campus* (1998). The surly Kyle (Jason Segel) tells Josh (Tom Everett Scott) that he's taking the single room in the suite. The third roommate, Cooper (Mark-Paul Gosselar), wakes up Josh to tell him he's having a few friends over; about *twenty* friends show up to drink alcohol and smoke marijuana. By disturbing Josh's studying and sleeping with his parties, video games, and sexual escapades, Cooper causes him to do badly on his midterms.[5] Conflict is also present in *First Daughter* (2004), in which a student who has just gotten rid of a roommate who practices her trombone four hours a day is jealous of the attention paid to her new roommate, the daughter of the president of the United States.

Another traumatized roommate is Paul (Jason Biggs) in *Loser* (2000). The naïve freshman is excluded from a drinking party and ignored when he politely asks the revelers to turn down their music so he can study. His roommate bluntly asks if he hasn't noticed that no one likes him. When Paul asks why, he's told it's because he talks weird, wears lame clothes, doesn't drink beer, and studies all the time. He's advised not to be "so you." In a meeting with their black resident adviser, Paul's roommates complain they have to do his chores for him, disparage his personal hygiene, and accuse him of being a racist. The RA tells Paul to make more effort, but Paul says he'd rather live alone, so he gets a job and a room at a nearby animal hospital. His living quarters there are even worse than the typical freshman dorm room, one example of which causes the mob boss in *The Freshman* (1990) to comment: "So this is college. Heh, heh. I didn't miss nuthin'." The valet to a Danish prince who enrolls at the University of Wisconsin in *The Prince and Me* (2004) makes a similar comment on first seeing their room: "I thought you had to be convicted of a crime before you lived somewhere like this."

One of the few movies to present living with a roommate in a positive light is *Brown of Harvard* (1926). Tom (William Haines) turns down an invitation to lunch with some dorm mates when they refuse to include his new roommate, the socially awkward Jed (Jack Pickford). When Tom asks Jed to join him in cutting a class, Jed says they ought to make the most of their opportunities or they might regret it later. Tom goes to class with him. Roommates' loyalty and positive influence are less common in college movies than angry words and fighting, even though the actual effects of dorm life are generally positive. Residence halls allow new students to meet a lot of people and select from them a group of friends who grow closer but fewer in number over their years in college. These friends help students to get more from their education, choose careers, and develop as people.[6]

Until the late 1960s, institutions of higher learning relied on the principle of *in loco parentis* to separate males from females in their residential facilities. *Mona Lisa Smile* (2003), which takes place at Wellesley College in 1953, refers to a rule that no male visitors are allowed in the girls' dorm rooms. This restriction is employed as a comedic device in *The Plastic Age* (1925), *She Loves Me Not* (1934), and its musical remake *How to Be Very, Very Popular* (1955). Violation of the rule is central to the plot of *Snafu* (1945). When a soldier follows a journalism student into her dorm to apologize for a mix-up that occurred when she tried to interview him, his presence causes a ruckus among

"Honest, girls... I was waiting for a street car and..."

The hullabaloo that follows the intrusion of Pfc Danny Baker (Jimmy Lloyd) into a women's dormitory in *Snafu* (1945, Columbia) seems old-fashioned by today's standards, which permit male visitors and coed housing.

the girls and is so shocking that a newspaper runs a front-page headline about an intruder in the all-female dorm. Students today would wonder what all the fuss was about.

Coed dorms are now commonplace, though many colleges segregate the sexes by floor and few permit males and females to live in the same room. However, the dramatic possibilities of a mixed-sex roommate situation have been too appealing for filmmakers to pass up. In *Happy Together* (1990), when Chris (Patrick Dempsey) tells his assigned roommate Alex (Helen Slater) that she's living in an all-male dorm, she confesses to causing the confusion by filling out her roommate questionnaire randomly. Chris tries to get the housing office to find him a different room, but he's told it will take three weeks, giving romance with Alex time to develop. In *Threesome* (1994), Stuart (Stephen Baldwin), Eddy (Josh Charles), and Alex (Lara Flynn Boyle) are thrown together as suitemates because of a housing office error based on Alex's gender-neutral name (the same one used in *Happy Together*). She tells Stuart and Eddy to inform the housing office that they need a different room, arguing she was there first, but the office claims a severe housing shortage. Because Alex can't afford an off-campus apartment, she has to live with the boys until another room becomes available.

Students of the opposite sex are deliberately assigned to be roommates in a few movies. When she enters her dorm room at an all-male engineering college in *Cinderella Jones* (1946), a girl surprises a bespectacled nerd. He says, "You're a girl, aren't you?" and mentions that his mother told him he'd run into one someday. The mixed-sex roommate situation gets a different spin in the sexually liberated 1970s. In *The Harrad Experiment* (1973), the head of the school tells the new students that their male-female roommate pairings were carefully thought out. He describes the school as a "controlled group experiment in premarital relations" and encourages them to experience sexual intimacy in both a spiritual and physical sense. The students are required to spend at least a month with their assigned roommate before requesting a change.

College movies look at social class differences between roommates less often than at sex differences. Most of the films that do deal with social class were made before World War II. A working-class Italian-American is taunted by his patrician Yale classmates in *Huddle* (1932), but eventually he's befriended by one who isn't troubled by his humble background. The two become roommates. The 1919 version of *Daddy Long Legs* strikingly contrasts Judy's (Mary Pickford) background as a poor orphan with that of her college roommates, one a descendant of a *Mayflower* family and the other a "true American aristocrat" whose father is a millionaire. In the 1955 musical remake, when French orphan Julie (Leslie Caron) arrives to start her first year of college, she's effusively greeted by her new roommates with no trace of class snobbery. The three will live in a large, sumptuously decorated suite, and Julie's benefactor has bought her a luxurious wardrobe. The theme of social inequality that is prominent in the 1919 version is all but absent from the 1955 one, perhaps reflective of greater access to higher education and more optimism about the possibility of upward mobility during the 1950s.

Roommates from different racial and ethnic backgrounds get along quite well in several college movies. Two young women who live together are practically the only people of different races who do get along in *Higher Learning* (1995). A white student and his black roommate co-exist in *College Kickboxers* (1990), any racial differences being overridden by a shared interest in the martial arts. In *Sunny Skies* (1930), the WASPy Jim (Rex Lease) gets along fine at first with his Jewish roommate Benny (Benny Rubin), a delicatessen owner's son who hangs a picture of his rabbi grandfather on the wall of his dorm room, though he later replaces it with one of a young woman after learning from Jim how to be a ladies' man. *American Desi* (2001) explores diversity among four Indian-American roommates. Kris (Deep Katdare), a culturally assimilated freshman at a New Jersey college, has three roommates

The social class differences between an orphan who goes to college and her roommates, central to the 1919 version of *Daddy Long Legs* (Mary Pickford Company/First National), are largely absent from this 1955 remake by Twentieth Century–Fox. Here Julie Andre (Leslie Caron, center) is warmly greeted in her sumptuous dorm room by roommates Linda Pendleton (Terry Moore, right) and Sally McBride (Charlotte Austin).

who are quite different from one another: one is a Sikh, another a Muslim, and the third is immersed in hip-hop culture and "talks street." The four live in a suite decorated with Indian imagery and redolent of the cuisine of their parents' native land.

An age difference between roommates is used as a plot device in several movies. Despite being thirty years older than his roommates, Harv (Bing Crosby) in *High Time* (1960) gets along well with them after explaining that he, not his son, will be living with them. An even larger age gap among dorm residents is overcome with little difficulty in *Someone to Remember* (1943). The elderly Sarah (Mabel Paige) refuses to move when she learns a university has bought her building and will convert it into a men's dorm. The administration accedes to her demand to stay and, in the fall, students are surprised to find a "little old woman about a hundred years old" in their dorm. They adapt quite easily, having tea with her in the afternoon and setting up an alarm system to keep her from running into naked boys in the hallway.

The generation gap is also present in *Blondie Goes to College* (1942). Dagwood Bumstead's (Arthur Lake) desire to go to college is sparked when he catches a football during a game on campus. He and his wife Blondie (Penny Singleton) got married years earlier rather than attend college, but now they decide to enroll because a degree will enhance his job prospects. Arriving on campus in a raccoon coat, Dagwood rhapsodizes about college traditions, romance, and the opportunity to learn. At the end, the couple leaves school, telling the younger students they (the Bumsteads) were wrong to crash into the students' lives because their own college days have passed them by and they just hadn't realized it.

Movies released following World War II reflect the influx onto campuses of older students whose education had been interrupted by military service. These veterans were supported by the Servicemen's Readjustment Act of 1944 (the G.I. Bill), which was part of a long tradition of government-supported benefits for returning soldiers, though this one required them to enroll in college to collect a stipend.[7] A veteran in *Kilroy Was Here* (1947) is refused admission to a college because he is a half-credit short, but a female journalism student convinces the dean to accept him. As he registers for classes in *The Big Fix* (1947), a 32-year-old veteran is described as rather old to be matriculating. He tells the basketball coach he just wants an education and will not play on the team. Another veteran, said to be the greatest forward ever to play for the school before he joined the armed forces, says he doesn't have enough time to play *and* attend to his studies. He's convinced to join the team but regrets it when he becomes involved with gamblers in a point-shaving scheme. Yet another movie about the problems faced by returning veterans is *Apartment for Peggy* (1948), in which a man is torn between his devotion to his studies and his need to support himself and his pregnant wife, who finds them housing in the attic of a professor's home. Veterans also face the problem of finding a place to live in *Campus Honeymoon* (1948). Two men are assigned to live with twins who are incorrectly assumed to be their wives. Because none of the four can register for classes without proof of housing, the twins live in one unit and the men in the unit next door, and they switch places each morning to maintain the illusion they are married.

The shortage of student housing is a plot device used in many movies other than those about returning veterans. In *Wild on the Beach* (1965), Lee (Sherry Jackson) plans to turn a beach house she has inherited into a rooming house for female students to pay her way through college, but she finds the house already occupied by young men who can't find other housing. She and a male student vie for a permit from the dean so they can open a rooming house, with the students who will be displaced from the single-sex residence in danger of suspension if they can't find other living quarters. In the end, Lee gets a permit to house female students, and her neighbor, a music producer and university lecturer, gets a permit to rent to the young men. A housing shortage also sets the stage for *Revenge of the Nerds* (1984). After football players burn down their Alpha Beta fraternity house, the coach convinces the dean the fire was caused by a wiring problem. The dean kicks freshmen out of their dorm so the ABs will have a place to live. Because their assigned quarters in the school gym are woefully inadequate, the freshmen are allowed to join fraternities immediately. The nerds who aren't pledged by any house start their own fraternity and eventually get their revenge on the ABs.

Campus housing shortages are used in horror and slasher movies to explain the willingness of students to live in unconventional places. In *The Silent Scream* (1980), a last-minute transfer student learns that all campus housing has been filled for months, so she has to rent a room in a seaside house that seems far from the school. Two roomers there are killed by a demented member of the owner's family, but she gets away. Five women in *Sorority House Massacre II* (1990) buy an old house to renovate, the property's low price being the result of a man's grisly mass murder of his family there five years before. In *Voodoo* (1995), a transfer student who is a late arrival on campus can't find a place to live and is advised to join a fraternity; he ends up pledging a house of zombies. Zak (Jamie Gannon) in *Shrieker* (1997) offers Clark (Tanya Dempsey) free housing as long as she agrees to no guests, no cell phones, no mail delivery, and no smoking. He takes her to a room in a deserted hospital where seven people were murdered years earlier by a monster from another dimension. The beast returns, killing four of the student squatters, but Clark and Zak escape. Another film in which common sense is abandoned in the search for housing is *The Doorway* (2000). Four students are promised money and free rent for a semester if they'll fix up a house that stands on the site of seventeenth-century satanic rites. Two students, a professor, and several others are killed, and the two surviving students are convicted of their murders.

The housing and roommate situations of undergraduates have been used to good dramatic effect by filmmakers, but they frequently bear little resemblance to the reality of campus living, because most freshmen live in residential halls with roommates of the same sex and a similar age.

Freshmen who separate smoothly from family and friends, survive hazing, adjust to living in a dormitory with a roommate, and settle into a routine are finally able to turn their attention to what is ostensibly the reason they came to college, their academic work.

3

HIGHER LEARNING

High school students are sometimes surprised when their excellent grades and high SAT scores do not result in admission to the college of their choice. After all, they picked the school because of its sterling academic reputation, and isn't education what college is all about?[1] When they start their freshman year somewhere else in a few months, many of these students will again be surprised, this time at the unexpectedly small role that intellectual matters play in campus life.

To an even greater degree than real colleges, the ones in the movies slight the academic side of undergraduate life in favor of romance, sports, and parties. Scenes of students listening to a lecture, reading in the library, or writing a paper are uncommon, and brief when they *do* appear. In the movies, grades are important only when a student is threatened with expulsion or in jeopardy of becoming ineligible for a big game. Students who work hard, get high grades, and are rewarded with a good job or acceptance into graduate school rarely appear on the screen. Because much academic work is visually uninteresting, movie audiences are more likely to see undergraduates pursuing romance, scoring touchdowns, or drinking beer than doing what they supposedly came to college for in the first place.

To some extent, the movies' inattention to academic work mirrors the reality of students' lives. Owen Johnson's *Stover at Yale*, a novel originally published in 1911 but still in print today, suggests that undergraduates around the time that the first college movie was released spent most of their time on nonacademic matters. Harold T. Shapiro describes the 1920s and 1930s as a time when "most undergraduates still did not consider their college education a serious intellectual affair. This was the era of 'the gentleman's C,' college friendships, and 'living it up' on campus. Regular class attendance and intensive study were frowned upon. For most students, college life seemed best described as a way to postpone adult responsibilities."[2] Helen Lefkowitz Horowitz gives the same impression, describing the culture that dominated American campuses until the 1960s as follows:

"After the big game, we're going to announce our engagement!"

Despite the presence of books in this scene from the musical comedy *Good News* (1947, Metro-Goldwyn-Mayer), the real focus of the film is revealed by the caption: "After the big game, we're going to announce our engagement." Pat (Patricia Marshall, center) and Tommy (Peter Lawford) are the couple about to get engaged, but Tommy really loves his French tutor Connie (June Allyson).

> In the competitive world of peers, *college men* could fight for position on the playing field and in the newsroom and learn the manly arts of capitalism. As they did so, they indulged their love of rowdiness and good times in ritualized violence and sanctioned drinking. Classes and books existed as the price one had to pay for college life, but no right-thinking college man worried about marks beyond the minimum needed to stay in the game. Faculty and students faced each other across the trenches. If cheating was needed to win the battle, no shame inhered in the act. No real college man ever expected to learn in the classroom, not at least the kind of knowledge that bore any relation to his future life in the world. No, college life taught the real lessons; and from it came the true rewards.[3]

The daily lives of undergraduates are filled with activities unrelated to their academic work. Classes typically occupy ten to fifteen hours a week, assuming none are missed, and course preparation usually takes another twenty or so hours. During the remaining seventy or eighty waking hours, students are likely to do the things that most interest film audiences, so the lack of attention to curricular matters by the movies is not surprising.

Choosing Courses and a Major

When undergraduates in the movies register for courses, they often pick them to be near a particular professor or student, rather than for their educational value. The classroom of a mathematics professor in *She Wrote the Book* (1946) fills up after she wins notoriety for a racy bestseller written under a pseudonym. In *Mother Is a Freshman* (1949), when middle-aged Abby (Loretta Young) is asked at registration what her major will be, she asks what Professor Michaels (Van Johnson) teaches and then declares an English major to observe the instructor on whom her daughter has a crush. One classmate says she signed up for the course because Michaels is handsome, and another declares she'll pass the course this time if she can keep her mind on her work. Three young women in *Raiders of the Lost Ark* (1981) stare dreamily at Professor Indiana Jones (Harrison Ford) as he lectures; "love you" is visible on the eyelids of one of them when she blinks. In *Quiz Show* (1994), a professor's

After she enrolls in the English literature class taught by Professor Richard Michaels (Van Johnson) in *Mother Is a Freshman* (1949, Twentieth Century–Fox) in order to observe the man her daughter has a crush on, Abigail Fortitude Abbott (Loretta Young) finds herself irresistibly attracted to him as well.

lecture hall is packed with students who have enrolled because he has become a television celebrity.

In the movies, taking a course to be near another student is more common than enrolling because of the instructor. In *Maker of Men* (1931), a boy talks to a friend about doing as little coursework as possible and especially avoiding Botany A, but when an attractive girl asks where to register for that course, he tells her he's taking it too and offers to show her the way. When a professor aggressively recruits students for his course on Greek mythology in *Mr. Doodle Kicks Off* (1938), the pretty daughter of the college president agrees to take it, and several young men enroll to be near her. In *The Affairs of Dobie Gillis* (1953), Dobie (Bobby Van) signs up for the same courses as Pansy (Debbie Reynolds) to be close to her, Lorna (Barbara Ruick) registers for the same courses as Dobie to be near him, and Charlie (Bob Fosse) takes the same courses because he likes Lorna. June (Jane Fonda) in *Tall Story* (1960) makes a bad impression on a professor when she enters his classroom and asks, "I'm

In a round-robin of mutual attraction, these four students (from left to right, Bobby Van, Bob Fosse, Barbara Ruick, and Debbie Reynolds) sign up for the same courses to pursue romance in the musical comedy *The Affairs of Dobie Gillis* (1953, Metro-Goldwyn-Mayer).

sorry. Am I late?" He replies, "Either that, or the rest of us are a little early." She nonetheless convinces him to abandon his alphabetical seating plan and put her next to the basketball star on whom she's set her sights. Students also take courses for non-academic reasons in *Fresh Horses* (1988), in which a boy who signs up for a required health course says the class is a good way to meet first-year girls, and in *Boys and Girls* (2000), in which the only boy in a dance class is apparently there just to meet girls.

Two films manage to mix romance with class discussions of some substance. In *First Love* (1977), when Elgin (William Katt) learns that Caroline (Susan Dey) is taking a course on religious philosophies, he lies to her that he's also taking the course but hasn't been to class yet because of his job in the cafeteria. He then convinces Professor Oxton (Tom Lacy) to let him join the class, even though the semester is three weeks old. Oxton tells Elgin that every spring he's approached by male students who want to get into his courses on obscure topics because of their interest in a female, but he'll let Elgin into the class in the hope that he'll absorb some knowledge. In class, Oxton calls on Elgin as he whispers to Caroline and mentions that he just signed him into the course, causing Caroline to smile at Elgin's deception. At first, Elgin stumbles in answering Oxton's question about Dante's conception of love, but then he quotes knowledgeably from a scholarly book. The professor calls his response excellent. In *Little Sister* (1992), Bobby (Jonathan Silverman) decides to stick with a course on women in history, even though he's the only male in the class, because he's attracted to a classmate, Diana (Alyssa Milano). In a class discussion he argues that presenting famous women as equal to famous men is good, but that women are different and the emphasis should be on what sets them apart from men. Diana counters that women are not intrinsically different from men, and that whatever differences might seem to exist were created by society to hold them back. Later, the instructor commends Bobby for his insightful comments and asks, "Do you think she liked them?" Bobby admits to playing to Diana in class rather than responding directly to the instructor's question, but he claims to believe what he said.

Few students experience conflict with their parents over the choice of a single course, but some encounter opposition when they have to declare a major. The dramatic possibilities of such differences have been exploited by filmmakers, especially since the mid–1980s when parents began to take a more hands-on approach to their children's education. In *Dr. Alien* (1988), Wesley (Billy Jayne) tells Leeanne (Olivia Barash) that he's majoring in economics to become an accountant, but he admits to second thoughts about this plan, which he says is really his parents' idea. Leeanne wants to major in music, but her parents think that it's impractical. Wesley pursues his true interest, which is also music. After his father watches Wesley's band perform in a club, he encourages him not to stifle his musical interests. Wesley and Leeanne complete their degrees and take the band on the road.

Students encounter parental opposition to their choice of a major in several other movies. A girl in *Down to You* (2000) tells her boyfriend that her parents don't want her to major in fine arts, because they think art is only good for graduate school or the weekends. In *Drumline* (2002), a student majors in philosophy even though she loves dance, explaining that her parents are paying for school and don't see dance as a real major; she later majors in dance anyway.

Two films released in 2001 revolve around a similar conflict between students and their parents who migrated to the United States from India. In *American Chai*, Sureel (Aalok Mehta) can't let his parents know of his love for contemporary music, so before they visit him he scatters around his dorm room several textbooks appropriate for the pre-med student they think he is. He observes that all Indian-American students seem to be studying engineering, pharmacy, or pre-med, but he wants to play guitar, keyboards, and sitar. When he admits that he's majoring in music rather than pre-med, his father hits him and says he just wants a good life for his family. Sureel replies that a good life includes the freedom to choose what kind of a life to lead. His father tells him to leave the house, but later he shows up at a band contest in which Sureel is performing. After watching the audience enjoying his son's music, he hugs him, apologizes, and admits that he also rebelled against his father by moving to the United States. In *American Desi*, Jagjit (Ronobir Lahiri) pays for his textbooks with his father's credit card, but he hides his true love for art by paying for his supplies with his own money. His father wants him to be an engineer and hopes he will join his construction company after graduating. At the end, the president of the student Indian Club publicly thanks Jagjit for his decorations for the Garba festival, and Jagjit's father asks him which of two engineering principles he used to animate one of his large figures, implying acceptance of his son's interest in art.

When students in the movies disagree with their parents over their choice of a major, the parents typically want the education they are paying for to lead to a financially rewarding career, while the children usually desire the personal satisfaction they get from expressive activities such as art, music, and dance. Disagreement over a major is really a generational conflict between parents espousing the responsibilities of independent adulthood and young people reluctant to give up emotionally rewarding activities for the practical aspects of a grownup's life.

Serious Students

Few college movies feature socially well-adjusted students who are committed to academic excellence. The few who do appear are usually female. In *Daddy Long Legs* (1931), an orphan whose education is being paid for by a benefactor is described by her roommate as the only person she knows who takes college seriously. In the 1955 remake, the orphan reports that she's twelfth in her class and writes to her benefactor that she loves college and loves him for sending her. Kay (Bonita Granville) tells Andy (Mickey Rooney) in *Andy Hardy's Blonde Trouble* (1944) that she's thrilled to go to her first class, saying that's what she came to college for. Andy wins a study date with Kay by pretending that he too is a serious student. Don (Donald O'Connor) is at first a weak student in *Top Man* (1943), but his grades improve dramatically after his father is called to active military duty and he has to assume new family responsibilities. Noting the extraordinary improvement in his grades, the head of his junior college asks Don if he's been cribbing, but Don startles him by replying that he's been studying harder. In *The Girl in White* (1952), a pre-med student makes several errors on an anatomy quiz and is urged by her professor to spend more nights in the lab getting acquainted with the skeleton; she ends up graduating second in her class. In *The Bell Jar* (1979), which takes place in the 1950s, a young woman who wins a writing prize responds to her boyfriend's suggestion that she support them while he finishes medical school by asking, "What about me and school?"

College students' wives who are not enrolled in school prove to be two of the most enthusiastic learners in the movies. In *Apartment for Peggy* (1948), the wife (Jeanne Crain) of a World War II veteran who has returned to college tells Professor Barnes (Edmund Gwenn) how hard it is for married couples when only one of them is educated. She points out that many G.I. Bill couples are from disadvantaged backgrounds and that as the husbands get more educated, they become embarrassed by their uneducated wives and leave them for other women. Barnes is convinced by Peggy to run a lecture series for the veterans' wives and is amazed at how intellectually engaged they are at his first lecture, asking him about books they might take out of the library and keeping him beyond the allotted time. He comments that he felt he was really educating his audience rather than just instructing it, and he's surprised that the women were able to apply the abstract ideas of the great philosophers to their daily lives. A colleague remarks, "Maybe the wrong people are going to school. Perhaps the husbands should stay home with the children, and the wives should go to class." This suggestion sharply contradicts the implicit message of many other post–World War II films that women who had worked in factories during the war should get married, have children, and stay home.

Support for greater access to higher education for women also shows up in *Joy in the Morning* (1965), which was released just as the modern feminist movement was emerging. Annie (Yvette Mimieux), the wife of a law student, is reprimanded by the dean for listening to a lecture and taking notes while sitting outside a classroom. When she says she finds the lectures interesting, he replies that the university doesn't grant listening privileges and stu-

Lovely Yvette Mimieux is a very informal nonpaying student who listens to lectures outside the classroom.

In *Joy in the Morning* (1965, Metro-Goldwyn-Mayer), Annie McGairy Brown (Yvette Mimieux) is a law student's wife who is so intent on getting an education that she takes notes outside a classroom and does the assigned work even though she is not registered for the course.

dents have to pay to take classes, because otherwise the classrooms would be empty and the halls full. Annie's husband tells the dean she has an undeveloped aptitude for learning and has been writing down the titles of books the professor discusses, taking them out of the library, reading them, and doing the assigned essays. The dean reverses himself and lets her sit in on the class.

Though some movies portray women as bright and eager learners, others convey the message that women can't be both serious students and physically attractive. A song in *My Lucky Star* (1938) questions the sex appeal of the academically inclined by asking whether you can pass in love if you do well in Greek and Latin. *Her First Romance* (1940) opens with the frumpy Linda (Edith Fellows) reading a book as she walks down the steps of a campus building. Her friend Susie (Marlo Dwyer) says that Linda gets good grades, but she should be more concerned about getting invitations to social events and acquiring fraternity pins. Susie advises, "Handsome is what makeup does." Linda eventually wins the man of her dreams after learning from a book how to display her charms. A student in *Dreamboat* (1952) is insulted when a young man describes her as a "museum type" and sets out to prove herself a "worthy woman" in his eyes. After she's been properly "feminized," they fall in love and plan to marry. In *All That Heaven Allows* (1955), when a bespectacled girl explains her boyfriend's interest in football as a sublimated means of winning the love of others, he asks how she can be so smart and yet so pretty, the two being incompatible in his view. Dowdy clothing, unstylish hair, and glasses have long been used as visual cues that a female student is an intellectual, setting up a physical makeover that transforms her into the stereotypical feminine ideal.

The message that females can't be both attractive and smart, which is analogous to the message in other movies that males can't do well both in the classroom and on the field, didn't disappear from the screen with the development of the modern feminist movement. A pretty girl in *Primal Rage* (1988) says her IQ is 184, but she has to hide her intelligence to attract guys. In the cult film *Cannibal Women in the Avocado Jungle of Death* (1989), a female professor tells a sexy but dim-witted student that every woman should get as much education as she can, but in her case there's no point.

College movies are more likely to deflate intellectual pretension than to portray serious students as worthy of admiration. In *Spring Madness* (1938), when a student tells her friend that a young man is a thinker, the friend replies, "A thinker at Harvard?" In *Dirty Harry* (1971), when his new partner tells police inspector Harry Callahan (Clint Eastwood) that he went to San Jose State, Harry remarks, "Just what I needed, a college boy.... Oh, you'll go far. That's if you live.... Just don't let your college degree get you killed. I'm liable to get killed along with you."

The Computer Wore Tennis Shoes (1969), the first of Walt Disney Productions' Dexter Reilly trilogy, features an undergraduate (Kurt Russell) who at first glance seems to be a serious student, but on closer inspection turns out to be nothing more than a weak student who is able to pose as an intellectual after an electrical shock infuses his brain with the contents of a computer. Before his fortuitous accident, Dexter takes multiple-choice exams by looking for letter patterns in the answers, citing the impossibility of three consecutive "A" answers as a reason for choosing "C" on one question. After he becomes a human computer, he can complete long tests perfectly in a few minutes, answer complex questions posed by academic experts, and win the "College Knowledge" television quiz show. The movie pretends to revere Dexter's genius and includes scenes of a New York tickertape parade in his honor and a meeting at which he speaks with United Nations delegates in their own languages. In fact, the implicit message of this and several other Disney movies is that technological shortcuts rather than intelligence and hard work are the way to succeed in college.

Though Dexter Reilly (Kurt Russell, center) poses here with books, in *The Computer Wore Tennis Shows* (1969, Walt Disney Productions) he gains all his knowledge from a fortuitous accident that injects the contents of a computer into his brain. Dexter also finds shortcuts to achieve his goals in *Now You See Him, Now You Don't* (1972) and *The Strongest Man in the World* (1975).

Weak Students

Academically deficient undergraduates abound in college movies, probably because audiences find it more entertaining to watch them struggle with their coursework or figure out ingenious ways to cheat than it is to see highly motivated students get excited about new ideas, study for exams, or write papers. Despite a sign on the "Grainbelt University" campus that proclaims, "Learn, Learn, Learn; Work, Work, Work," the title character in *The Affairs of Dobie Gillis* (1953) answers "women" when asked what he's interested in, causing the registrar to ask if he wants to sign up for obstetrics. Dobie says he's not that interested. He worries that history, law, and physiology seem like too much work and says he's an "enjoyer" rather than a "worker." His girlfriend says her father disapproves of enjoyers, but later she complains that she's working too hard and wants more fun and romance. Because her father doesn't want her to go out with him, Dobie suggests they have their fun in the daytime. When she worries about missing classes, he says they'll go to class when it rains. Nearly fifty years later, a student in *Road Trip* (2000) dismisses his coursework in much the same way, saying he's "starting to question this whole college thing. No one told me there was gonna be this much reading involved."

Poor students show up in many other movies. A boy in *The Day It Came to Earth* (1979) says too much studying can cause a mental block that might hurt his performance on an upcoming exam, so he and his friends skip class and go on a picnic. In *Final Exam* (1981), a young man asks, "What do I have to take chemistry for anyway? I'm going into advertising." His girlfriend answers, "Well, that is a problem with education. They do keep trying to teach you all that stuff." Another student in the film says that once you're out of school, nobody cares what your grades were, and she'd rather spend her time having fun and flirting than studying. Slackers in *Animal House* (1978), *Son in Law* (1993), *Kicking and Screaming* (1995), *PCU* (1999), and *Van Wilder* (2002) have been in school for six years or more without earning a degree. In *Up the Creek* (1984), the dean tells Bob (Tim Matheson), who has been expelled from sixteen universities, that their university is the single worst educational institution in the country. He complains that none of its students has ever won a prize or trophy, so they need to win this year's intercollegiate white-water rafting race to enhance the school's reputation. He tells Bob and three other students that they are the worst students in the country and have nothing left to lose. They agree to race after he offers them a degree in a major of their choice.

Some students who have the ability to get good grades fail to do so because they are too disaffected to focus on their work. *The Young Lovers* (1964), which was released just prior to the escalation of the war in Vietnam, features two students who are more concerned about the draft than their studies. The alienated Eddie (Peter Fonda) isn't paying attention in class when his history professor asks him a question, and he gives an inappropriate response. The professor asks why Eddie is taking up space that others would like to have and calls him a second-rate student who is contemptuous of what he doesn't understand. He drops Eddie from the class, but later readmits him after Eddie says he needs the course to graduate. Eddie passes the final exam but doesn't seem to care. Another character in the film, Tarragoo (Nick Adams), is described as a "scholastic bum" who's been in and out of four colleges. He admits that he likes the academic life and doesn't want to take a job, but when he and his girlfriend decide to get married, he plans to quit school and sell used cars for her father while she finishes her degree.

Student alienation is also the subject of *Summertree* (1971). Jerry (Michael Douglas) wants to transfer from liberal arts to his university's conservatory, explaining to his father that the concepts he's been studying are just theories that mean nothing to him. His disaffection is underscored by a brief classroom scene in which a group of bored students watch a videotaped lecture on a television monitor. Jerry has an impressive audition at the conservatory, and the professors acknowledge his talent, but they're concerned about his lack of formal training and will admit him only as a first-year student rather than as a transfer student. This results in the loss of Jerry's student deferment and he's drafted and sent to Vietnam.

Academic Dishonesty

Undergraduates in the movies seem more likely to cheat, negotiate, blackmail, or even kill to get good grades than they are to study hard for an exam or work long hours on a paper. Academic dishonesty has long been common on American campuses, according to Helen Lefkowitz Horowitz, who writes that in the 1920s and 1930s, "[f]aculty and students formed two streams that ran parallel but seldom mingled. As in the nineteenth century, cheating provided a key measure of the seriousness of the divide. Students, honest in their other relationships, submitted work not their own, brought 'cribs' to exams, and gave each other information during tests."[4] Academic dishonesty is still commonplace, with one recent survey concluding that two-thirds of all undergraduates admit to some kind of cheating.[5] There is no reliable evidence that cheating has increased over time, though the reasons for it may have changed. In the 1920s and 1930s, students were likely to cheat to stay in school or help their classmates do so, but cheating today is more likely aimed at getting the best possible grades in order to have an edge in the competition for a good job.[6]

Negotiation for a better grade gets a lot of screen time in *Night into Morning* (1951). After his wife and son die in a house fire, an emotionally distraught Professor Ainley (Ray Milland) gives a tougher-than-usual final exam. When Chuck (Jonathan Cott) fails the course, he says that he has to finish his degree in order to get a job as a football coach. His girlfriend begs Ainley to change the grade, claiming their marriage hangs in the balance. Ainley refuses, saying he wanted Chuck to pass, even to get an A, and he'll show her the exam and if she can convince him that Chuck passed, he'll change his grade. When Ainley asks Chuck if he honestly thinks he passed, Chuck says no, causing the professor to say that at least he's honest. Ainley then gives Chuck a written exam that he passes. A student in *The Dorm That Dripped Blood* (1981) tries a different approach, telling a classmate that the best way to get a good grade is to make the teacher like you. He claims that he got an A in a geography course, even though he didn't read the textbook or take the final exam, because he told the professor how much he respected him. In *Evolution* (2001), two community college students complain about their C- grades on their biology papers on cells. Their professor, who has just told the class that nearly everyone got an A, admits his standards have fallen, but not so low as to give them A's. Their identical essays read: "Cells are bad. My uncle lives in a cell. It's ten foot by twelve and he has to read the same old boring magazine every day. The end." When a student in *13 Conversations About One Thing* (2001) asks his professor if he can retake his exam, because he needs a better grade to get into medical school, the professor says he hasn't finished grading the exams and maybe the student did better than he thinks. Anxious over his grade, the student commits suicide the night before the exams are to be returned.

Negotiation for better grades sometimes includes threats. In *Soak the Rich* (1936), a student at a university built and supported by her father uses his influence to persuade her professors to give her better grades than she deserves. A young woman in *Witches' Brew* (1980) warns a professor to look out after he refuses to raise her grade; she later fires a rifle at him from the top of a building. A professor in *The Girls' Room* (2000) tells a student that even if she gets an A on her final exam, it's up to him to determine whether she passes his course. She responds to his thinly veiled come-on by saying she aced the final and should pass, and if he passes her she'll ignore his sexual harassment. He acquiesces.

In *Red Letters* (2000), a black girl complains to white Professor Burke (Peter Coyote) that he has given her the first C she's ever gotten on a college essay exam, and she asks him to reevaluate it. He says it's just one test and he's been impressed with her classroom performance and is sure she'll do better on the next exam. She insists that the grade "has to be straightened out right now." He threatens to change it to a D, and after more argument from her, says she's just worked her way down to an F and to get out of his office. She swears at him and says she's going to take the matter to somebody above him. Later the dean tells Burke he's changing the girl's grade to an A, because she's one of their best students and he wants her to go to Harvard for graduate school. He also mentions that she's filed a complaint with the Office of Minority Affairs. Burke disagrees with the grade change, but acknowledges that he's only a visiting professor and the dean is the dean.

In the movies, pressure for a good grade sometimes takes the form of blackmail. A student in *The Wild Party* (1929) vows to get something on her anthropology professor, because she thinks he doesn't like her and wants to flunk her. When she brings her paper to his house at night and pointedly tells him she just saw another girl leaving, he replies that he'll grade her paper on its merits. Later he changes his mind and gives her a passing grade, but he also gives everyone else in the class a good grade, even though he worries that doing so will earn his course the reputation of being a "soft snap." Students also try to negotiate and blackmail their way to better grades in *Loser* (2000). Paul (Jason Biggs) begs Professor Alcott (Greg Kinnear) to raise his grade so his GPA will be better. Alcott says he realizes it's a crazy idea that a grade should represent a student's grasp of the material rather than his negotiating skills, and that while Paul's skills are amazing, he really needs to pay more attention to his work. When Paul's former roommates learn that Alcott has been having an affair with a student, they drop the course in which they're getting their lowest grade and transfer into his European literature course after telling him they'll keep quiet about his affair in exchange for an A. Alcott offers Paul the same deal his friends got, but Paul is unaware of their blackmail scheme and refuses the A.

Students in a few movies are even willing to kill for good grades. Two 1998 films are based on the urban legend that if a student commits suicide, the surviving roommate will be awarded a perfect grade point average for the semester because of the impossibility of studying while grieving. When a student in *The Curve* gets a B+ in an ethics course, he is sure it will keep him from fulfilling his lifelong ambition of going to Harvard Business School. He and a roommate joke about killing their third roommate to assure themselves of perfect GPAs for the term. In the end, one of the roommates dies and the other two get the straight A's and will go to Harvard for graduate school. In *Dead Man on Campus*, Josh (Tom Everett Scott) and Cooper (Mark-Paul Gosselaar) learn that their school's policy is to award straight A's for the semester to students when their roommate commits suicide. Rather than kill their roommate when they get into academic trouble, they search for a suicidal student to become their roommate, something Josh can arrange because he conveniently works on room transfer requests in the campus housing office. They are unable to find a suitable roommate, but they discover that a dorm mate has taken an overdose of pills and left a suicide note. Cooper says this is what they've been praying for and begins to move the unconscious student's possessions into their room, but Josh has a change of heart and calls for help.

Negotiation, blackmail, and murder to get better grades are most likely to show up in movies released since the mid–1990s, but cheating in its myriad forms has appeared on the screen regularly since the 1920s. A lazy undergraduate in *Collegiate* (1926) cheats on an exam but casts the blame on another student, who is declared ineligible for a football game. In *Extortion* (1938), a young man described as a class leader with a great academic record kills a proctor for trying to blackmail him to keep secret that he's been getting his high grades by purchasing exams and papers. A girl in *Class of '44* (1973) instructs a classmate on how to hide notes in his shoes and attach a card to a string that he can pull up his sleeve if an instructor approaches him during a test. In *Splatter University* (1984), one student has the answers to an exam written on his wrist, and another is selling copies of an upcoming midterm for $10. After a student is caught looking at notes written on his arm cast during an exam in *Happy Together* (1989), a faculty committee votes to expel him and give him no course credits for the semester. In *The Program* (1993), the daughter of the football coach is expelled when she's caught taking an exam for her boyfriend. The coach kicks the boy off the team and out of school, saying he has embarrassed his family, the team, and the university. Later the boy is reinstated under pressure from alumni boosters. The coach says the penalty should fit the crime, and although cheating is bad, it shouldn't lead to an excessively severe punishment.

The cover of the videocassette box of *Slackers* (2002) carries the tag line, "When all else fails ... cheat." Sam (Jason Segel) and Jeff (Michael C. Maronna) steal official university blue-books by diverting a delivery truck with a staged bicycle accident. Their friend Dave (Devon Sawa) records the test questions in one of the blue-books during the final exam for a physics course in which he is not enrolled. After persuading the teaching assistant to let him go to the men's room, Dave passes the blue-book to Sam and Jeff, who pay a fourth student to provide the correct answers. Sam, who is enrolled in the physics course, goes to his professor's office after the exam, explains his tardiness and his crutches and bandages by a bicycle accident he says happened on his way to the exam, and he gets permission to take the exam in the office. He waits until no one is looking and substitutes the completed blue-book he has brought with him for the blank one the professor has given him. Cheating is also central to the plot of *Learning Curves* (2003). Brad (Rodney Scott) works on a take-home exam at the apartment of Lisa (Lindsay Frost), a professor with whom he's having an affair. She shows him the textbook from which his professor takes all of his exam questions. Brad studies the book and gets a 98 on the exam. Fearing he will be found out, Brad confesses to his professor, who gives him a failing grade on the exam but says he has the rest of the semester to salvage his course grade.

Undergraduates who cheat, both in real life and in the movies, sometimes show ingenuity in their use of technology. In *Strike Me Pink* (1936), Eddie (Eddie Cantor), who runs a shop near the campus, helps his friend Butch (Gordon Jones) pass an exam so he can graduate after seven years in college. Eddie outfits Butch with earphones and a lapel microphone that allow Butch to hear the answers Eddie relays to him during the exam. Butch gives the wrong answers when he unwittingly repeats comments Eddie is making to a telephone caller about his laundry. Butch manages to pass anyway. There is cheating of a similar sort in *College Swing* (1938). Gracie (Gracie Allen) cannot take ownership of "Alden College" until she passes a graduation exam. For her tenth and last chance to pass, she hires Bud (Bob Hope) to tutor her. He steals a copy of the exam and writes the answers on the back of a laundry ticket and gives the "cheat sheet" to Gracie, but during the exam she answers questions by reading from the list of laundry items on the front of the ticket rather than from the list of answers on the back. When this somehow produces the right answers, Hubert Dash (Edward Everett Horton), a descendant of the college's founder, questions her passing grade and she has to take another exam. This time, Gracie wears glasses with hidden earphones so Bud can look up the answers and relay them to her. She answers some questions correctly, but when she takes off the glasses, his voice can be heard speaking the answers. She turns over ownership of the school to Dash and admits she answered the questions with Bud's help, but she praises her method of taking exams and says it will soon be used in all good colleges.

While Gracie's method hasn't become the standard way for undergraduates to take tests, it has shown up in several movies, being modified somewhat over the years as technology has advanced. In *The Monkey's Uncle* (1965), the board of regents discusses the troublesome practice of cheating, especially by football players. One regent tells of a halfback who used the classic method of writing on his cuffs until the instructor caught him by sneaking up in tennis shoes; the student went on to become a senator and might run for president. Another player wrote his answers on gum that he chewed when the proctor approached; he was expelled before a big game and his team lost badly. When one regent suggests they deal with cheating by abolishing football, another who was on the team as an undergraduate says, "Getting grades is only part of acquiring an education, unless your idea of an education is to turn out memory machines. I prefer men and women who can think." The board votes to keep football but decides to increase surveillance of students during the upcoming exam period, causing one player to complain that the extra vigilance is equivalent to abolishing the sport. When Merlin (Tommy Kirk), the tutor for a fraternity, refuses to help its players cheat, one of them says it's unfair to put students of different levels of intelligence in the same classroom and expect them all to pass the same exam. He urges Merlin to fight this injustice. Instead of helping the players cheat, Merlin uses an electronic helmet he has invented to help them absorb course material at night through "sleep learning." When a player gives answers during an oral exam in the voice of the female student who recorded the tapes played through the helmet, the players and Merlin are accused of cheating and have to take a written exam to pass the course. During the exam, a proctor thinks Merlin is signaling answers to the players because he twitches a lot, so Merlin and the players are given F's, though it's hard to imagine how signaling would work for the essay exam in English literature. When the players and Merlin attribute their identical essays to learning the material from the same tape, the regents vote not to expel them, award them A's on the exam, and declare sleep learning "an honest way to cheat." This is one of several Disney movies that treat shortcuts that border on the unethical, if they are not outright dishonest, as acceptable ways for college students to accomplish their academic and athletic goals. Other Disney films that subvert the values of working hard and playing by the rules include *Blackbeard's Ghost* (1968), the Dexter Reilly trilogy (*The Computer Wore Tennis Shoes* [1969], *Now You See Him, Now You Don't* [1972], *The Strongest Man in the World* [1975]) and the three "Flubber" films (*The Absent-Minded Professor* [1961], *Son of Flubber* [1963], *Flubber* [1997]).

Ingenious ways to cheat continue to show up in college movies. Computer hackers change students' grades in *Interface* (1984) and *Campus Man* (1987). In *I'll Be Home for Christmas* (1998), a student arranges to have a copy of a history exam thrown out a window during the test and have a friend supply the answers, and then uses a beeper to transmit the correct answers to students taking the exam. To pass an exam in *The Prodigy* (1999), a twelve-year-old runaway, who is fraudulently registered as a student by members of the fraternity where he is being harbored, is rigged with a transmitter because he doesn't read well enough to use crib notes. In *Old School* (2003), a group of men living near a campus try to win university certification as a fraternity by taking a test using earphones to receive correct answers from helpers in a van outside.

Today's undergraduates make use of the latest technology to cheat. Students at the University of Nevada at Las Vegas photographed test questions with their cell phones, sent the pictures to students outside the building, and received back text messages with the correct answers. A student at the University of California at Los Angeles stored class notes on an e-mail device and referred to them during an exam.[7] With the recent growth in wireless access to the Internet, laptops provide students with even more ways to cheat, prompting some professors to add to their syllabi warnings about the consequences of inappropriate use of technology.[8] To some degree, college movies reflect the methods of cheating used by real students, but today's films seem to lag behind the techniques already in use on some campuses.

Plagiarism is a form of academic dishonesty with a long history in the movies. Students in *Eadie Was a Lady* (1945), *Vamp* (1986), and *Threesome* (1994) enlist others to write papers for them. When the title character in *The Affairs of Dobie Gillis* (1953) spots the essay section in the campus library, he tells his girlfriend that just this once he's going to plagiarize so he can stay in school and be with her. A student in *'68* (1988) is suspended for plagiarizing a political science paper from an article in an underground newspaper; his professor says he wishes he could send him to prison instead.

Today, plagiarism often involves the use of unreferenced Internet sources or the purchase of term papers from websites. Businesses that sell these papers disingenuously claim they're only offering "research assistance" and do not approve of their clients submitting the papers as their own. They promise the papers they sell are custom-written for each client, though often they aren't, and sometimes they guarantee an A, a claim rarely backed up with a refund in the event of a lower grade. Most of the papers available for purchase on the Internet are poorly organized, awkwardly written, padded, and full of spelling errors and redundancies.[9]

If modern technology has increased plagiarism or made it easier, it has also increased the chance that cheaters will be caught. Google searches and plagiarism-detecting software such as Turnitin are more efficient ways to catch dishonest students than the methods used in the past. A student who downloads an essay and passes it in as her own in *Man of the House* (2005) would have been caught even before the latest tools became available, because her paper was a journal article written by her instructor. The professor gives her an F on the paper and warns that her next one had better be good or she'll be off the cheerleading squad. Many colleges would have expelled or suspended her or placed a letter about her academic dishonesty in her file.

Only a few students in the movies express regret about cheating. In *Take Care of My Little Girl* (1951), Chad (Jeffrey Hunter) tells Liz (Jeanne Crain), a naïve freshman, that he has turned in a nearly empty blue-book for his French exam. He asks her to fill in a blue-book with the correct answers so they can go to the professor's office and exchange it for the one he turned in. She fears this is risky, but he says everyone cheats and he has to graduate so he can prove himself to his father. She agrees to help, and they go to the professor's office, where Chad successfully makes the exchange. Liz is praised by the members of his fraternity and rewarded by being chosen Queen of the Frosh Frolic.

Liz (Jeanne Crain) distracts Professor Benson (Grandon Rhodes, right) with her charm in *Take Care of My Little Girl* (1951, Twentieth Century–Fox) so that Chad (Jeffrey Hunter) can surreptitiously exchange a filled-in blue-book for the nearly empty one he turned in at the end of a French exam.

When her boyfriend and a sorority sister criticize her for helping Chad, Liz realizes she was wrong and says she wouldn't do it again. In *Senseless* (1998), Darryl (Marlon Wayans), a working-class black student, competes against his well-to-do white classmates for a position as a junior analyst with a Wall Street investment firm. A representative of the firm tells Darryl's economics class that the successful candidate will need a high GPA, participation in sports, and old-boy ties through a fraternity. Darryl tries out for the hockey team but proves inept. He's kicked out of a rush party by the fraternity's president, another candidate for the job. Darryl is then transformed by a sense-enhancing drug he's taking as the sole participant in a neuropsychology experiment. The drug enables him to excel at hockey, though he fails an important economics test while his senses are in overdrive. Learning how to focus his senses, he becomes a finalist for the position and is eventually offered the coveted job. He then experiences remorse and admits he cheated by using a drug that gave him an unfair advantage over the other candidates. After he graduates, the firm offers him a second chance, hiring him to sort mail and giving him a year to work his way up to junior analyst.

Even though the majority of today's undergraduates cheat at some time, for most of them academic dishonesty is probably sporadic rather than routine. This is not, however, the impression left by college movies. Few students in the movies work hard for their grades, because outwitting a professor is more entertaining to the young people who make up the largest part of today's audiences. Conflict is dramatic, whether it is between students and their professors over grades or between students and their parents over what major to choose.

4

TEACHER'S PET

Undergraduates usually interact with their professors in class or during office hours, but the movies suggest they are just as likely to go out with them on a date or sleep with them. Though Hollywood films slight teaching and mentoring in favor of the more entertaining fare of intergenerational romance and sex, quite a few films include classroom scenes, and several deal insightfully with faculty members nurturing the intellectual and social development of their students.

In the Classroom

Interactions between students and instructors sometimes highlight differences in their values and behavior. In her history of campus life, Helen Lefkowitz Horowitz writes that undergraduates at the University of North Carolina in the early 1800s "horsewhipped the president, stoned two professors, and threatened the other members of the faculty with personal injury."[1] According to Robert Cooley Angell, in the 1920s many students believed that "a state of war exists between faculty members and students—no mere game, where the canons of sportsmanship prevail, but a downright, ruthless struggle in which any method of overcoming the foe is justifiable."[2]

Undergraduates in the movies are more likely to be bored with their professors than openly hostile toward them. In *The Blot* (1921), a professor has to cope with students who are drawing a caricature of him, reading a newspaper, and playing with a leashed salamander. He addresses the students as follows: "I am giving you the best service in my power. May I not in the future expect at least the courtesy of your attention in return?" When the school president in *Horse Feathers* (1932) proposes tearing down the college but keeping its football stadium, he's asked where the students will sleep then. He replies, "Where they always sleep, in the classroom." A professor in *I Met My Love Again* (1938) throws an eraser at several football players who aren't paying attention to his lecture on polymorphism in ants. He then wins them over by comparing the roles in ant colonies to the behavior of students and faculty. When a professor in *The Male Animal* (1942) declares that a college education should be concerned with all kinds of ideas, and a conservative trustee expresses his concern that students might begin to believe some of those ideas, a second faculty member comments that he hasn't seen students much affected by what he teaches. In *Bathing Beauty* (1944), a professor asks a student, "Are we keeping you awake, Mr. Elliott?" He replies, "Barely." Napping students also show up in *Now You See Him, Now You Don't* (1972), *Didn't You Hear...* (1983), *Campus Man* (1987), and *Freshmen* (1999). Lack of interest in what their professors have to say is apparent in other films as well: students roll a marijuana cigarette in *End of the Road* (1970), listen to a Walkman in *Camp Fear* (1991), and drink from a bottle of whiskey in *The Land of the College Prophets* (2005).

Several movies suggest that student apathy is the result of the faculty's unwillingness or inability to engage their students in learning. *Freshman Year* (1938) features a professor who has been using the same exam questions for

Napping in class has long been a part of college movies. Here a sleeping student draws the attention of his classmates in *Sweetheart of Sigma Chi* (1946, Monogram).

twenty years, prompting a student to write an article in the campus newspaper accusing him of being old-fashioned, a position the student successfully defends before a disciplinary board. A professor in *Class of '44* (1973) asks a question about Eugene O'Neill, but he answers his own question instead of calling on a student whose hand is raised. The size of his class dwindles over the course of the semester as he continues this practice, as the few remaining students listlessly raise their hands with no hope of being called on. Fewer students also show up for class as the semester wears on in *Real Genius* (1985); eventually, a tape recorder plays the professor's lecture to an empty classroom of students' tape recorders. After an instructor excuses a student from class for answering a question rudely in *Killer Party* (1986), two of her friends also leave. When he asks if anyone else would like to go, all but one student walk out, and the professor sends that one away when he asks about the subtext of sexuality in *Madame Bovary*. A student in *Surviving Desire* (1991) becomes so incensed that his instructor never discusses anything or answers any questions that he grabs him and demands that he teach the class something they can use to pass the final exam. In *The Nutty Professor* (1996), a professor who is twenty minutes late for class tells the dean waiting in the empty lecture hall that he wanted to see how his students would react to a teacherless environment.

Criticism and sarcasm by faculty members drive a wedge between them and their students in movies from all eras. Irritated that only two of his students have passed an exam, an instructor in *Louisiana* (1947) suggests their poor performance means he's a failure as a teacher, but then he scolds them for making a travesty of education and showing no respect for their parents who pay the faculty to teach them. A professor humiliates a student in *Dreamboat* (1952) when he calls on him to read from *Hamlet*. When the young man reads "Ham" before a line of dialogue, the professor says that stands for Hamlet and is not to be read. The student reads in a halting monotone until the professor interrupts his "unthinking desecration" with a dramatic reading of his own. Even more callous are the comments of a professor in *The Affairs of Dobie Gillis* (1953): He calls the title character asinine, suggests his brain has been affected by puberty, and describes him as "a presumptuous driveler, a cretinous barbarian, a thick-tongued oaf, and an ill-bred churl." Insensitive treatment of a student has disastrous consequences in *Meatcleaver Massacre* (1977). When Mason (Larry Justin) mocks a demon discussed in class, Professor Cantrell (James Habif) gives him an angry look and says he doesn't have to believe the legend, just turn in a term paper, which can even be about why he doesn't believe the legend. Cantrell humiliates Mason in front of other students by telling him to grow up. The student and three friends retaliate by breaking into the professor's home, knocking him out, and killing his wife and children. To avenge the deaths, a comatose Cantrell summons the demon to kill Mason's friends and drive Mason insane.

Jimmie Davis, playing himself as a Dodd College professor who later became governor in the biographical *Louisiana* (1947, Monogram), talks with his students after chastising them for their poor performance on an examination.

In the movies, faculty insensitivity often occurs in creative writing courses, where criticism cuts especially deeply because students are often writing about intensely personal matters. A Berkeley professor in the biographical film *Jack London* (1943) reads his class a story by his yet-to-be-famous student (Michael O'Shea), and then describes it as "raw, almost brutal to the point of unbelievable" and as "batter[ing] good taste with a sledgehammer." Jack asks, "Just what is it that's so wrong with my writing?" The professor replies that it has "too much imagination, too much exaggeration." Jack replies that he actually saw what he wrote about, but the professor questions how far Jack will get writing about poverty, cruelty, and brutality and asks if he's a writer or a crusader. Jack says he had to work hard to get to college and he wants to develop his mind, and if the professor intended his comments to make him think, it worked. He walks out of the classroom and quits college, commenting later that he'll write what he wants and not what professors and editors tell him to write.

Another writing student is treated badly in *D.O.A.* (1988). When Nick

(Robert Knepper) quotes Shakespeare in response to a question by Professor Dexter Cornell (Dennis Quaid), the professor warns, "Don't one-up me in public. I haven't graded your independent project yet." After class, Nick asks Dex if he's read his book manuscript yet, threatening to stop work on his novel if Dex doesn't like it. Dex dismisses him without an answer. After Nick dies, Dex tells a colleague he gave him an A without even reading his manuscript, because he couldn't stand to "wade through 400 pages of flatulent student fiction." In a similar vein, a screenwriting instructor in *Happy Together* (1989) gives Chris (Patrick Dempsey) a D-, telling him he didn't understand his play. He criticizes it for being too linear and for reflecting Chris's insecurities, and he advises him to let his characters get angry and break loose. Chris worries that he has no talent, but with his female roommate as his muse, his grades on revisions of the script improve significantly. The instructor praises Chris for learning to write with passion and inspiration, but at the end Chris says he can write anywhere and asks, "Who goes to college to learn how to write?"

The threat to fail a student appears regularly in college movies and is central to the plot of *Make a Million* (1935). During the Great Depression, a professor answers a student's question as follows: "The only thing that's wrong with money in this country today is that the wrong people have it. Fortunes are being amassed by nincompoop millionaires, who have attempted to set up an aristocracy of wealth instead of achievement." As he speaks, the daughter of a wealthy banker draws a caricature of him and writes in her notebook that he's full of importance but earns only $25 a week to tell everything he knows about money. When the professor proposes a 90 percent inheritance tax to limit the antics of the children of the wealthy, she disagrees with him. He asks to see her notes and finds the caricature and critical comments. He asks what she thinks is wrong with the country, and she replies that people should just go out and get jobs. He says she'll have to change her ideas to get her diploma, and he gives her the only failing grade in the class. She insists that he change her grade, which he awarded simply because she disagreed with him, but he refuses, calling her a "campus menace" who has a demoralizing effect on male students who want to get rich by marrying her rather than working hard.

A few films show professors successfully engaging their students in learning. Professor Daniels (Roland Young) in *Here I Am a Stranger* (1939) asks his class who has read Joseph Conrad's *Victory*. David (Richard Greene) and Tom (Russell Gleason) speak up and discuss the book intelligently. After class, Daniels tells them he likes having students who know Conrad, and he invites them to tea. When David tells Daniels he plans to study law, the professor says he writes very well and encourages him to write more. In *She's Working Her Way Through College* (1952), a professor who encouraged a burlesque performer to return to college praises a play she's written as much better than he had expected. When students in *Confidentially Connie* (1953) learn their professor will be leaving the school, they give him a handsomely bound volume of Shakespeare's works and praise him as the best teacher they've ever had, saying they owe him a lot for helping them to love poetry and better understand life.

Professors in the movies express different ideas about the importance of an engaging teaching style. In *A Reason to Believe* (1995), an instructor tells students on the first day of class that learning is a two-way street and they must listen and participate, because teaching isn't about him entertaining them. Two professors reach a different conclusion in *The Mirror Has Two Faces* (1996). Gregory (Jeff Bridges) demonstrates a proof to his math class, some of whom are yawning. One girl says he's cute and asks a classmate if she thinks he's gay; the classmate replies that he's too boring to be gay. Observing Rose (Barbra Streisand) giving a class in a large lecture hall packed with attentive students, Gregory notices that she spices her comments with humor and references to sex and seems to know every student by name. When Rose sees Gregory lecturing with his back to the class, she says, "It's like you're giving a math party and you only invited yourself." She advises him to relax, get some fun out of teaching, and relate better to his students by telling stories, injecting humor, and wearing more casual clothes. He introduces an example from baseball into an otherwise dull lecture and finds he has created "tangible energy" in the classroom.

Katherine Ann Watson (Julia Roberts) also finds a way to capture the attention of her students in *Mona Lisa Smile* (2003). In her first class, she follows another professor's syllabus as she's been told to do, but her students already know everything that she tries to teach them, and they leave the room as she lectures. In the next class, she shows them a slide of a Soutine painting that no one has seen before and asks them if it's any good, pointing out they now have no textbook to tell them what to think. One student says the painting is grotesque, and another describes it as aggressive and erotic. By discussing the standards used to judge art, the students are exposed to different points of view and learn to become more analytical in their approach to art.

Mentoring

What goes on in the classroom is but one aspect of the professor's role in fostering the development of undergraduates. Professors also advise students on their choice of courses and majors, offer them career guidance, and help them deal with personal problems.

An early example of mentoring appears in *The Age of Consent* (1932). A young man complains to his professor that he doesn't have enough money to show his girlfriend a good time, and asks, "What good is education if it interferes with your happiness?" The professor says he once nearly made the mistake of sacrificing his education for love and tells the student not to be too hasty, because he might just end up unhappily married. When the boy's girlfriend asks her housemother, who is also a professor, if she should let her boyfriend give up college for her, the woman reminisces about her failed romance with the male professor and suggests to the girl that her relationship might also fall apart if she waits too long. At the end, the students quit school and get married. Mentoring takes a similar form in *All Women Have Secrets* (1939). Professor Hewitt (Lawrence Grossmith) advises John (Joseph Allen) to limit his dating, saying that pretty girls and test tubes are like oil and water. He tells John he's fallen behind in his studies and he won't be able to recommend him for a coveted scholarship if his work doesn't improve. John marries Kay (Jeanne Cagney) anyway, and she asks the professor if it would be bad for John to quit school. Hewitt says it would be criminal, because it's the work that counts, and he wants John to carry on after he's gone. When John tells Hewitt he's leaving college, the professor says his decision shows the selfishness of youth, but when he learns that Kay is pregnant, he agrees to pay John's expenses so he can finish his degree and become his assistant. Faculty members mentor returning World War II veterans in *Kilroy Was Here* (1947), in which the professor is appropriately named Shepherd, and *Apartment for Peggy* (1948), in which a professor convinces a young man who has quit school to support his family that he should return to his studies.

The most extended treatment of mentoring is in *Saturday's Hero* (1951). Professor Megroth (Alexander Knox) announces to his freshman English class that he has no interest in sports, then asks his advisee Steve (John Derek), a football standout with a working-class background, if he's read all the assigned poems, implying that he's a slow reader. Steve has read only one of the poems, but he's read it ten times, and he begins to recite it from memory. Megroth is pleased and admits to trying to make Steve look like "a dumb ox." Later he tells him that his paper was quite good and he's been improving in his other courses as well. Steve replies that football starts up again in the spring, but he'll try to keep his grades up. At the end of the academic year, Megroth gives Steve *Leaves of Grass* to read over the summer, saying he'll like Whitman. In another scene, the two discuss novels by Balzac and Dostoyevsky, which Steve has read over winter break. He says he found their characters real, alive, and true, and Megroth observes that you see yourself as you really are when you read them. This movie is a rarity among college films for the attention it gives to a professor's intellectual nurturing of a student outside the classroom.

A well-intentioned but unsuccessful effort at mentoring opens *Where the Boys Are* (1960). A professor tells her class on courtship and marriage that for many women, college is their introduction to adult heterosexual society and their first opportunity for unrestricted contact with men. She warns that this can lead to random dating and premature emotional involvement. One of the students, Merritt (Dolores Hart), complains that their textbook is old-fashioned and irrelevant to modern college life, claiming that if a girl isn't a little

Professor Megroth (Alexander Knox, seated) epitomizes the faculty mentor in *Saturday's Hero* (1951, Columbia). Here he advises Steve Novak (John Derek), who struggles to reconcile his commitment to football with his desire to be a good student.

emotionally involved on a first date, she won't have a second one, and that a girl will be considered antisocial if she doesn't make out. She starts to cite Kinsey's research but is stopped by the professor, who asks if Merritt thinks girls should "play house" before marriage. She says yes, and the shocked professor sends her to the dean, who worries that she's overly concerned with sex, to which Merritt responds, "Dean Campbell, I'd say there were probably half a million coeds in this country. I imagine 98 percent of them are overly concerned with that problem, so in that respect I guess I'm fairly normal."

    A similar generation gap separates professor from student in *Young Warriors* (1983). Professor Hoover (Dick Shawn) speaks of the erosion of values and how a sense of duty has been replaced with "doing your own thing." He's critical of recreational sex and the desire to satisfy immediate impulses, and assails the "let it all hang out" mentality. In a reversal of the usual generational differences, a professor in *The Sure Thing* (1985) criticizes her students' writing for being too dry and not containing "enough you" and tells them to be free and experience life. Value differences between a faculty member and an undergraduate also show up in *With Honors* (1994). A senior meets with his adviser to discuss his political science thesis, a conservative critique of the masses. After the student becomes more liberal as a result of befriending a homeless man, he informs his adviser that he's changed his thesis because his beliefs have changed. The conservative professor says the student is foolishly optimistic and he disagrees with him, but he admires the intent of his thesis and says few people agree with him anyway.

One noteworthy mentor is MIT's Gerald Lambeau (Stellan Skarsgard) in *Good Will Hunting* (1997). The professor writes on a blackboard a difficult math problem it took him and his colleagues more than two years to solve, promising recognition to anyone who solves it. When he catches Will Hunting (Matt Damon), a building custodian who got his job through his parole officer, solving a second math problem that he's posted, Lambeau realizes Will also solved the first one. He gets a judge to release Will to his supervision in exchange for Will's promise to see a therapist and meet weekly for math instruction. Lambeau later tells Will he'll be offered jobs at think tanks where cutting-edge math is being done, but Will isn't sure he wants that kind of career. Another mentor, a professor who is also Will's therapist, tells him his book learning can't provide him with certain experiences and feelings, such as what it smells like in the Sistine Chapel.

Learning Curves (2003) features a complex relationship between Beth (Sophia Bush), a senior who hopes to do graduate work at Cal Tech, and her mentor, Professor Lisa Ducharme (Lindsay Frost), a professor who does research on breast cancer. The two are co-authoring a paper, which Ducharme asks Beth to revise because the results are not significant enough. Beth is conflicted because she needs her mentor's recommendation for graduate school but thinks she's been told to falsify the data. Beth fakes the data and the paper is accepted by a journal, but she has second thoughts and tells Ducharme she can't go through with the deception. Ducharme says she merely asked her to re-run the data, not to fake it, but Beth threatens to ask the journal to withdraw the article and report the situation to the head of their division. When Ducharme speaks of the importance of her laboratory's research and threatens Beth's acceptance into graduate school, Beth says that without her integrity she has no future anyway. She does get into Cal Tech and tells her mentor she doesn't want to become like her, caring only about her career.

Faculty members advise students about their career plans in other movies. A professor in *Campus Man* (1987) praises a student's entrepreneurial skills, but says he needs to pace himself and maybe take some time off. The student says he can't do that, because his scholarship requires him to work three years in Tokyo after graduating. The professor says he'll become a successful businessman once he finds the missing ingredient. In *The Stand-In* (1999), an instructor tells a student he could be a very successful actor and urges him to pursue that career. When the student says he plans to go to law school, the professor responds that it's arguably a noble profession, but he wonders if it arouses the same gleam in his eye that acting does. The student follows his mentor's advice. A professor in *Art School Confidential* (2006) is more discouraging, telling his students that if they want to make a living, they should look for another school or program, because only one in a hundred of them will ever make a living at art.

Several films released since 1990 deal with the mentoring of black students by black professors. Professor Sinclair (Georg Stanford Brown) in *House Party 2* (1991) tells his class that black Americans have always had to define themselves in relation to others, never as their own selves, and he refers to Ralph Ellison's *Invisible Man*. Confusing the novel with the unrelated science-fiction movie *The Invisible Man* (1933), Kid (Christopher Reid) observes that people only see black guys if they're wrapped in white bandages. Sinclair calls this comment very insightful and says Kid has taught him something. After class, he asks Kid if he has the gift he thinks he does or if he's just charming him. He gives Kid a week to do a twenty-page paper on Ellison, Baldwin, and other black writers. Kid turns in his paper, saying that he's quoted from Sinclair's excellent book, and the professor commends him for his "ass-kissing." He grades the paper A-, joking that he had to take off for a coffee stain, and says Kid is a talented writer. Another effective educator is Professor Phipps (Laurence Fishburne) in *Higher Learning* (1995). When he discusses with track star Malik (Omar Epps) the C- he gave him on a paper because of his poor grammar, spelling, and punctuation, the professor says the paper would have been better if Malik could spell as well as he runs. Malik calls him an "Uncle Tom," and the professor asks what that has to do with his poor grammar. He tells Malik he needs to change his attitude that the world owes him something and stop being so lazy. The paper Malik turns in after working with a tutor is so much better that Phipps questions whether he wrote it himself. At the end of the semester, he praises Malik for overcoming a lot of obstacles, saying he has his utmost respect.

Several movies heighten dramatic tension between undergraduates and their professors by making them of different races. In *The Prodigy* (1999), a white professor asks a black twelve-year-old runaway pretending to be a college student to read his paper on dysfunctional parents to the class. When the boy can't read the paper, which was written by the fraternity members who are sheltering him from his abusive parents, the professor tries to ease his embarrassment by asking him what a parent does. The boy uses simple terms to describe abuse, transfer of guilt, ambivalent sentiment, childhood insecurity, and phobias. The professor praises him for stating complex ideas in the lucid vernacular of the street. A similarly supportive professor appears in *Freshmen* (1999). At first too intimidated to speak up in his black professor's English class, a white student is praised by her when he offers his reactions to

Ayn Rand's *The Fountainhead*. His analysis of Dom DeLillo's *White Noise* in a later class goes on too long but again pleases the professor. Eventually he decides to major in English. In *Divided We Stand* (2000), Troy (Jaxon Ronin), a black student, tells his white professor that he's interested in attending law school at Harvard, Georgetown or Howard. The professor questions the inclusion of Howard on the list, suggesting that Troy not "limit himself at a black school," and he mentions a prestigious internship for which he has recommended him. When the militant Black Student Coalition, of which Troy is a member, gets involved in a campus racial incident, the professor tells Troy he's bragged about him to his colleagues, but they've begun to question his judgment since the incident and so he's going to tell the sponsors of the internship that he was mistaken about Troy. That black students might fare better with professors of their own race is suggested in *How High* (2001) by a student who declares that a white man teaching a black history course is "bullshit" and urges the other black students to walk out of the class.

Romance and Sex

Movies since the late 1920s have featured romantic and sexual relationships between students and professors that institutions of higher education have increasingly defined as unacceptable. Opponents of faculty-student intimacy argue that such relationships are inherently coercive, because a professor has the power to give a low grade or refuse to write a good letter of recommendation if the student refuses to get emotionally or physically involved or continue an existing relationship.[3] Others believe that faculty-student intimacy is acceptable, because undergraduates over the age of eighteen are adults who have the right to make their own decisions about relationships.[4] Students over eighteen do have such a legal right, but colleges also have the power to establish administrative policies prohibiting such behavior by their employees. Most parents of undergraduates probably support these policies, believing that professors who become romantically or sexually involved with their children, even if they are over eighteen, are exploiting their inexperience and violating what was once a guiding principle in American colleges, *in loco parentis*.

What is extraordinary in the sixty college movies that include a romantic or sexual relationship between an undergraduate and a faculty member is that male professors are rarely shown exploiting their female students. In thirty of these films the partners appear to have played an equal role in beginning the relationship. In the other thirty, when it is clear who initiated the relationship, it is a female student in eighteen and a male student in one. Male professors initiate intimacy with female students in seven films and with a male student in one. Female professors initiate romance or sex with a male student in the other three movies. The strong impression conveyed by college movies is that professor-student intimacy is often the result of a decision that is mutually arrived at, but when one partner makes the first overture, it is most often a female student.

In only eight of the sixty movies featuring faculty-student intimacy is there an exchange of sexual favors for grades. In three of those films, it isn't clear who suggested the exchange, in three a male professor is the first to suggest the exchange, and in two a female student offers sex for a better grade. Looked at another way, three of the seven male professors who initiate an intimate relationship with a female student in the movies explicitly exploit their power to give grades. More surprising is that in only two of the eighteen movies in which a female student initiates intimate relations with a male professor does she do so for a better grade. Most of these young women apparently begin their affairs with professors because they are interested in a romantic or sexual relationship with an older man. College movies thus present faculty-student intimacy either as the result of a decision that is mutually made or as initiated by a female student looking for romance or sex with an older professor, but rarely as the result of the exploitation of young women by older male instructors. This depiction of faculty-student intimacy, which is at odds with popular perceptions of how and why such behavior occurs, may be the product of the culture's fascination with relationships between older men and younger women, but it also reflects the fact that most of the screenwriters, directors, and producers of these films are men. These movies rarely acknowledge the underlying principle of institutional policies that, even when such intimacy is consensual or initiated by a student, the professor has an obligation not to enter into such a relationship.

One of the first films to feature an intimate relationship between a student and a professor is *The Wild Party* (1929). Stella (Clara Bow) and her classmates enthusiastically welcome the arrival at their all-women's college of a handsome new anthropology professor, James "Gil" Gilmore (Fredric March). In the first class for his course, ironically titled "The Study of Man," Gil announces to a lecture hall packed with giggling girls, including Stella, that the enrollment is larger than he'd expected. As the girls in their short skirts flash their legs, he remarks, "Some of you seem to think this is a course in anatomy." Later he rescues Stella from three aggressive men in a tavern. Holding her hand as they walk up a hill and look down on the campus, he tells her the school's founder built it to bring true freedom to women, but Stella and others like her have turned it into a four-year country club for "jazzing around" in search of "cheap sensation." He concludes, "Life for you is just one wild party." He warns her that by being together, they are risking scandal, maybe even his job. When she apologizes for her behavior and asks why he hates her so much, he takes her in his arms and kisses her. In class, Gil passes back the students' papers and says they need rewriting; he singles out Stella's as "a

The caption on this lobby card from *The Wild Party* (1929, Paramount) reads: "Courage, girls, he's a hard-boiled professor." The flirtatious Stella Ames (Clara Bow) is the student closest to Professor James "Gil" Gilmore (Fredric March).

shoddy piece of work" that cribbed his lectures and blended in material from a paper by Darwin. She's humiliated and angry and says to her roommate, "But if he loved me, he would make allowances. How could any girl know what she was writing about after that kiss?" Gil tells Stella that after their kiss he thought he'd found "the real you," but she's still shirking her work and expecting him to betray his values. He says he both hates and loves her, but at the end of the film he leaves his job and she quits school so they can be together "for keeps."

Female students were portrayed as seducers of their professors even after strict enforcement of the Production Code began in 1934. In *I Met My Love Again* (1938), Brenda (Louise Platt) attempts to seduce Professor Towner (Henry Fonda) by telling him that her rich father knows of his splendid reputation as a scientist and could make it easier for him to do his research rather than waste his time on students. Towner rejects her offer and says she's play-acting just a little, and she slaps him. Later he takes her to a tavern, gets drunk, and kisses her, but then tells her he could never love her. A male student jealous of Towner's attention to Brenda makes a comment about the paramecium feeding on its young. He later reports that she has tried to kill herself in despair over being spurned by Towner, but the professor correctly claims she was just faking it. In *Young Ideas* (1943), Susan (Susan Peters) bets her classmates she can get a date with Professor Tom Farrell (Richard Carlson), even though college rules prohibit professors from dating students. In class she says she knows the author of the next play on the reading list. To avoid being shown up by a student who knows more than he does, Tom invites her to dinner to learn what she knows. Later, he gets angry at the trustees for making rules that keep him from seeing her, telling her, "I've broken one rule they didn't think of. I've fallen in love with you." They kiss, and she remarks, "I wonder what the trustees would say about that." They argue, reconcile, and then marry, all before they have sex. Another unconsummated relationship appears in *Andy Hardy's Blonde Trouble* (1944). When Professor Standish (Herbert Marshall) tells Kay (Bonita Granville) about a college tradition that a girl has to kiss a boy if they're sitting on a certain bench, she kisses him, but immediately apologizes for her impulsive action. Later she tells the perplexed professor he has nothing to be sorry about and perhaps she's younger than she thought. He confesses to a friend his near-foolishness with a young lady, saying he mistakenly thought he was as young as he felt. The friend replies that now that the college is coeducational, every year there will be many fine young girls to whom the professor's "culture and poise seem romantic." Standish says he's already noticed "a half-dozen or so of them in class, gazing soulfully at me." The friend says they're probably just reacting to boys of their own age putting too much emphasis on "spooning." This possibility is reiterated in *Overnight Delivery* (1998) by Reese Witherspoon's character, who says she once had an affair with a professor because she wanted to hide behind an older man to be safe from the guys her own age who had been taking advantage of her.

Mother Is a Freshman (1949) features two professor-student romances, one involving the adolescent Susie (Betty Lynn) and Professor Richard Michaels (Van Johnson), and the other involving Richard and Susie's mother Abby (Loretta Young). Susie informs her mother of her infatuation with Richard, but she assures her there is no longer a "caste system" between professors and students. Richard doesn't reciprocate Susie's interest. He asks Abby, who has enrolled in his class to see if he's suitable for Susie, why with her sophistication and maturity she thinks there's anything left for her to learn in college. At one point he closes his office door, tells Abby to take a seat, and says he didn't understand her essay, adding that "she'd better" have dinner with him at his house so he can help her with her work. When she arrives, he tells her to call him Richard rather than professor and offers her a martini to help her relax and loosen her inhibitions. She's uncomfortable with his behavior, but apparently just because her daughter is in love with him. He tells Abby he's glad she's weak in English literature because it gives him a chance to get to "know her very well." As he walks her back to her dorm, he tells her that faculty-student barriers no longer exist, and they kiss. His treatment of Abby before their romance blossoms is treated lightly, perhaps because she's his contemporary, but colleges today would regard similar behavior as sexual harassment if a student filed a complaint.

In contrast to *Mother Is a Freshman*, two films released in 1951 acknowledge that faculty-student intimacy violates institutional policy. In *Goodbye, My Fancy*, Congresswoman Agatha Reed (Joan Crawford) tells Virginia (Janice Rule), the daughter of the college's president, James Merrill (Robert Young), that Merrill was her favorite professor when she was an undergraduate. She reveals that when she was eighteen, she was caught climbing in a window at 5 a.m. after a night out with Merrill. She tells Virginia the scandal that would have ensued had their relationship become known would have been costly to Merrill's career, so she refused to implicate him and was expelled from school. *Elopement* also makes it clear that professor-student intimacy is forbidden. The night after she graduates, a young woman is approached by a former professor at a dance. He asks her to a concert, telling her that it's permissible now that she's no longer a student. He says he waited for her to graduate after falling in love with her the first time she walked into his classroom five months earlier. He admits to writing her thousands of notes he never sent because the university frowns on instructors who fraternize with their students.

College movies present intimate relationships between an older student and a professor, such as the one between Abby and Richard in *Mother Is a Freshman*, as more socially acceptable than those between a younger student and a faculty member. In *Teacher's Pet* (1958), Erica (Doris Day) tells Gannon (Clark Gable), a middle-aged journalism student she doesn't know is really a newspaper editor, that the dean was impressed by a story Gannon wrote for Erica's class and thinks Gannon should have the chance to take on extra work, which would mean working very closely with her at night. When he kisses her, she says the relationship between a teacher and a student is complex, friendly but requiring distance and discipline, and they kiss again. Another romance between an older student and a professor involves Harv (Bing Crosby), a widower and restaurant chain owner in his early fifties, and Helene (Nicole Maurey), an unmarried French professor. In *High Time* (1960), when Harv pays Helene to tutor him during the summer after his sophomore year, his daughter mistakenly reports to the college president that her father has been having an affair with a faculty member. The president says it was improper for the two to have spent the summer together, but Harv says they did nothing wrong—that is, they didn't have sex—and argues that students should be able to socialize with their professors. The president later tells protesting students that Helene has submitted her resignation but he won't accept it, and he sets a date for an investigation of the matter that is after Harv's scheduled graduation. As a senior, Harv describes his relationship with Helene as just companionship, but a friend tells him the two are really in love. Helene asks Harv to marry

Thornton Melon (Rodney Dangerfield) is a middle-aged student who gets romantically involved with Dr. Diane Turner (Sally Kellerman) in *Back to School* (1986, Orion).

her, and he says he's too old, but in his graduation speech he indicates that he'll marry her. There is no suggestion in the film, released several years before the Production Code was formally abandoned, that the middle-aged couple has sex while Harv is still a student.

Young women behave seductively toward their professors in two films released in the early 1960s. In *Tammy Tell Me True* (1961), the title character (Sandra Dee) is an unsophisticated first-year student from the backwoods who is attracted to her handsome public speaking instructor, Tom (John Gavin), but whenever she encourages him to kiss her, he excuses himself by saying he has papers to grade. She tells him she gets queasy when he's near and realizes she never really loved her absent boyfriend, who made her feel like a child while Tom makes her feel like a woman. Implicit in Tom's resistance to Tammy's advances is his awareness that intimacy with a student would be improper, but she overcomes his reservations by the end of the film. In *Bachelor Flat* (1962), female students warmly greet a professor as he drives onto the campus. Girls in his class apply makeup in anticipation of his arrival, but they're dismayed

For most of *Tammy Tell Me True* (1961, Universal International), public speaking instructor Tom Freeman (John Gavin) is able to resist the advances of his unpolished student Tammy Tyree (Sandra Dee).

to learn that he's just gotten engaged. One of them lets the air out of the tires of his sports car so she can offer him a ride home, telling him on the way that she can't sleep at night because she thinks about him. She hugs and kisses him as she recklessly steers her car, and she says she signed up for his class just to be near him.

Seductive behavior by female students became more commonplace as well as more sexually explicit in movies released in the 1970s. This was the result of the sexual revolution, which included abandonment of the Production Code in 1967, and the feminist movement, which encouraged the liberation of women from traditional gender roles. After teaching a class in *Getting Straight* (1970), Harry is approached by a student who says she really likes him. He replies that teachers don't get involved with their students in that way and recommends that she read de Sade instead. She says her high school teacher told her the same thing. In *How Do I Love Thee?* (1970), a distracted instructor teaches a class as his student and future wife displays her breasts, legs, and panties to him. After class, she chides him for ogling her, but admits that she's been wondering about him, too. He immediately takes her to a secluded spot, grades her kissing a B+, and they go to his place for sex. This is the most open acknowledgment of faculty-student sex since an instructor unquestionably accepted his student-lover's claim that she was pregnant in *All of Me* (1934).

In *The Swinging Cheerleaders* (1974), a student tries to keep her grades up and retain her scholarship by seducing a professor by showing cleavage and sitting in the front row of his class without panties. In similar fashion, a blonde seductively crosses her legs as her professor gives his last lecture of the semester in *The Eiger Sanction* (1975). After class she comes to his office and tells him she'll lose her scholarship if she doesn't maintain a B average. She's afraid of not doing well on his final exam and says she's willing to do anything for a good grade, pointing out that she isn't busy that evening and her roommate is away for the weekend. The professor tells her the best way to maintain a B average is to go home, break out her books, and "study her ass off." He pats her on the bottom, tells her not to study it off, and sends her on her way.

Faculty-student relationships appeared regularly in movies throughout the 1980s. In *A Change of Seasons* (1980), the middle-aged Karyn (Shirley MacLaine) observes that the girls on campus all look like *Playboy* centerfolds and says to her husband Adam (Anthony Hopkins), a professor, "You're having an affair, aren't you?... You're sleeping with one of your students." He denies it at first, but then admits that he is. Asking "Do you love the child?" she points out that the girl must be about the same age as their daughter and wonders why every middle-aged man acts like he wants to sleep with his daughter. Adam claims to love Karyn but to be infatuated with Lindsey (Bo Derek), saying he's going through a phase but is capable of loving two women at once. Lindsey's father agrees with Karyn in describing Adam as "an aging professor groping a student who's young enough to be his daughter," but Lindsey calls her father a hypocrite because he has been sleeping with younger women for as long as she can remember. Even though she says she still loves Adam, Lindsey ends their affair, believing that he'll never leave Karyn. Another affair shows up in *Dirty Tricks* (1981), with a professor telling a student that he's given her term paper a C, even though she gets an A in bed. She tells him another professor she slept with gave her an A, but she doesn't care that he's only giving her a C. Later she reconsiders and ends the affair because it isn't helping her grade. The perception that faculty-student sex was commonplace in the 1980s is suggested by a professor's comment to his wife in *D.O.A.* (1988): "I'm probably the only professor on campus who's not screwing a sophomore." When he awakens with a hangover in the bed of a student and worries that they had sex, she assures him they didn't, commenting that he mumbled something about rules and ethics as he passed out the night before. Later they do have sex.

Four slasher movies from the 1980s feature sexual relationships between students and professors. In *Final Exam* (1981), a student flirts with a profes-

The fact that Lindsey Rutledge (Bo Derek) is half the age of Professor Adam Evans (Anthony Hopkins) evokes negative comments about their affair from both her father and his wife in *A Change of Seasons* (1980, Twentieth Century–Fox).

sor in his office, saying he loves the sweet young girls who throw themselves at him. She calls his wife over the hill at thirty and arranges to meet him in a studio for "art in the dark," but she's murdered before he gets there. A police lieutenant in *Night School* (1981) investigates the brutal murders of two students at a women's college in Boston. He sees Professor Millett (Drew Snyder) kiss his teaching assistant Kim (Elizabeth Barnitz) while the professor's live-in partner Eleanor (Rachel Ward) watches jealously. A waitress remarks to Eleanor that the only thing college girls ever talk about is sex and asks if it's true that Millett fools around with his students, observing that he's a good-looking guy and she wouldn't blame him with all those "horny coeds" around. After Kim is murdered, the lieutenant tells the professor he's heard rumors about his affairs with students, but Millett claims he has a strict rule never to get involved with them. When Eleanor complains that Millett was having affairs when they first met, he replies that in that case she should have known what to expect from him. In another slasher movie, *Pieces* (1983), a young woman bares her breasts to her anatomy professor and asks him where her pectorals are; she giggles when he shows her. A girl in *Primal Rage* (1988) tells her roommate she's beginning the semester late because she had an abortion, apparently the result of an affair with the middle-aged, balding Professor Jenkins (Turk Harley). In class, Jenkins directs a question at a young woman, who seductively crosses her legs but can't come up with the correct answer. Later, he drives her into the woods and tells her she's been doing much better in his course but is still behind. She says she needs a C to stay in school and asks what it will take. He answers, "A lot of hard work."

Two films from the 1980s feature female professors seducing their male students. In *They're Playing with Fire* (1984), a beautiful blonde who wears pearls, a suit, and spiked heels to her lecture on *Macbeth* hires a young man to work on her yacht. She offers him a drink, and soon they are making love. When he asks if she's ever done it with a student before, she says no, though she did have an affair with her husband when she was a student and he a professor. In *Dr. Alien* (1988), a biology class is taken over by an alien in a sexually provocative human disguise. She lectures about foreplay, penetration, and ejaculation and then chooses a nerdy freshman to be her research subject. He asks a friend, "But why would she be interested in me? I'm a student. She would be violating her professional ethics." The friend replies that some older women like younger guys. When the alien injects the freshman with a green fluorescent chemical, a penis-like appendage grows out of the top of his head and they have intercourse on a laboratory table as her assistant takes notes. The experience transforms the freshman into a swaggering stud.

Movies released in the 1990s continued to emphasize faculty-student intimacy. In *Necessary Roughness* (1991), thirty-four-year-old college quarterback Paul (Scott Bakula) meets Suzanne (Harley Jane Kozak) while she's playing racquetball. When he goes to his first journalism class, the students mistake him for their professor, but then Suzanne, who is actually teaching the course, enters the room. She announces that she gives no special treatment to football players, but later tells Paul that she worshipped him in high school. The dean feigns shock when he sees the two kissing, but he's simply jealous. Suzanne tells the dean that she and Paul are consenting adults, but he warns that her involvement with a student is jeopardizing her career. A student in *Psychic* (1992) asks his teaching assistant to dine with him, but she declines, explaining that the university has strict guidelines on faculty-student relations. He then asks her to sign a form so he can drop the course, saying he likes it but they can go out if he's no longer her student.

College movies as old as 1929's *The Wild Party* suggest that professors can suffer negative consequences if they become intimate with their students, but the threat of disciplinary action or job loss got little attention until the 1980s. When the young woman in *Oleanna* (1994) learns that she's failing a course, she goes to her professor's office. He says her work isn't good, and she replies that she's been doing what he tells the class to do. He offers to let her start the course over and give her an A if she'll meet with him a few more times. Believing that she's being sexually harassed, she files a complaint that he asked her to his office because he "liked" her, moved as if to embrace her, and promised her an A if she'd stay alone with him in his office. She tells him she'll let his tenure committee deal with her complaint, but he wants to settle the matter immediately. He grabs her in anger, and she runs from his office, yelling for help. Later she informs him that the committee decided to deny him tenure and suspend him for his behavior. Her threat to press criminal charges for attempted rape and battery enrages him, and he slaps and punches her.

The repercussions of faculty involvement with a student are also dealt with in *Mind Games* (1996). When the student-lover of Professor Jarvis (Brian Krause) commits suicide, he's forced to find a new job. The dean at his next place of employment tells him the faculty board wants him to sign an agreement to abide by the school's rule of no dating of students by the faculty. Jarvis offers to resign, saying he can't teach at an institution with such a McCarthy-era policy, but the dean refuses to accept his resignation. A colleague who got pregnant by a professor when she was an eighteen-year-old student sees Jarvis as a predator and tries to get him fired for his involvement with a student who is intent on seducing him. The dean suspends Jarvis out of fear that a scandal would hurt the school, and the faculty board votes to dismiss the professor. He's later cleared of all charges, but he quits to find a job where his colleagues will trust him. A professor in *The Misadventures of Margaret* (1998) tells his wife that his college once tried to deny tenure to a married professor who was having an affair with a student, but he defended him. He claims that adultery is necessary to human evolution because it allows superior married men to perpetuate the best of the species. In *Among Brothers* (2005), a professor who has been charged with harassment in the past is fired after being falsely accused of murdering a female student to whom he had made a sexual overture.

The new century saw no abatement in the number of movies dealing with faculty-student affairs. Professor Alcott (Greg Kinnear) in *Loser* (2000) delights in humiliating Dora (Mena Suvari), a student in his class, even though he's sleeping with her and she's grading his tests and typing his papers. He tells her he's risking his job by being involved with her, mentioning a professor who lost tenure because he took advantage of impressionable students. She claims she has the right to choose her own sex partners because she's over eighteen. At the end, he is sent to prison for having sex with a seventeen-year-old. *Red Letters* (2000) begins with a nude female reading to Professor Burke (Peter Coyote) from his erotic novel. She's upset that he's ending their affair and says, "Expect a sexual harassment suit, professor.... The university doesn't like its students getting fucked ... or fucked over." She wishes him good luck finding a new job. Later, at a different college, the daughter of the dean flirts with Burke during his lecture on Nathaniel Hawthorne and guilt, sin, and temptation. When he finds her in his office, he asks her to open the door that she's closed. She calls his novel the most erotic and disturbing piece of literature she's ever read, and then she propositions him. He tells her the book is fiction and was written more than twenty years ago, and says he was never the man in the book and certainly isn't now. He says he's flattered by her offer, but she's off-limits because she's a student.

Other professors in recent movies are less reluctant to get involved with their students. A male professor has an affair with a female student in *Gossip* (2000), and a female professor carries on a sexual relationship with a male student in *Harvard Man* (2001). A professor in *Mona Lisa Smile* (2003) ends an affair with his student to pursue a female colleague, who tells him after they've had sex that if they are to continue their relationship he has to promise not to sleep with any more students. In *Man of the House* (2005), a professor comments that her ex-husband teaches at the college because of its endless supply of young females. A newly separated professor in *The Squid and the Whale* (2005) tells his son he's never had an affair with a student, though he's had opportunities, but when a young woman in his writing seminar says she's wondered what it would be like to have sex with him, he unsuccessfully tries to persuade her to perform oral sex.

Two movies look at intimate relationships between faculty members and students of the same sex, and a third, *Stay* (2005), makes a passing reference to a male art professor who seduces his cute male students. In *Lianna* (1983), the thirty-three-year-old title character (Linda Griffiths) falls in love with Ruth (Jane Hallaren), the professor in her child psychology course. As a student years before, Lianna had had an affair with a professor she married after she quit college so as to prevent damage to his reputation. Ruth tells Lianna she was frightened to initiate their affair, because if she'd been wrong about Lianna's intentions and it had gotten around campus, she would have been embarrassed. When Lianna tells her husband of the affair, he says, "So you're still fucking your teachers." She replies, "And you're still fucking your students," having observed him having intercourse with one at a faculty party. He responds, "At least they're the right sex." Ruth tells Lianna they can't live together after Lianna's husband kicks her out of the house, explaining that she has to convince parents to volunteer their children for her research and that their relationship would soon be known all over town. Ruth then admits that she's still involved in a relationship with a woman back home, and she returns to her old job. Another same-sex relationship appears in *Eden's Curve* (2003). A male poetry instructor, who is also a graduate student, cares for an undergraduate after he is assaulted, and the two become romantically and sexually involved. When the dean learns of the affair, he expels the instructor, telling him his career is over because he won't be getting a recommendation.

Faculty-student intimacy in the movies often fits institutional definitions of sexual harassment, but usually it doesn't meet the legal standard for sexual assault. One exception is *The Accused* (1949), in which an attempted rape of a psychology professor by her student leads to her killing him in self-defense. The 1966 film *Penelope* treats a professor's sexual assault on a student as humorous rather than criminal. A compulsive thief tells her psychiatrist that the first time she stole anything was during her last week in college. She was dressed for her prom when an anthropology professor lured her into his laboratory, where he ripped off her dress and chased her before he was knocked out by a falling stuffed gorilla. During the attack, which she describes as a "session in primitive anthropology," she grabbed the professor's watch fob, which she decided to keep. A professor's assault on a student is treated more seriously in *The Private Public* (2000). When Maddy (Kelly Lynch) goes to the home of Professor Hass (Ross Brockley) with questions about his course, he touches her shoulder, takes her hand, and tries to kiss her. She fights him off. In a student-made documentary that is aired on the campus television station, Maddy says Hass lied to her that other students would be at his house. She claims to have been so traumatized by his behavior that she can't go to his class or even be around him. A dean says the number of nationally known professors at the school can be counted on one hand, and Hass, though "a little eccentric," is one of them. Worrying that publicizing the incident would hurt Hass and the school, he buries Maddy's complaint.

College movies convey the erroneous impression that professors are as likely to interact with their students in the bedroom as in the classroom. When classroom scenes appear, they are usually brief and more likely to show students bored with their instructors rather than intent on learning. College movies occasionally do a good job of portraying faculty members mentoring their students, but in general they pay more attention to romantic and sexual relationships between professors and students than they do to teaching and mentoring. These intimate relationships are often presented as consensual; when it is clear who initiated the relationship, it is more often a seductive female student than a predatory male professor. Despite the frequent appearance of faculty-student intimacy in college movies, far more of them show students looking to their peers rather than their professors for romance and sex.

5

LOVE STORY

Finding a romantic or sexual partner does not require enrollment in college, but the process is affected in important ways by being a student. Today's undergraduates meet potential partners from many countries, regions, and racial and ethnic groups, but the high cost of a college education means they are unlikely to meet many students from low-income families. Because the students at many schools are similar in age, and because most marriages are between people close in age, campuses provide a larger selection of potential mates than students are apt to encounter in a single place after graduation. However, intimate relationships among undergraduates are impeded by the pressure of coursework, the need to hold a job, and commitment to extracurricular activities.

Pursuing Romance and Sex

College movies suggest that some students find romance soon after arriving on campus. No film shows a freshman meeting a partner during an orientation program, but first-year students begin relationships at registration in *Sunny Skies* (1930), *The Quarterback* (1940), *Take Care of My Little Girl* (1951), and *Trick Dribble* (2001). In *Boys and Girls* (2000), a couple who met on a plane and didn't get along four years earlier run into each other at freshman registration at Berkeley. They become platonic and then romantic partners over the course of their years in college.

Freshman mixers have faded in importance over time, but two movies that take place around 1950 show first-year students meeting romantic partners at these social events. In *The Affairs of Dobie Gillis* (1953), two young men check out their female classmates at a mixer, though their conversation is devoid of sexual bantering. The Amherst College mixer that opens *Carnal Knowledge* is a stark contrast to the sexual revolution that was in full swing when the movie was released in 1971. Timid Sandy (Arthur Garfunkel) talks with his roommate Jonathan (Jack Nicholson) about what to look for in a

Mike Nichols, Jack Nicholson, Candice Bergen, Arthur Garfunkel, Ann-Margret and Jules Feiffer. Carnal Knowledge.

Jonathan (Jack Nicholson, center) and Sandy (Arthur Garfunkel), Amherst freshmen in the late 1940s, discuss how to seduce a Smith College student in *Carnal Knowledge* (1971, Avco Embassy).

woman. When Susan (Candice Bergen), a Smith College freshman, walks into the room, the two students discuss the best way to approach her. After one false start, Sandy awkwardly talks to Susan about how much they hate mixers. Sandy and Jonathan later consider the best way for Sandy to "put the moves" on Susan, but Jonathan takes his own advice and has sex with her before Sandy can, though Jonathan remains jealous of the greater intimacy of Sandy's relationship with her. This film both captures the innocence of freshmen of an earlier era and takes advantage of the liberal sexual mores of the early 1970s to offer what is perhaps a more realistic picture of the way students behaved in the 1940s than did movies that were made then. Sandy and Jonathan actively pursue sex, while *The Affairs of Dobie Gillis*, restricted by the Production Code and public standards of the time, had to limit itself to the search for romance.

Couples in the movies meet in a variety of academic settings. In *Kicking and Screaming* (1995), a boy and a girl begin a relationship after their creative writing class when she apologizes for criticizing his paper, though she says it did have a lot of spelling errors. Two students meet in a Columbia University language lab in *The Magic Garden of Stanley Sweetheart* (1970). In *Loser* (2000), a boy enters a class late and disrupts the lecture by falling down the aisle. He takes a seat next to a girl who is having an affair with the professor, a formidable obstacle to his romantic pursuit of her. A professor in *The Human Stain* (2003) reminisces about how he picked up girls in the library stacks as an NYU undergraduate.

Students also search for intimacy off campus. Ft. Lauderdale, Florida, became a popular destination for undergraduates from the North just a few years after Colgate University's swim team traveled there over the 1934–1935 winter break to keep in shape in the city's new pool. Filmmakers took a while to exploit this tradition, but in 1960 *Where the Boys Are* solidified "the city's image as a student playground."[1] The movie begins on a snowy, windswept Midwestern campus with four women planning a spring vacation in Ft. Lauderdale, where each hopes to meet the love of her life, or at least have a bit of fun. They prioritize their male targets, with one of them remarking, "I think they're Yalies, maybe even Harvard." One girl sets her sights on a suave, wealthy Brown University senior, telling him that Ivy Leaguers have a certain cool look, like they couldn't even bother to perspire. At 140, his IQ exceeds hers by two points, barely making it possible for their relationship to conform to the tradition that women shouldn't be smarter than the men they marry. The remake of this movie, *Where the Boys Are '84* (1984), starts on a campus with Chip (Howard McGillin) telling Carole (Lorna Luft) they've now slept together for five years and it keeps getting better. She apparently disagrees and suggests they take separate vacations. A friend who plans to accompany her to Ft. Lauderdale says all you need there is a string bikini and a diaphragm. The young women in this version of the story are looking for sex, not necessarily with someone who'll become a long-term partner, rather than for romance that will lead to marriage, as in the 1960 movie. Sex is also the goal of male students vacationing in Ft. Lauderdale in *Spring Break* (1983) and *Can It Be Love* (1992).

The shift from the pursuit of romance in the 1960s to the pursuit of sex in the 1980s is also evident in two spring break movies set in Palm Springs, California. A college basketball team visits the desert town in *Palm Springs Weekend* (1963), and its captain and the daughter of the local police chief fall in love. Just before he leaves, he says he wouldn't be able to finish his education if they got married, and she vows to wait for him until he does. *Fraternity Vacation* (1985), which uses the post-sexual revolution formula, features a pledge who is easily identified as a nerd by his glasses, open fly, and admiration for Wayne Newton. Two fraternity brothers agree to teach him the tricks of the trade with the opposite sex in exchange for his father's donation of a Jacuzzi and a sauna to their house. The boy gets a make-over, wins a bet by being the first to bed an attractive woman, and delights in his newfound reputation as a stud.

The pursuit of sex was prominent in *Where the Boys Are '84* (1984, TriStar), a remake of 1960's *Where the Boys Are* (Metro-Goldwyn-Mayer), which emphasized the search for romance with an eye toward marriage.

Husband-Hunting

You Can't Ration Love (1944) reverses the usual storyline of boys competing for girls by having females vie for the attentions of the few males remaining on campus during World War II. The film begins with a chart showing the proportion of men in the student body declining from 50 percent in 1939 to only 5 percent in 1944. The women cope with the shortage by devising a system to register every eligible male student and rate him on a point scale. Adopting the system used to distribute scarce consumer goods during the war, each girl is given a ration book with points she can use to get her "fair share of the available dates." Pete (Bill Edwards) complains to his girlfriend Betty (Betty Jane Rhodes) that he feels like a can of tomatoes because he has to go out with any girl who has enough points. When Betty runs out of points and can't date him, she plots to remodel the nerdy John "Two Points" Simpson (Johnnie Johnston) into a twenty-five pointer, trade him in for a twenty-three point profit, and use the extra points to date Pete. She takes John for a

John "Two Point" Simpson (Johnnie Johnston, center) questions his low rating on a point scale devised by female students to ration dates with the few men remaining on campus during World War II in the musical comedy *You Can't Ration Love* (1944, Paramount). Big man on campus Pete Allen (Bill Edwards) is graded 24 in one scene in the film, but here he wears a button with a score of 30 as Betty Hammond (Betty Jane Rhodes) evaluates the men.

haircut and new clothes, coaches him on "the art of making love," and teaches him modern music and dance. He's transformed into a dream man who heptalks, discards his glasses, sports a bow tie, and drives girls into a frenzy with his crooning. Betty falls in love with him, but only after concocting a scheme to win him away from his crowd of admirers does she succeed in getting him to marry her.

You Can't Ration Love is based on a recurrent theme in college movies: a young woman's search for a husband. The men targeted by "husband-hunters" are usually resistant or indifferent to marriage; for them, the college years are about having fun rather than settling down. In *Good News* (1930), football hero Tom (Stanley Smith) tells his tutor Connie (Mary Lawlor) that he loves her, but he has to marry another girl because he proposed to her first. Eventually he marries Connie, but he epitomizes the passive college male buffeted by external forces compelling him to marry someone against his true wishes. In the 1947 version of this film, husband-hunters Connie (June Allyson) and Pat (Patricia Marshall) plot to trap the befuddled Tommy (Peter Lawford) into marriage. In *Too Many Girls* (1940), Connie (Lucille Ball) is told she can pledge a sorority if her answer to one question indicates that she's their type of girl: "What do you consider your ultimate goal in life?" Connie correctly answers, "A man," and the sorority president replies, "Why, that's downright brilliant, honey. You're pledged." Curiously, the husband-hunters in these three movies are all named Connie, a name suggestive of conniving and con artist.

Young women also go to college for their "MRS. Degree" in two movies from the early 1960s. In *Tall Story* (1960), June (Jane Fonda), a home economics major, transfers to "Custer College" to pursue Ray (Anthony Perkins), a cute basketball star and brilliant science student. After accidentally crashing her bike into two professors, she says she was on her way to see them to register for their courses, which Ray is also taking. She plans to attract Ray by

June Ryder (Jane Fonda, center) is the epitome of the husband-hunter in the romantic comedy *Tall Story* (1960, Warner Brothers), transferring schools to pursue a basketball star, who is also a brilliant student, and joining the cheerleading squad so he will notice her legs.

becoming a cheerleader so he can get a good look at her legs. She also tries to get his attention by pretending to read unassigned books out of intellectual curiosity. After Ray tells Professor Sullivan (Ray Walston) that June is eager to learn and isn't just looking for a husband, Sullivan comments to his wife (Anne Jackson), "Just because he's a scholar doesn't mean he's stupid. He'll wake up to what she's doing." When June and Ray end up together, Mrs. Sullivan tells Ray he's lucky to have a girl strong enough to come after him. The title character (Sandra Dee) in *Tammy Tell Me True* (1961) also has her eyes on marriage and sees college as a place where an uneducated country girl can become "ladified" and thus more attractive to a potential mate.

Before the mid–1960s, many people supported women going to college to acquire the education and polish that would attract a suitable husband. Others opposed husband-hunting, arguing that educational resources should be reserved for men who would become their families' breadwinners. In the 1960s, the reasons that women went to college began to change. Single-income families were gradually replaced by dual-income ones because of economic necessity, as high rates of inflation and lagging salaries eroded buying power. Women's increased participation in the labor force was reinforced by the emergence of modern feminism, which was critical of a society that kept women economically dependent by discouraging them from working outside the home. The development of the birth control pill around the same time made it easier for families to plan their work lives by controlling the arrival of children. These social changes increased women's access to higher education and made it easier for them to pursue careers.

The declining use of the husband-hunting theme in college movies reflected these changes. Of the forty-five college movies that portray undergraduate women as husband-hunters, twenty-nine were made before 1966; of the sixteen released since then, five take place before 1966. In *Everybody's All-American* (1988), much of which takes place in the 1950s, a woman who is dating the campus football hero comments, "I'm majoring in Gavin and me." She refuses to enter a Miss Louisiana contest because she'd have to promise not to get married for two years. *Heart of Dixie* (1989), which takes place in Alabama in the late 1950s, looks at the impact of the civil rights movement on a group of sorority girls, but it also focuses on their search for an ideal husband. Maggie (Ally Sheedy) is conflicted between doing something about the mistreatment of blacks in the South and marrying her handsome and well-to-do boyfriend. Delia (Virginia Madsen) tells Maggie she'd kill for a marriage like that and won't work after graduation because she doesn't have to, concluding, "I'm gonna marry Jenks, end of story." Maggie grows increasingly alienated from her sorority's husband-hunters, one of whom comments after getting pinned, "I'm safe." Only non–sorority girl Aiken (Phoebe Cates), who gets pregnant but refuses to marry, unambiguously rejects matrimony, quitting college to move to Greenwich Village.

In *Mona Lisa Smile* (2003), which also takes place in the 1950s, young women are instructed on how to further their husbands' careers by entertaining the boss. Betty (Kirsten Dunst), who has just gotten married, tells her instructor Katherine (Julia Roberts) that she had to miss some classes because she was on her honeymoon and then had to set up her home, but she claims most faculty members consider these valid excuses. Katherine tells Betty to come to class or she'll fail her, and Betty warns her of consequences if she carries out her threat. At the end, Betty files for divorce from her unfaithful husband and plans to attend law school, while her classmate Joan (Julia Stiles), who has been accepted at Yale Law School, gets married so she can put dinner on the table for her husband while he gets his law degree. Joan says that Katherine sees the life of a housewife as shallow and boring, but that's the life she wants.

A recent movie that in the end rejects husband-hunting is *The Prince and Me* (2004). Paige (Julia Stiles), a senior at the University of Wisconsin, falls in love with Eddie (Luke Mably), a student who is actually Prince Edvard of Denmark. She plans to go to Johns Hopkins Medical School and then work in Latin America for a humanitarian organization. Eddie asks her to marry him, and the prospect of being queen is enticing. She leaves school for Denmark to get married, but at the last minute backs out and decides to follow her dream of becoming a physician. Eddie shows up at her graduation and tells her he'll wait for her until she's fulfilled her dream, apparently assuming that her career will not be a lifelong commitment. Paige's putting a fairy tale-like marriage on hold to become a doctor is in sharp contrast to the husband-hunting of older movies.

Pinning, Pregnancy, and Marriage

Romantic involvement and sexual attraction lead in various directions in the movies. Some students get pinned, a pre-engagement or "going steady" practice that indicates serious commitment. A few get pregnant out of wedlock, and occasionally undergraduates get married.

Pinning shows up in twenty-eight movies released between 1927 and 1966, but in only eight films since then, and four of those take place before 1960. Pinning does not appear in any film made about contemporary college life after 1988. Girls in *So This Is College* (1929), *The Age of Consent* (1932), and *Sex Kittens Go to College* (1960) wheedle fraternity pins from unsuspecting boys by claiming they need safety pins, and then they keep them as symbols of mutual commitment. *Fraternity Row* (1977), which takes place in 1954, includes a sorority ceremony for two girls who have secretly gotten pinned. The sisters pass a lighted candle among themselves, and the pinned girls blow it out when it comes to them, eliciting screams from the less fortunate. Fraternity members outside the house serenade the lucky girls with a song that mentions losing one's virginity.

By the 1920s, a girl's reputation on campus depended on her popularity, which was measured by the number and desirability of the boys she dated.[2] Because fraternity members were at the top of the status hierarchy at most colleges, fraternity pins were a measure of popularity. In several films from the 1930s, girls accumulate a collection of pins from different boys, each believing she is his alone. In *The Sweetheart of Sigma Chi* (1933), a boy gives a girl his pin, which she had bet her sorority sisters she could get, but he's upset to learn she also has the pins of several of his fraternity brothers and is nicknamed the "sweetheart of Sigma Chi" because of her history with members of his house. In *Two Minutes to Play* (1936), when a girl asks a boy why he hasn't called her in a while, he says there's too much competition for her. She asks him to a dance and he gives her his fraternity pin, which she adds to her 1935–1936 collection of pins, apparently having collections from other years

This title card from the 1933 version of *The Sweetheart of Sigma Chi* (Monogram) suggests that Bob (Buster Crabbe) has the upper hand in romance, but he gets upset when he learns that Vivian (Mary Carlisle) has a collection of fraternity pins acquired from other members of his house.

as well. Later she accepts a pin from another boy, and at the end she announces she's going to marry a third student who has just struck it rich. When a young woman in *Sorority House* (1939) wears her boyfriend's pin to a rush party, the house president snidely comments that the girls who have worn his pin are thinking of starting a club. A minor character in *Those Were the Days* (1940) is pinned to half a dozen men in addition to her supposed boyfriend. This recurring theme of accumulating fraternity pins seems to have been a coded way to convey a girl's promiscuity without violating the Production Code by explicitly mentioning sex.

Undergraduates who get pregnant out of wedlock in college movies are always romantically involved with one partner rather than promiscuous. Thirteen films released since 1952 feature a pregnant but unmarried student, but there was only one movie with such a character before then. In the pre–Code *Confessions of a Co-ed* (1931), Pat (Sylvia Sidney) tells her sorority sisters that she approves of premarital sex if the partners are in love. She gets pregnant after spending the night in a mountain cabin with a young man while they're on a school skiing trip. He's expelled for an unrelated reason and leaves campus unaware that she's expecting a child. She decides not to have an abortion, though that word is not spoken, and then she marries a different student in the mistaken belief that he knows she's pregnant. She drops out of school, while he apparently finishes his degree.

Beginning in 1952, fifteen years before the Production Code was formally abandoned, college movies began to deal with out-of-wedlock pregnancy more often and at the same time take an increasingly skeptical view of the institution of marriage. A middle-aged chiropractor in *Come Back, Little Sheba* (1952) reveals to a boarder that he quit medical school years before because he got his girlfriend pregnant and they had to get married. In *A Kiss Before Dying* (1956), Bud (Robert Wagner) is distressed when his wealthy girlfriend Dory (Joanne Woodward) tells him she's going to have his baby. He doesn't want a family and decides to kill her, first by shoving her down the stadium steps, then by trying to poison her, and finally and successfully by pushing her off the roof of a building. Eddie (Peter Fonda) tells Pam (Sharon Hugueny) in *The Young Lovers* (1964) that girls study Freud, Marx, and T. S. Eliot in college but end up over a hot stove wishing they looked like Princess Grace. Pam says she can't imagine standing over a hot stove, and Eddie tells her she's different from the other girls, who just wanted to get married. Pam gets pregnant, but before she tells Eddie the news, she says they should get married. He says married students live like gypsies, that the two of them need to finish college first, that he's been offered a scholarship to continue his study of art, and that he has to worry about serving in the armed forces. Pam's doctor talks about abortion's physical and psychological risks, tells her to think it over, and says to let him know if she needs his help. When Pam suggests terminating the pregnancy, Eddie says he doesn't want to be responsible for that. She goes to have an abortion but can't go through with it, drops out of school after finishing the semester with good grades, and plans to move back east with her mother.

An even more negative attitude toward marriage is expressed in *The Harrad Experiment* (1973). When Sheila (Laurie Walters) asks Margaret Tenhausen (Tippi Hedren), wife of the school's director, if two people can fulfill one another in marriage, Margaret says that it's possible but unusual, because a husband and a wife are more likely just to share their loneliness. She describes marriage as a legal contract that encourages the expression of jealousy. Her husband (James Whitmore) asks the students why society is so critical of adultery, claiming that traditional marriage causes partners to stagnate, and he touts group and open marriage, ideas widely discussed during the sexual revolution, especially in Nena and George O'Neill's bestseller *Open Marriage*.[3] Sheila doesn't want to share the man she loves with other women and remains unconvinced by the Tenhausens' arguments against monogamy.

Eddie's reluctance to marry Pam in *The Young Lovers* is based in part on his assumption that getting married will keep them from completing college, a belief rarely questioned in college movies. In *The Age of Consent* (1932), the undergraduate Michael (Richard Cromwell) walks a café waitress named Dora Swale (Arline Judge) to her home, where they're found the next morning by her father. Mr. Swale (Reginald Barlow) insists that the two get married or he'll prosecute Michael for seducing a minor. Michael says they don't love each another, and a professor who is his mentor tells Swale that marriage isn't supposed to ruin lives. Swale criticizes universities for teaching bad morals and threatens to ruin the school's reputation if Michael doesn't marry Dora. Michael agrees to wed, even though he knows it will mean dropping out of college and facing a bleak future. At the last minute, Dora says she doesn't want her whole life laid out for her by others and refuses to get married. A student in *The Band Plays On* (1934) tells his girlfriend the year and a half of college he has left plus the three years of law school after that are too long to wait to get married. She replies that it's not smart to marry while in college because nine out of every ten students who do never finish school, and she wants him to complete his education so they'll have enough money to live on. Marriage does end a college education in *Love, Honor, and Behave* (1938), in which a Yale student marries his childhood sweetheart and, as a result, can't finish his senior year and go on to medical school as his mother had planned for him since he was ten. *Cynthia* (1947) begins with a woman remembering her first year in college seventeen years earlier, when she met her future husband. They spent the summer apart but got married when they returned to campus in the fall. After she became pregnant, they canceled their plans for graduate study and settled down in a small town to care for their frail daughter.

In contrast to movies that assume that marriage effectively ends a college education are a few that show undergraduates struggling to reconcile their roles as students with their roles as spouses or parents. In *All Women Have Secrets* (1939), Kay (Jeanne Cagney) tells her boyfriend John (Joseph Allen) not to quit school, because they can get married later. Later he tells her his coursework has improved now that they're seeing less of each other. They get married, John's academic work suffers, and Kay feels guilty, so she goes to work so he can quit his job and concentrate on his studies. Marriage and parenthood are also obstacles for veterans returning to school in *Apartment for Peggy* (1948) and *Yes Sir, That's My Baby* (1949). In the latter film, a woman tells her husband he has to complete his degree and has no time for football, a fraternity, or the prom. In *All the Fine Young Cannibals* (1960), an undergraduate tries to complete his education despite having a pregnant wife. After the baby is born, he says he may never attend another class.

Hooking Up

Most college movies released before the mid–1960s present the search for a partner in terms of romance and marriage; those made since are more likely to emphasize the pursuit of sex, with love and matrimony downplayed or absent altogether. The modern idea of "hooking up" can refer to a variety of sexual acts but is defined by the casual nature of those acts and the lack of commitment to a partner. As a young woman in *Inexchange* (2006) tells her virginal lover, "It's just sex." She adds that he shouldn't make more of it than it is, it doesn't mean they're in love, and she hasn't been in love with most of the guys she's slept with.

This recreational approach to sex rarely appears in college movies made between 1935 and 1959, but it shows up in a toned-down version in several pre–Code films. A football player in *The Plastic Age* (1925) adds a photograph of each girl he kisses twice to the wall of his dorm room, an early form of "scoring." In *Brown of Harvard* (1926), Tom (William Haines) cuts a notch in his "sheik belt" each time a new girl "falls for him." He offends a girl at a dance by kissing her aggressively, and a classmate calls him a "mucker" for kissing someone about whom he has no serious—that is, matrimonial—intentions. In *Hot Stuff* (1929), an heiress who is sent to college to find a husband wins acceptance by the school's "fast set" by smoking, drinking and suggesting that she's loose sexually. This impression is revealed as a pretense by a young man who gives her his fraternity pin and tells her it's still the nice girls who get the wedding rings. A young woman who actually is the kind of person this heiress pretends to be is the flirtatious Babe (Bessie Love) in *Good News* (1930); she tells a young man, "I'm not hard to get, but I'm hard to get away from." Several references to sex appear in *The Age of Consent* (1932). Duke (Eric Linden) says that for spending time with a girl, his car is better than a hotel, because he doesn't have to register. When he tells a dancing partner to loosen her morals, she tells him to loosen his grip. He speaks of free love and playing the field and warns the dean that if he can't take a few liberties at the school, he'll find another one.

Campus sex began to be treated more openly in the early 1960s, but for several years the use of veiled language, off-camera behavior, and negative repercussions for the sexually active suggested uncertainty about how to deal with the subject. In *Where the Boys Are* (1960), Merritt (Dolores Hart) speaks out in class in favor of premarital sex, but in Ft. Lauderdale it's Melanie (Yvette Mimieux) and not Merritt who looks for sex and ends up being raped, an endorsement of the contemporary belief that unmarried women should remain chaste.[4] Ambivalence about premarital sex surfaces in 1964's *Get Yourself a College Girl*, in which the respectable Joanie (Mary Ann Mobley) is working her way through college by making hit records under another name. She provocatively performs her newest song, "Help Stamp Out Men," which mentions "s-e-x," and a college trustee declares it trash, accusing Joanie of ruining the school's reputation and threatening her with expulsion. A girl tells her boyfriend in *The Young Lovers* (1964) that engagement is a ploy that guys use to lure girls into temporary sexual relationships, and she refuses to sleep with him until they're married. Later she says two years is too long to wait and offers to have sex, but he wants to wait.

Movies released since the late 1960s have treated sex among college students as rampant. A young man in *3 in the Attic* (1968) is rumored to have had sex with more than fifty girls by the time he was a sophomore. When three women discover he has been deceiving them by sleeping with the other two, they lock him in a dormitory attic and have sex with him in shifts. He becomes delirious and describes himself as one of the first casualties of the sexual revolution. In *Didn't You Hear...*, which was made in 1970 but not released until 1983, a young man who is doing survey research asks a fellow student if he's ever had sexual intercourse. The student says no, and the researcher says he's his first virgin. In *Road Trip* (2000), a boy tells a girl that her smoking of marijuana might affect her decision-making abilities and lower her inhibitions; she replies, "Good, uh, that's the plan." By 2002, a musical director in *Drumline* can tell the members of his band to play their instruments like they make love and assume they'll know what he means. Recent movies such as *Inexchange* (2006) show "sexiled" students forced out of their rooms so their roommates can have some "private time."

The apparent increase in student sex was accompanied by growing pressure to hook up. In *Carnal Knowledge* (1971), a freshman comments, "I feel the same way about getting laid as I feel about going to college. I'm being pressured into it." His remark is more appropriate to the year the film was released than to the late 1940s when it is spoken. A football player in *The Swinging Cheerleaders* (1974) says a teammate is giving the squad a bad reputation by not scoring with his virginal girlfriend. Pressure to have sex is central to the plot of *The Sure Thing* (1985). Gib (John Cusack) travels across the country for casual sex with a beautiful blonde provided by his friend Lance (Anthony Edwards). When Gib questions the morality of their plan, Lance encourages him by claiming, "Every relationship starts with a one-night stand." The importance of peer pressure is made clear in the "rule of three" from *American Pie 2* (2001): To determine the actual number of sex partners a girl has had, multiply what she tells you by three; to get the actual number for a boy, divide what he tells you by three. Contradicting the notion that women don't want to flaunt their sexual experience, a student in *Prozac Nation* (2001) throws a party to celebrate the loss of her virginity. Her partner is offended by her invasion of his privacy, but she says what he's really objecting to is a girl taking the same casual approach to sex that he does. Sex as a recreational activity preoccupies a student in *Learning Curves* (2003). He estimates that he wouldn't be caught dead with 100 of the girls on campus, 200 wouldn't be caught dead with him, and that leaves about 200 he can ask to bed without any preliminaries. He calculates that if only 5 percent say "yes," he'll get ten "hits." He concludes, "Those who strike out the most also hit the most homers," one of many sports metaphors for sex that show up in college movies.

Sexual Assault

Long before sex became a common theme in college movies, males were sometimes presented as boorish, even criminally aggressive, in their treatment of women. A "college cad" who molests a young woman in *The Freshman* (1925) has to be restrained by a meek but chivalrous student. A girl in *The Spirit of Notre Dame* (1931) carries a police whistle whenever she dates football players. A boy in *Mother Is a Freshman* (1949) tells a girl he's in love with her, but she says he's being silly and should be a man. To demonstrate his sincerity, he kisses her twice against her will and then suggests that maybe she needs "a little mussing up." A girl in *Come Back, Little Sheba* (1952) asks a track athlete to her off-campus room to pose for a poster she's doing for a contest. He comes over a second time to help her with chemistry. They kiss, he becomes insistent, and when she resists his advances, he says women have to pretend to be offended by aggressive men, but that she'd be offended if he didn't try. She concedes that he's right.

Occasionally the pursuit of sex leads to rape. In *Daughters of Today* (1924), a girl from the country is assaulted during a party at her fashionable urban college. When her attacker is found dead, she's suspected of his murder. Fraternity members pressure their brothers to "score," even if it means committing rape, in *Animal House* (1978); one boy who decides not to force himself on an unconscious girl is called a "homo." In *Higher Learning* (1995),

Harold "Speedy" Lamb (Harold Lloyd) comes to the rescue of his admirer Peggy (Jobyna Ralston) when she is attacked by "the college cad" (Brooks Benedict) in the classic 1925 comedy *The Freshman* (Harold Lloyd Corporation/Pathé).

a boy is mocked for failing to overpower a girl who resisted his attempt to have sex without a condom.

The most violent sexual assaults in college films involve multiple offenders. In *The Swinging Cheerleaders* (1974), Ron (Ian Sander) invites Andy (Cheryl Smith) to his apartment and they have consensual sex. She then tells him she wants to try everything, and he calls his friends and tells them they're going to "gangbang a cheerleader." Early the next morning, a battered Andy is taken in by her boyfriend, who goes to Ron's place and beats him up. Three fraternity brothers in *Primal Rage* (1995) describe girls as "fresh party meat" and force one into their car, make her drink beer, and take her to their room for a gang rape. *Train Ride* (2000) involves the efforts of three students to cover up a gang rape in which the victim was slipped a date-rape drug. *Going Greek* (2001) presents gang rape as a pledge prank, the "game" of "rodeo" in which one fraternity brother after another has intercourse with a girl from behind, the goal being to see who can most successfully resist her efforts to buck him off.

The question of how a woman should respond to a sexual assault by an acquaintance comes up in several movies. In *Heart of Dixie* (1989), a student described as "a nice girl" is raped after her boyfriend gets her drunk. She's urged to report the crime but is conflicted because she thought he was going to give her his fraternity pin, and she's a senior desperate to get married. Other sexual assault victims are also reluctant to define the use of force as a crime. A girl in *Higher Learning* (1995) doesn't want to report a rape attempt by a boy she knows out of fear that other students will think she "asked for it." A first-year student in *Freshmen* (1999) says she can't report being raped because she was drunk and should have been more careful, but a classmate says she isn't to blame and convinces her to report the crime to the campus police.

Other rape victims also take action against their attackers. A young woman in *Dream Trap* (1990) defends herself against repeated assaults by an insistent fraternity member and football player who has bet $100 he can score with her. She closes a door on his hand, fights back, and finally pushes him, wheelchair-bound because of injuries she has inflicted, into a swimming pool. In *Divided We Stand* (2000), Jennice (Andrea Lia), who has a white mother but identifies with the black students, is raped by Jarib (Crayton Robey), president of the militant Black Student Coalition. He denies the allegation at first, but then tells Troy (Jaxon Ronin) he never thought she'd dare tell anyone of the rape. Two other girls reveal that Jarib also sexually assaulted them, and Troy plays Jarib's tape-recorded admission that he raped Jennice. Jarib eventually serves three years in prison for rape.

Students deal with rape in different ways in other movies. Taryn (Jennifer Connelly) in *Higher Learning* (1995) educates first-year student Kristen (Kristy Swanson) about the blue lights on campus that mark emergency call boxes to be used in the event of an attack. Warning Kristen that the campus isn't safe, Taryn urges her to join Students for a Nonsexist Society, which holds a rally loudly proclaiming that "no means no." In *A Reason to Believe* (1995), the most in-depth consideration of rape on campus, Wes (Danny Quinn) tells his girlfriend Charlotte (Allison Smith) that he can't go to his fraternity's party because he has to attend a funeral. She goes alone, and there she and Jim (Jay Underwood) have too much to drink and he rapes her. Later, Wes overhears one of his fraternity brothers comment that he can't believe Jim "tagged" Wes's girlfriend. To save face, Wes announces that he broke up with Charlotte a few days before the party and says he's glad that Jim had the "first taste" of her. He refuses to believe Charlotte's claim that Jim raped her. Jim acknowledges that he may have misread Charlotte's signals, but he says she had sex voluntarily to make Wes jealous, and when it didn't work, she cried rape. Charlotte admits to the dean that she was wearing a sexy toga and kissing Jim at the party, but she says that doesn't mean she wasn't raped. The administration fears that bad publicity from the case might reduce donations and applicants, but it nonetheless convenes a disciplinary board to hear the case. At the hearing, Jim says that men, and especially fraternity men, are not the source of all evil and asks why women don't also have a responsibility to remain sober and make correct decisions. A feminist responds that women should be able to get drunk at parties without having to fear rape. The board finds that Charlotte was raped and offers to support her in prosecuting Jim. He's expelled from school, and his fraternity is put on probation for the remainder of the semester. The board promises to make the campus safer by publishing crime reports in the newspaper and by implementing programs to educate fraternity members. Charlotte tells Wes it's too late to resurrect their relationship and she's afraid she won't ever be able to be affectionate again.

Gays, Lesbians, and Bisexuals

Romance and sex in college movies were entirely heterosexual until 1966, and on-screen physical intimacy between partners of the same sex did not appear until the 1990s. College films have included cross-dressing since the 1920s, but wearing the clothes of the opposite sex rarely had anything to do with homosexual desire or behavior. Instead, it was most often used as a device for one of the following purposes:

- to hide a woman in a men's dormitory
- to give men access to dormitories and sorority houses limited to women
- to humiliate freshmen or fraternity pledges in hazing rituals by forcing them to pretend to be members of "the subordinate sex"
- to entertain an audience in a theatrical production or variety show
- to comment on gender roles

Though included just for its entertainment value, drag in early college movies did present a challenge to traditional gender roles that helped pave the way for the more substantial changes wrought by feminists and gay rights activists.

Except for a fleeting remark in *She Loves Me Not* (1934), drag was not explicitly linked to homosexuality until 1979. In *Fast Break*, Roberta (Mavis Washington), who is called "Bobby" and nicknamed "Swish" for her basketball skills, but also as an allusion to homosexuality, dresses as a male so she can play on the City College of New York team. When teammate DC (Harold Sylvester) starts to fall in love with her, he's confused and resists his feelings, thinking he must be gay because Bobby appears to be a guy. When he learns that Bobby is a female, he pretends to come on to her as a gay man. This makes her uncomfortable, but then he calls her Roberta and hugs her. A player who finds them kissing in the locker room is shocked at what he thinks is his teammates' homosexual behavior, unaware that Bobby is a female. In *Nobody's Perfect* (1989), a boy dresses as a girl so he can join the women's tennis team and spend time with a girl he likes. They win a tennis championship with their

On the run from gangsters in *She Loves Me Not* (1934, Paramount), Curly Flagg (Miriam Hopkins) seeks refuge in a Princeton men's dormitory, where Paul Lawton (Bing Crosby) gives her a short haircut, dresses her like a boy, and hides her from her pursuers and college officials.

doubles victory, declare their love, and kiss passionately on the court, raising eyebrows in the audience at what seems to be lesbian love. A young man in *Happy Together* (1989) dresses in women's clothing and comes on as an aggressive gay man to drive away a potential roommate. In *Sorority Boys* (2002), a girl rejects the advances of a boy because she's suspicious of boys who take women's studies courses to impress girls with their sensitivity. The boy gets a friendlier response after dressing in drag, but when the girl kisses him, he's confused because his feelings for her are as a straight man and not the lesbian he imagines she thinks he is.

Homosexuality became a more common theme in college movies after the mid–1960s as a result of the sexual revolution, the abandonment of the Production Code, and the emergence of the gay liberation movement. Only seven college movies released between 1966 and 1992 included a gay, lesbian, or bisexual student, but twenty-six films released between 1993 and 2006 had one. Nineteen movies released between 1966 and 2006 included a lesbian student, fourteen had a gay male student, two had a bisexual student, and none had a transgendered student.

The first college film with an openly gay, lesbian, or bisexual character is *The Group* (1966). One of the Class of 1933 graduates of an exclusive women's college is openly lesbian years later and admits to having engaged in same-sex behavior in college, though she refuses to tell a man if she and his deceased wife had an affair. In *The Bell Jar* (1979), Joanie (Donna Mitchell) tells Esther (Marilyn Hassett) that two instructors at their women's college were apparently fired for being lesbians. When Esther replies, "Good," Joanie is startled because she's sexually interested in Esther. Both are later institutionalized in the same mental hospital, and Esther finds Joanie in a field where she has committed suicide by hanging, the implicit message being that lesbians are psychologically unstable and come to a bad end.

Threesome (1994) is probably the college movie that is most open-minded about sexual orientation. Because of a mix-up by the campus housing office, Stuart (Stephen Baldwin), Eddy (Josh Charles), and Alex (Lara Flynn Boyle)

Joan (Donna Mitchell, right) is unhappy to learn that Esther (Marilyn Hassett) is homophobic, because she hopes to seduce her in *The Bell Jar* (1979, Avco Embassy).

are assigned to room together. Alex grows to like Eddy, but he doesn't respond to her because he lusts after Stuart, who in turn pursues Alex, though she says she feels no magic with him. When Eddy tells Alex he's "ambivalent about sex with girls," she says she had suspected it, but because he has yet to have sex with a man, he's really a blank slate rather than definitely gay. Stuart accuses Eddy of "checking out my butt" and asks if he's a "homo," saying it wouldn't bother him because he's secure in his sexuality and his mother has a lot of gay friends. Eddy believes gay sex is best because you know how your own type of equipment responds. Stuart counters that straight sex is better because the Bible says so, but he also claims that everyone knows lesbian sex is best for women. The three roommates agree to be just friends, but erotic tensions persist and they fall into bed together and make out naked outdoors.

Gay, lesbian, and bisexual students in other movies encounter more hostile responses when they reveal their sexual orientation. In *I Shot Andy Warhol* (1996), a radical feminist's come-on to a female psychologist who is administering a word-association test to her is strongly rejected. *I Think I Do* (1997) begins with George Washington University seniors Bob (Alex Arquette) and Brendan (Christian Maelen) roughhousing in a dorm room. Bob starts to kiss Brendan, but they break off. At a party, Bob attacks and wrestles with Brendan, who reacts this time by punching him hard on the mouth. Several years later, Brendan apologizes to Bob for hitting him and startles him by trying to kiss him. They have sex, and Brendan says he's been out of the closet for two years and now realizes that he loves Bob, explaining that he was confused in college but now wants to pick up where they left off, which the final scene suggests they do. *Ordinary Sinner* (2003) deals with the consequences of remaining closeted. Peter (Brendan Hines) is straight but awkward around Rachel (Elizabeth Banks), because he is sexually inexperienced. Alex (Kris Park), a male student who is attracted to Peter, behaves in a way that causes the death of a priest he thinks is pulling Peter away from him and Rachel, threatening his plan for the three of them to live together after graduation. This movie looks critically at homophobia, some of it religiously inspired, including one scene in a church in which a student quotes from the Bible and argues that gays should be put to death, prompting the priest to announce that he's a homosexual and to ask the student if he thinks that he should be put to death.

A gay-themed film that begins with conflict but ends with love and commitment is *Defying Gravity* (1997). Pete (Don Handfield) has moved out of his fraternity house and stopped paying dues in order to pursue a gay lifestyle. His closeted lover Griff (Daniel Chilson) occasionally stays overnight with Pete but continues to live in the house, where he has to tolerate a lot of heterosexual bantering. When Pete tells Griff he's tired of his ambivalence, Griff replies that he's interested in Pete more for sex than for a relationship. After Pete nearly dies from a gay bashing, Griff's hand is forced. A fraternity brother asks him if he's in love with Pete, and Griff says he is and has never been so sure of anything in his life. In the hospital, he vows to Pete and Pete's parents that he'll stand by him and they'll go on "defying gravity" together. At one point, Griff tells a black lesbian that he's afraid to come out, and she says it's the same with her, but by the end of the film they're both open about their sexual orientation and go to a tailgate party with their lovers and a group of straight friends. The gays and lesbians in this movie have to rely on their straight classmates for a sense of community, because the only other available support is an off-campus café catering to gays and lesbians. This is somewhat surprising because at the time the film was made, most colleges had organizations of gays and lesbians.[5]

The Last Year (2002) takes place at a coeducational Christian college where some of the students are gay (though open about it to varying degrees), some are straight, and others are gay-bashers who are encouraged by the homophobic Dean Saunders (Rand Smith). Saunders reports his suspicion that Paul (Ron Petronicolos) is gay to the student's father, but the man already knows it because his son was once arrested for an incident in a men's room. When the dean tells Paul that the school has a strict code of sexual behavior, and that he must repent of his wrongdoing and change his ways, Paul replies that he doesn't need counseling. The dean's henchmen beat up one openly gay student and tell him to leave the campus. They trash the room of Paul and his straight friend Robby (Patrick Orion Hoesterey), plant gay pornography there, and hand them dean's infraction slips for having the material. Two openly gay students are expelled, Robby is suspended, and Paul is put on probation with a warning from the dean that he needs Christian discipline but can stay in school if he obeys the rules. In his office, the dean tells Paul that he's one of his favorite students and touches him on his shoulders and leg, making it clear he's been repressing his own homosexual desires. At the end, Paul accuses the dean of murder after one of the expelled students kills himself, announces that he's leaving school, and reveals that the dean made sexual advances toward him.

Few college movies deal with bisexuality. A student in *The Girls' Room* (2000) remarks that she's had her "lesbian summer," and another one says she's bi until she graduates; both comments imply that the college years are a time for sexual experimentation. In *The Private Public* (2000), Laina (Traci Bingham), a black student, breaks up with her white lover Auggie (Jason Cornwell) by announcing that she's involved with a girl and doesn't love him anymore. In a student-made documentary, Auggie talks about how depressed he is about the breakup, and Laina praises her female lover's sexual skill.

Social Class, Race, and Ethnicity

College movies frequently use romantic and sexual relationships to introduce the themes of social class, race, and ethnicity. Compared to the neighborhoods and high schools from which most undergraduates come, campuses are places where they are less supervised by adults and more likely to meet peers from different backgrounds. Because many parents want their children to settle down with someone with a background similar to themselves, campus living increases the chance of intergenerational conflict over a student's choice of a partner. Conflict between partners sometimes develops from incompatibility caused by background differences.

Differences in the social class backgrounds of romantic partners surfaced just one year after the appearance of the first feature-length college movie. A well-to-do student in *The Thousand Dollar Husband* (1916) quits college after his father goes broke. He marries the maid in his boarding house so she can claim an inheritance, but soon he rejects her as his social inferior. Later, he returns to college and finds her transformed into a lady, and they start their marriage over. In *Plain Jane* (1916), a boy regards as beneath him a pretty girl who works in his boarding house and is in love with him. After she wins a beauty contest, he turns from studying and earning money to romancing her. Love also blossoms between young women who are working in boarding houses and the privileged students who live there in *Sweet Lavender* (1920) and *The Freshman* (1925).

These early films introduced students to romantic partners from less privileged backgrounds in off-campus residences, but this way of meeting disappeared from the screen as more undergraduates began to live in college dormitories. When students in movies from the 1930s and 1940s get romantically involved with lower- or working-class partners, they frequently meet them in other kinds of off-campus settings: taverns, gambling joints, and dance halls. *These Glamour Girls* (1939) opens with New York socialites receiving engraved invitations to house parties from the "glamour boys" at "Kingsford College." Carol (Jane Bryan) is engaged to Phil (Lew Ayres), the most desirable—that is, the richest—of the boys. A drunken Phil meets Jane (Lana Turner), a taxi dance girl, and asks her to his house party, forgetting he's already invited Carol. At a formal dinner and dance, Jane hears the other girls talking about the importance of family background, something they stress because they know of her disreputable occupation. After the dance, Jane berates the rich girls and their dates for their empty lifestyle and their snobbery.

Undergraduates in more recent movies also get romantically and sexually involved with less privileged people they meet in off-campus settings. In *Goodbye, Columbus* (1969), a Westchester (New York) County country club is where a well-to-do Radcliffe student meets a man who served in the army before taking his current job in a library. Her parents' disapproval of their relationship is obvious when the young man says that he's also sold shoes and worked in real estate and has no definite plans for the future. An Indiana University student in *Breaking Away* (1979) is attracted to a boy she thinks is from Italy, but she angrily rejects him when she learns that he's really a working-class "townie." *Fresh Horses* (1988) has privileged male students meet working-class girls who aren't in college in a disreputable off-campus location, a "perpetual house party" in the country. One student falls in love with a married sixteen-year-old high school dropout. She's sensitive to his slumming and complains that his lack of respect for her is the reason he brings her to his fraternity house only at night when everyone is asleep. Class differences also arise in *Good Will Hunting* (1997) when an MIT custodian who is on parole accuses a wealthy Harvard student of just wanting a fling with someone from the other side of the tracks. She replies that he's obsessed with her money and says she'd rather have her father alive than have his money.

College students meet people from different social classes on campus as well as off. In *The Heart of Ezra Greer* (1917), the daughter of a butler who has saved to send her to college falls in love with a wealthy student whose guardian refuses to let them marry. A young man in *Ashamed of Parents* (1921) is sent to college by his shoemaker father and his father's two friends. He falls in love with a society girl and sends the three men an announcement of his engagement party, but he tells them not to come. They show up anyway and learn that he is embarrassed by his humble background. In *The Snob* (1921), a girl strikes the name of the campus football hero from her dance card when she learns that he's working his way through college. She later takes a job as a waitress to atone for her behavior. The young man proposes marriage and will take over her father's oil business. The wealthy heroine of *Collegiate* (1926) is sent to college to keep her from marrying, but she falls in love with a football star who's working his way through school.

College movies continued to look at the consequences of class differences between romantic partners during the Great Depression. In *Huddle* (1932), Tony (Ramon Novarro), a steel mill worker and the son of Italian immigrants, wins a company scholarship to attend Yale. There Tom (Kane Richmond), the son of the mill's owner, gets angry at what he thinks is Tony's insulting treatment of his (Tom's) sister Rosalie (Madge Evans). Tony and Rosalie fall in love, but Tom and his father strongly oppose the relationship and the father convinces Tony that his daughter won't be happy living in poverty. Rosalie tells Tony she doesn't care about money and wants to marry him despite her family's objections. Another Depression era film that looks critically at class through the medium of romance is *Most Precious Thing in Life* (1934). A well-to-do student marries the working-class Ellen (Jean Arthur) over his parents' objections. When he asks her for a divorce, she agrees to let him and his parents raise their baby. Twenty years later, Ellen is working as a maid in a college dormitory when her son Chris (Richard Cromwell) arrives for his freshman year. She oversees his well-being but doesn't reveal that she's his mother. When he becomes romantically involved with the daughter of another maid, the issue of class differences resurfaces. Chris's father wants his son and the girl to wait a year or two to marry, hoping their relationship will dissolve, and Chris feels that he owes it to his father to wait. Ellen tells her ex-husband she couldn't have done a worse job than he and his wife did in raising the conceited and snobbish Chris. She calls Chris a coward for acceding to his father's demands, and in the end he sees that she's right and decides to marry the maid's daughter.

Parents oppose the marriage of their children to those from less privileged backgrounds in many other movies. In *That Hagen Girl* (1947), Mary (Shirley Temple), a junior college student whose parentage is in question, is pleased at the attention she gets from a rich boy, but his mother insists that he take his upper-class girlfriend to a fraternity dance because she's "more like one of us." Gay (Jill Corey) in *Senior Prom* (1958) is immediately attracted to Tom (Paul Hampton) when he sings at her sorority's open house, angering her rich boyfriend Carter Breed III (Tom Laughlin). When Carter learns that Gay has fallen in love with Tom, a scholarship student who holds a job, he accuses him of being attracted to the $1 million she's about to inherit, something Tom didn't know about. Gay's mother tells her that Tom isn't good enough for her, but when a song he recorded some time ago becomes a big hit, the woman is impressed and the future looks rosy for the couple. In *For Those Who Think Young* (1964), the wealthy "Nifty" Cronin (Robert Middleton) adamantly opposes his grandson Ding's (James Darren) relationship with sorority girl Sandy (Pamela Tiffin), whose education is being paid for by her guardians, two ex-vaudevillians who run an off-campus bar and comedy club. Cronin fears for the decline of his family's genes if Ding marries Sandy, but when he's revealed to be an ex-convict rather than the blueblood he pretends to be, one of Sandy's guardians acknowledges that people can rise above their past mistakes, and Cronin agrees to the couple's marriage.

Maligned by some critics for its sentimentality, *Love Story* (1970) does deal astutely with social class differences. After Oliver Barrett IV (Ryan O'Neal) meets Jenny Cavalleri (Ali MacGraw) in the library, she says he looks stupid and rich, while she's smart and poor. She connects his name with a campus building named after his great-grandfather, and she responds to her first view of his family's mansion with "Holy shit!" Oliver tries to minimize the importance of the difference in their backgrounds, his father being a successful lawyer while hers owns a bakery. His mother suggests that if money is so unimportant to him, he can give back the family fortune when he inherits it. Jenny tells Oliver that rebellion against his father is part of the reason he's attracted to her, and she admits that she loves him partly for his name and numeral. When Oliver asks his father whether he finds Jenny's class background or her Catholicism more offensive, his father asks Oliver which attracts him more. Over the Barretts' objections, but with the support of Jenny's father, Oliver and Jenny marry. Their relationship ends tragically, as does the romance in *Four Friends* (1981) between a wealthy young woman and a student who chooses college over his immigrant father's work in a steel mill.

Social-class differences between wealthy Oliver Barrett IV (Ryan O'Neal) and working-class Jennifer Cavalleri (Ali MacGraw) pose an obstacle to romance for the two Harvard University students in *Love Story* (1970, Paramount), but they get married anyway.

Racial and ethnic differences between romantic partners, differences that are often associated with social class, show up in fifteen college movies. Seven of them were released between 1915 and 1928, though only *Braveheart* (1925) is available for viewing today. White students are involved with Native Americans in three of these early films, with Latinos in two, and with an African American and a Chinese in one each. In *Betrayed* (1916), Heart of Oak (Robert Whittier) leaves his Indian reservation in the Pacific Northwest to attend college in the East, where he becomes friends with the rich and white Granville (Roy Pilcher). When Heart of Oak's sister Little Fawn (Grace de Carlton) comes to college the following year, she and Granville fall in love. After telling her she can't marry a white man, Heart of Oak finds Granville with her in a cabin and threatens to kill him, but before he can carry out the threat, Little Fawn commits suicide. Another movie dealing with an Indian-white romance is *Braveheart*, an extended version of the short film *Strongheart* (1914). Dorothy (Lillian Rich), the daughter of a mill owner, is rescued by Braveheart after her horse throws her. Three years later, he is helping his tribe pay for his college education with royalties from a novel he's written. Dorothy's brother Frank (Arthur Housman), a football teammate of Braveheart's, says it's too bad that not all the players on the team are white, and Braveheart replies that he may be red but Frank is yellow. The Indian encounters more racism at a party, where a butler stares at him for being out of place and a student suggests he's acceptable on the field but not at social gatherings. At the end, Braveheart tells Dorothy the difference in their races makes love impossible, and so they must return to their own people with just a sweet memory. That romance between an Indian and a white was the basis of three college movies during the silent era is surprising, but even more unusual is that a romance between a black student and a white one appears in just one film about college life before 1988, *The Burden of Race* (1921).

Only two college movies released between 1929 and 1993 deal with romance between partners of different racial or ethnic groups; both involve a white student and a Native American (*Life Begins in College* [1937] and *Jim Thorpe—All American* [1951]). Six movies made between 1994 and 2006 deal with romance between students of different racial or ethnic groups; whites are involved with blacks in four of them and with a student of Chinese or Indian ancestry in the other two. Several of these films—*Freshmen* (1999), *American Chai* (2001), and *The Human Stain* (2003)—show non-white students struggling with their racial or ethnic identity while romantically involved with a white partner. In *Freshmen*, San (Tom Huang) is torn between the Chinese-American Grace (Mary Chen), who brings out his fear of being seen as part of a "cute Oriental couple," and the white Dana (Wendy Speake), with whom he immediately hits it off because of their common interest in Billy Joel's music and Ayn Rand's *The Fountainhead*. A black friend tells San to stop trying to figure out whether girls like him because he's nice or because he's Chinese, and Grace says he's just an American who happens to be Chinese.

Race intersects with social class to affect romantic relationships in two movies. In *The Program* (1993), Darnell (Omar Epps) gets angry at another black student, Autumn (Halle Berry), for thinking he's good enough for her to tutor but not good enough to be her boyfriend. She says her father expects her to be with someone more like Darnell's football teammate Ray (J. Leon Pridgen II), another black student. Darnell replies that Ray's "class" and he's not, and maybe he should find another tutor, because Autumn's father wouldn't want her to fall back to Darnell's level. After Darnell excels on the field and in the classroom, he wins over Autumn's father and his future with her looks promising. In *American Chai* (2001), Sureel (Aalok Mehta) is enchanted by another Indian-American student, and his parents are ready to have them marry after a single date because of her family's wealth.

Filmmakers have incorporated romantic and sexual relationships into the majority of college movies, and they have often used these relationships to cast light on social inequality in American society. Heterosexual romance has been a staple of college films since the first one was released in 1915, but intimacy between straight students became explicitly sexual only in the 1960s. No openly gay, lesbian, or bisexual student appeared in a college movie until 1966, and fully developed characters with a same-sex orientation did not show up with any regularity until the 1990s.

6

GOING GREEK

Life on many campuses was dominated by fraternities and sororities from the 1920s until the 1960s, though no more than one-third of undergraduates were members. Greek-letter organizations sponsored most of the parties and dances, supplied most of the leaders for extracurricular activities, and pledged most of the high-profile athletes. Students who remained independent, by choice or otherwise, looked up to the Greeks, whose greater wealth and commitment to having fun led them to spend more on entertainment, clothes, and drink.[1] In recent years, some colleges have banned Greek-letter societies; where they continue to exist, many students don't join them, so their importance to campus life has diminished. Because those who do join usually do so as freshmen, for them rushing, pledging, and initiation are important aspects of their first year of college. For many, the fraternity or sorority remains central to their social life until they graduate; for some, it continues to be important for years thereafter.

Greeks in the movies are usually portrayed as uninterested in academic work but intent on partying, drinking, and pursuing sex. Fraternity members and, to a lesser degree, sorority members have behaved more rudely in movies made since *Animal House* was released in 1978, probably because of a change in standards about what can be shown on the screen rather than because of any major change in the behavior of real students. Several older films are sharply critical of the elitism of Greeks, but recent ones are more likely to assume they are snobbish and boorish, traits that might seem mutually self-contradictory. Earlier movies present fraternities and sororities as useful for finding a romantic partner who will become a spouse, while recent ones are more likely to show them as places to get drunk and hook up. Fraternity and sorority members are more likely than students living in dormitories or off campus to engage in binge drinking, defined as five consecutive drinks for men and four for women.[2] Indeed, the leaders of these organizations are even more likely to binge-drink than members who are less involved in the organization.[3] Pledges are often required to consume potentially life-threatening quantities of alcohol during their initiation, though movies such as *Going Greek* (2001) treat their drunkenness and vomiting as humorous. Greeks are especially heavy users of alcohol; students who want to drink a lot are more likely to join fraternities and sororities, because to a large extent these organizations exist to party and today that means drinking, and because alcohol consumption in chapter houses is shielded from administrators and the police.

Cinematic depictions of fraternities and sororities can influence the way these organizations are perceived by prospective pledges, active members, alumni, faculty, administrators, and the general public. Freshmen who rush a fraternity after seeing *Animal House* (1978) or one of its imitators might think that drunkenness, vandalism, food fights, and sexual aggression are acceptable, even expected, behavior and model their own actions on what they saw on the screen. The president of the State University of New York at Buffalo said that property damage on his campus nearly doubled in the year after that film was released and claimed that other schools had also experienced an increase in vandalism.[4] Administrators and faculty members at many colleges have become more hostile toward fraternities and sororities in recent years, and some of that change might be attributable to the way that Greek life has been portrayed in the movies.

Rushing

The presence of fraternities and sororities on campus confronts first-year students with the decision of whether to "go Greek," assuming they get a bid to membership. They have to make this decision at a time when they are vulnerable: Many are away from home for the first extended length of time, and most have not yet found a comfortable niche in the campus community. Greek-letter organizations offer a family-like way of life, a place they can live and be part of a group that provides intimacy and support. Some first-year students refuse to join, complaining that Greek organizations choose their members on the basis of class background and physical appearance rather than character. Even those tapped for membership sometimes question the selection process.

Greek-letter societies offer their members friendship, housing, a dining facility, an active social life, access to alcohol, opportunities for community service, social contacts, and tutoring. Those who join derive varying degrees of prestige from belonging, the relative desirability of each house on campus being as clearly defined as the ranking of colleges by the *U.S. News and World Report*. Students are quick to show off their affiliations with both highly regarded colleges and their Greek-letter societies, as do young men at a country club party in *Goodbye, Columbus* (1969).

Some students do not rush a fraternity or sorority to avoid the emotional trauma they would suffer if they were rejected by all houses or got bids only from undesirable ones. Explaining why she never pledged a sorority, a student in *Final Exam* (1981) says the year before, a girl committed suicide after being turned down for membership. A rush party proves only somewhat less upsetting for Seth (Tom Brown) in *This Side of Heaven* (1934). A friend who expects an automatic bid from a prestigious house because his father was a member tells Seth that to get a bid he has to be more assertive, self-promoting, friendly, and talkative. The socially awkward Seth, who admits he isn't good at sports, brags about his family to an active member and pretends to be a friend of a quarterback who belongs to the fraternity. The active brothers think Seth is egotistical and don't extend him an invitation to join. He's embarrassed and feels something must be wrong with him. On his way home from college, he has a near-fatal car accident, but he tells his father he didn't intend to kill himself, because he wouldn't do that to the family. He does acknowledge that when his car turned over, he hoped he would die so he wouldn't have to face his friends again. Gnossos (Barry Primus) also fails to get a bid in *Been Down So Long It Looks Like Up to Me* (1971), but in this case his offensive behavior at a rush party is intentional. Repelled by the vapid brothers in their conventional jackets and ties, he smokes marijuana in the bathroom as they drink beer. He calls one brother, the crew's coxswain, a dwarf, suggests another is gay, and chants an Indian mantra at dinner. Gnossos's behavior reflects the antagonism toward fraternities that was common on many campuses during the Vietnam War era when the movie was made.

Petey (William Holden) in *Those Were the Days* (1940) is aggressively rushed by three fraternities as soon as he arrives on campus. The boys in one house sing to him, light his pipe, and tout their organization. A member of a second fraternity poses as a real estate agent and tells the first group they have to vacate their house because the rent hasn't been paid for six months. Other members of the fraternity try to set fire to the house and persuade Petey to join their organization. The brothers of a third fraternity, Beta Pi, disguise themselves as police officers and tell Petey they're arresting him for arson, but real officers arrive and arrest them for impersonating officers. They and Petey are taken to court, but when one of the defendants whistles his fraternity song, the judge recognizes the tune because he was once a member of that house, and he dismisses the charges. Petey joins Beta Pi.

Movies critical of Greek-letter organizations emphasize the criteria they use to select their members: economic privilege, race, physical attractiveness, athletic prowess, and popularity. Howie (Richard Long) in *All American* (1953) tells his influential father not to recommend the working-class Nick (Tony Curtis) for admission to his college, arguing that Nick's clothing and manner of speaking will be out of place on the genteel campus. Nick's skill at football wins him admission anyway. In a rush party at the Sentinel Club, an organization much like a Greek-letter society, Nick announces that he isn't going to play football. When Howie tells him he was only being rushed because he played football, Nick pays for his beer and walks out. He changes his mind

In *Been Down So Long It Looks Like Up to Me* (1971, Paramount), Gnossos "Paps" Pappadopoulis (Barry Primus) greets fraternity members at a rush party in such a way as to guarantee that he will not be asked to join. His hostile attitude toward Greek life was common on many campuses during the Vietnam War era when the film was made.

and joins the team, performs well on the field, and gets a more conventional haircut. The club again asks him to join, and he accepts. Then he changes his mind, saying he wants to be liked for himself and not for his prowess on the field. The ability to play football well is also a criterion for fraternity membership in *Going Greek* (2001). The nerdy Gil (Dublin James) is sure he'll get a bid from the coolest fraternity on campus because his father was a member. His cousin Jake (Dylan Bruno), an outstanding football player, goes to a rush party with Jake, even though he doesn't want to join. Jake is offered membership because he can help the house win a game against a rival fraternity, and Gil gets a bid to induce his cousin to join. Gil quits when he learns of the package deal, but after a member tells him he got the bid on his own and the other pledges beg him to return, Gil comes back. He catches the winning touchdown pass in the big game and is carried off the field, finally accepted by the brothers, though only after he's proved to be an asset to the house.

Another student who is offered membership because of what he can bring to a fraternity is war veteran Johnny Kilroy (Jackie Cooper) in *Kilroy Was Here* (1947). Johnny has the same last name as a famous cartoon character whose picture was seen everywhere during World War II, and a friend claims he was the model for the character. When Rodney (Rand Brooks) hears about "the real Kilroy," he invites him to dinner at his fraternity house. Johnny's roommate describes the fraternity as the snootiest bunch on campus, but Johnny replies that college is more than lectures and books, it's also the friends you make. Johnny pledges the house with another student, who is treated in demeaning fashion while Johnny is deferred to because of his fame. When the brothers learn that Johnny is a fraud, they consider blackballing him, but Rodney fears this might lead to criticism that they accepted him just because he was a celebrity. After Johnny is suspended from school for getting into a brawl at a dance, he complains about the fraternity's rules for deciding who is good enough to join, finally realizing he was wanted for his name and not for who he really is. He compares this to his experience in the army, where it was the man and not the name that mattered. Johnny is reinstated in the college by the dean, but he moves out of the fraternity house.

College movies also look critically at sororities for the way they choose their members. In *Sorority House* (1939), Alice (Anne Shirley) leaves her small town for college, which her father pays for with money he's borrowed using his small grocery store as collateral. One of Alice's roommates calls sororities "the most important thing in college," because membership means the right marriage and the right kind of life after college, and girls who don't get in are "simply nothing." When Alice's boyfriend convinces the sorority girls her father is a rich man who owns a chain of grocery stores, she's invited to all the rush parties. Her father shows up unexpectedly at a parents' night rush party, and she is so ashamed of him that she sends him away. She recognizes how insensitive she was and realizes she was rushed only because the active members thought that her father was wealthy. She rejects the bids she gets, and her roommate is so devastated when she doesn't get any that she tries to kill herself.

Take Care of My Little Girl (1951) also questions the effects of sorority rushing. Liz (Jeanne Crain), the daughter of a "Tri-U" alumna, begins her first year of college by living in the town's most expensive hotel in order to impress the members of the sorority. Actives evaluate rushees by their style of clothing and the brands of their handbags. Liz gets a bid from Tri-U, but she is upset when the members blackball a friend before she can be initiated. She says belonging to Tri-U would help her socially and professionally and acknowledges that there are some good things about sororities, but in the end she concludes that they don't outweigh the hurt that is caused. She quits the house, the first pledge to do so in more than a decade.[5]

Other pledges in the movies also see their friends wounded when they

Alice Fisher (Anne Shirley) seems to be having a good time at a sorority rush party dancing with Bill Loomis (James Ellison) in *Sorority House* (1939, RKO), but later she refuses to join a house because of the snobbery she finds there.

aren't offered membership. A boy is invited to join the best fraternity on campus in *Freshman Year* (1938), but he turns down the bid because his friends from less prominent families aren't considered. He later joins when one of the friends is offered membership. In *Saturday's Hero* (1951), when a student's roommate gets a bid and he doesn't, he is dejected and says fraternity life isn't for him. Fraternity members in *Freshmen* (1999) chat with a white student at a rush party but ignore his Chinese-American classmate; only the white student gets a bid. A friendship falls apart in *Followers* (2000) when a black student doesn't get a bid to an exclusive fraternity that two white friends are asked to join.

Snobbery based on differences in social class, race, and ethnicity is a charge often leveled against fraternities and sororities. In *Sis Hopkins* (1941), wealthy sorority girl Carol (Susan Hayward) is embarrassed when her hillbilly cousin Sis (Judy Canova) enrolls in her college. Envious of Sis when she gets into the Fall Frolics show, Carol plays a trick to get her expelled. She tells Sis her sorority wants Sis to join and instructs her to come to a secret initiation at the local burlesque house. Carol calls the police to report an indecent performance at the theater, where she pulls on a thread that causes Sis's dress to fall off while she's on stage. Sis escapes from the police, but the sorority members feel bad about the prank and offer her a bid over Carol's objection. Class bias in this movie is limited to Carol, while the others are open to pledging a girl from a less privileged background.

Social class and ethnicity are used to determine suitability for fraternity membership in *The Pride of the Yankees* (1942). Lou Gehrig (Gary Cooper), whose German immigrant mother is a cook at the fraternity house where Lou waits on tables, is supported for membership by most of the brothers, probably because his athletic skills are weighed more heavily than his social background, but one active member doesn't want to extend Lou a bid because he believes the house should "maintain a certain standard." Class and ethnicity are also considered in *A Swingin' Affair* (1963). Johnny Kwalski (William Wellman, Jr.) pays for college by boxing professionally, a disreputable job that he keeps secret from his fellow students. He tells his mother, a potential source of embarrassment because she works in the gym where he trains, that he wants to join a fraternity for the connections he can make with prominent people who will help him advance in his chosen career of engineering. When his rich girlfriend learns of Johnny's working-class background, she says he has his world and she has hers, asking, "Can you see your mother at my mother's club?" During his fraternity initiation, Johnny is verbally harassed by an alumnus who asks, when he hears Johnny's last name, "Are you sure you're not in the wrong school? Sounds like a player on the Notre Dame football team." Johnny says he wants to join the fraternity to be with gentlemen, and the man questions whether a working-class kid should belong to an organization of gentlemen. Johnny walks out of the initiation, but after he learns that the taunting was a routine part of the initiation and he is cheered by the fraternity brothers during a boxing match, he decides they would have supported him all along had he been more open with them, and he joins the fraternity. *Fraternity Row* (1977) also looks critically at discrimination, in this case during the 1950s at the "finest small, private college in the East." Gamma Nu Pi is said to have "the best athletes, the most devious politicians, and the brightest scholars. None of course [is] Jewish or black, Oriental or on the G.I. Bill." Nearly all the members are from affluent families and attended exclusive private schools, and the traditional pairing of the college's fraternities and sororities guarantees "a social hierarchy, inviolate, insensitive, and immaculate."

Class background is also a criterion for membership in a fraternal organization in *The Skulls* (2000). The movie's title refers to a secret society at an unnamed university, but it's obviously Skull and Bones at Yale, an organization and university that are also depicted in *The Good Shepherd* (2006). In *The Skulls*, Luke (Joshua Jackson) is a working-class townie who holds a job in a college dining hall and is shocked when he gets a $45,000 term bill. He resists joining the Skulls, but when he learns that its alumni can get him into Harvard Law School and will pay his way through, membership is more appealing. A friend warns him that if an organization is secret and elite, it can't be good, reminding him that they've made fun of "private school dicks" for three years and now he's planning to become one. The elitist pretensions of fraternal organizations are satirized in *Old School* (2003). Three thirtyish party animals who are not students set up a bachelor pad near campus. When they learn the area has been rezoned and their house can be used only for collegiate purposes, they decide to form a fraternity to avoid eviction. One of them says the organization will be a non-exclusive, egalitarian brotherhood in which social status and age play no role in the selection of members. True to their word, they pledge social misfits and even an old man they kidnap off the street.

In recent years, many fraternities and sororities have responded to the criticism that they are elitist by becoming more racially and ethnically diverse. This trend is poked fun at in *Animal House* (1978) by contrasting the worst fraternity on campus, Delta Tau Chi, with the best one, the staid and politically correct Omegas, whose rush party features a group of potential pledges that includes an African, an Arab, a Jew, and a blind student in a wheelchair. In similar fashion, *Pumpkin* (2002) satirizes sororities by having a house president admire its rushees, who include a "blue-chip" rich white girl and two "diversity girls," a Filipina with Caucasian features and a Whitney Houston lookalike.

Hazing

Fraternity and sorority pledges are required by active members to endure humiliations, pranks, and mean-spirited, even life-threatening acts before they become full-fledged members. This hazing, which can occur with or without the pledge's consent, encompasses all intentional acts that result in mental anguish, physical discomfort or injury, humiliation, or harassment.[6] A girl in *Sorority Babes in the Slimeball Bowl-O-Rama* (1988) calls hazing "institutionalized sadism."

There has been at least one recorded death from fraternity hazing every year since 1970. Even when hazing results in death, it is rarely punished, despite the fact that most colleges and states have banned it. An exception is the incarceration of four men who were involved in the 2005 death of Matthew Carrington by "water torture" during his initiation into a fraternity banned from the campus of Chico State University in California. Sororities are less likely than fraternities to haze pledges in life-threatening ways, relying instead on demeaning tasks and embarrassing stunts.

Those who do not belong to fraternities and sororities sometimes wonder why pledges willingly subject themselves to abuse and ridicule. Making membership difficult to attain confers prestige on these organizations by making them appear to be worth the sacrifice. The pledgemaster in *The Dream Machine* (1990) tells his charges that the harder it is to get in the fraternity, the more they'll love it. Even pledges who worry about hazing rarely change their minds about joining; those who try to quit before initiation are pressured by fellow pledges and active members to stick it out.

Hazing has a long history in the movies. A pledge is required to recite the Gettysburg Address in a nightclub while wearing only a towel in *Most Precious Thing in Life* (1934). His dorm maid, who is actually his mother, tells him that in his father's day, pledges were beaten with hoses and tied to railroad tracks and urges him to go through with the initiation when he wants to quit. The Hell Week that supposedly tests a pledge's character and integrity in *Take Care of My Little Girl* (1951) includes being called a "a lowly one" by the sorority sisters, shining their shoes, and eating off the floor. A middle-aged pledge in *High Time* (1960) has to scrub the floor, wash a car's whitewall tires, and dress like a woman and get an elderly college trustee to dance with him.

Fraternity pledge Chris Kelsey (Richard Cromwell) is forced to deliver the Gettysburg Address in a nightclub while wearing only a towel in *Most Precious Thing in Life* **(1934, Columbia).**

In *Class of '44* (1973, Warner Brothers), which takes place during World War II, pledges are stuffed into a telephone booth and have to answer the phone and pass it to the person who has been called.

In *Class of '44* (1973), pledges have raw eggs dropped on their heads and are stuffed into a telephone booth, where they have to answer the ringing phone and pass it to the right person or else be paddled. When the active members in *Final Exam* (1981) learn that a pledge has given his girlfriend his fraternity pin, they "tree" him, which consists of tying him to a tree in his underpants, covering him with shaving cream, and throwing ice water down his underpants. In *Rush Week* (1989), a professor lectures on the human digestive system, and when a cadaver is wheeled in, a fraternity pledge jumps up from the gurney and pretends to strangle the professor, causing shrieks of laughter. A pledge in *The Prodigy* (1999) has to check a children's book out of the library while wearing only underpants, bunny ears, and a tail. During Hell Week, the pledges in *Going Greek* (2001) are required to enter a classroom with beer kegs tied to each ankle and jog into another one in shorts and sing "I'm a Little Teapot" while standing on a table.

"Mooning" is a favorite prank in post–*Animal House* (1978) movies. In *King Frat* (1979), a university president dies from shock when fraternity brothers flash their bare buttocks at him. House members in *Fandango* (1985) turn out the lights and moon the front door to surprise a brother they are expecting, but a middle-aged couple enters instead; they explain that they just wanted to see how their son has been living for the past four years.

Fraternity members' obsession with buttocks, at least in the movies, also shows up in a form of hazing that first appears in *Class of '44* (1973). In that film, pledges are made to pick olives off a block of ice with their bare buttocks and move them around the room. Whether this stunt was really a part of fraternity initiations in the 1940s, when the film takes place, is uncertain, but it appears regularly in movies released since 1973. A pledge in *Young Warriors* (1983) has to pick an olive off a block of ice in the same manner and drop it into a martini and drink it. *The Dream Machine* (1990) replaces olives with marshmallows, with the pledges who lose a race having to eat the marshmallows they've carried between their buttocks. *Pledge Night* (1988) varies the stunt slightly by forcing two teams of pledges to pick up cherries from a block of ice with their bare buttocks and race to a designated spot; the captain of the losing team has to swallow the cherries deposited by the winning team.

Early college movies sometimes use pledges' interest in romance to humiliate them. In *Nobody's Fool* (1921), an unattractive girl is asked to a fraternity dance as an initiation prank. Members of the house become attracted to her when they learn she's inherited a lot of money, but she doubts their intentions and rejects them. A pledge is required to ask a frumpy, studious girl to a dance in *Her First Romance* (1940), but she turns the tables by getting a make-over, demonstrating her extraordinary singing voice, and rejecting him and his fraternity brothers for an older man. In *The Pride of the Yankees* (1942), a naïve Lou Gehrig (Gary Cooper) is tricked by a flirtatious blonde into thinking that she's attracted to him. The fraternity brothers who put her up to the stunt eavesdrop on their conversation and repeat it verbatim as Lou waits on their tables. When he realizes he was set up, he attacks the instigator.

Fraternities and sororities in more recent movies frequently embarrass their pledges with sexual stunts. In *Didn't You Hear...* (1983), a topless girl is pushed into a boy's dorm room, where she tells him that as part of her initiation he has to drop his pants or she'll yell "rape." She starts to scream, so he lowers his pants and she attaches her pledge pin to his underpants. Active members outside his window photograph the scene, laugh, and sing a sorority song. In *Dream Trap* (1990), sorority sisters evaluate each pledge's skill at faking an orgasm. Pledge Half-Pint (Spike Lee) is mocked for his virginity throughout *School Daze* (1988). The house's president and pledgemaster tells his girlfriend to prove her dedication to his fraternity by having sex with Half-Pint. She reluctantly goes along with the "Gamma slammer," but her hypocritical boyfriend rejects her for caring too much about his fraternity.

A stunt that first appears in *Class of '44* (1973) requires a pledge to wear a "pull me" sign that is attached to a bell around his genitals and hangs outside his pants. The prank is varied a bit in *Pledge Night* (1988), in which each pledge has one end of a string tied to his penis and the other end to a corn cob. He has to tell any girl who asks what the corn cob is for to pull it and find out, causing him great pain. Each pledge in *Young Warriors* (1983) has to drop his pants to have the size of his penis ridiculed. A string attached to a brick is then tied to his penis, and he has to drop the brick out a window. The string has plenty of slack, so no one is hurt. While the active brothers listen from another room as the pledges drop their bricks out the window, one boy screams in agony, but he has tricked the brothers and isn't really hurt. They commend him for his cleverness. *Going Greek* (2001) goes beyond these phallocentric shenanigans by having pledges participate in a "circle jerk," the last to "pop" being required to eat a cookie onto which they've all ejaculated.

The traditional way to humiliate pledges is to strike them with a wooden paddle that has the fraternity's or sorority's letters on it. This practice appears in *Most Precious Thing in Life* (1934), shows up again in *Campus Rhythm* (1943), and takes on sadistic overtones in *Sorority Girl* (1957). In the last film, an active member not only paddles a pledge and forces her to do sit-ups despite a sore stomach, she threatens to blackball her if she doesn't do her laundry and other personal favors, assignments that violate house rules. Fraternity members in *School Daze* (1988) hit their pledges with an outsize paddle. In *Pledge Night* (1988), after receiving a paddle stroke a pledge has to say, "Thank you, sir. May I have another, sir?" Several low-budget films associate paddling with sexual gratification. In *Sorority Babes in the Slimeball Bowl-O-Rama* (1988), sorority pledges wearing only panties are paddled hard while male voyeurs peer through a window. *Witch Academy* (1993) drops any pretense of hazing and has the only three members of a sorority paddle one another just because they enjoy it.

Theft and vandalism are sometimes required of pledges. In *The Initiation* (1984), sorority pledges have to steal a night watchman's uniform and badge from a closed shopping mall. Two girls in *Sorority Babes in the Slimeball Bowl-O-Rama* are told to break into a closed bowling alley and steal a trophy. Pledges in *The Skulls* (2000) risk their lives to steal a weathervane from atop the chapter house of a rival secret society. In *Night of the Creeps* (1986), a pledgemaster tells two pledges that before they can join the house they must steal a corpse from a laboratory and deposit it on the front steps of another fraternity. A pledge in *Voodoo* (1995) has to steal a corpse from a morgue; a fraternity brother jumps up from the body bag, scares him, and then makes him steal a real corpse.

Another form of hazing is to abandon pledges some distance from campus and require them to find their way back by a certain deadline. Pledges in *The Prodigy* (1999) are deserted in just their underpants nearly two hundred miles from campus and told to get back to the fraternity house by sundown. In *The Hazing* (1977), pledges in jock straps are dropped off in the mountains

134 Campus Life in the Movies

The paddling and other abuse of pledge Ellie Marshall (Barbara Crane) by sorority sister Sabra Tanner (Susan Cabot) in *Sorority Girl* (1957, American International) is crueler than the hazing seen in most college films.

and instructed to run five miles to a lodge in the near-freezing weather. When Barney (Charles Martin Smith) apparently dies, active members tell fellow pledge Craig (Jeff East) that hazing is prohibited and everyone could get into trouble for the accidental death. They fake a skiing accident to account for Barney's death.

The hazing of pledges in college movies has become less playful and more dangerous over time. A pledge in *Fraternity Row* (1977) chokes to death when forced to swallow raw liver without chewing it, much like the actual death of a pledge at the University of Southern California in 1959, about the time the movie takes place. In *Pledge Night* (1988), a zombie returns to take vengeance on the current occupants of a house that two decades earlier belonged to his fraternity, which disbanded after he died by being forced into a tub of acid during his initiation. Current residents of the house threaten blindfolded pledges with a hot branding iron. Ice is thrust against their bare bottoms, and they scream when they initially mistake the sensation for heat. Everyone is shocked when one pledge is actually branded with a hot iron. Initiates are also branded in *The Skulls* (2000), and because their organization is a secret one, they are given expensive wristwatches to cover the marks. In *Voodoo* (1995), a transfer student joins a fraternity to have a place to live, not knowing that he is being pledged so he can be sacrificed in a voodoo ritual and give the house president eternal life.

Horror and slasher movies often locate fraternity and sorority initiations in scary settings far from campus. A pledgemistress in *The Day It Came to Earth* (1979) tells prospective members that to become active they have to stay overnight in a haunted house, where a rampaging monster terrorizes them and a group of fraternity members who have shown up to scare them with pranks. In *Hell Night* (1981), a joint fraternity and sorority initiation takes place in an eerie mansion where years before a man killed his wife, his three children, and himself, but left a demented son alive. Three active members come to the house to play tricks on the pledges, and the mad son kills all but one of the intruders. Pledges in *Blood Sisters* (1987) have to stay all night in a haunted house, which was once a notorious brothel where a boy killed a prostitute and her client. The boy, now a college student, murders the pledges with repeated stabbings that simulate sexual intercourse. In *The Unnamable* (1988), fraternity and sorority members and pledges are killed by a creature from another dimension in a deserted house where their organizations are holding a joint initiation.

The repeated use of remote settings for initiations and the recurrence of the same stunts from movie to movie might be due to the simple fact that they accurately mirror the practices of real fraternities and sororities. However, the similarity of these scenes could also be due to filmmakers' recycling of material from earlier movies. The places where real fraternities and sororities hold their initiations and the stunts they require of their pledges might even be influenced by what imaginative screenwriters and directors put on the screen.

Sexism, Rape, and Homophobia

Bluto (John Belushi) first appears in *Animal House* (1978) holding a beer, belching, and urinating into the bushes and then on the shoes of two freshmen who have shown up for a rush party. The film, which is based on one of the screenwriters' experiences at Dartmouth in the early 1960s, is reportedly less offensive, misogynistic, and racist than earlier versions of its script, but it nonetheless set a new standard for vulgar behavior in college movies.[7] One-upping *Animal House*'s perhaps unintentional allusion to female genitalia in naming its fraternity the Delta house, the imitative *King Frat* (1979) doubles the pun and calls its fraternity members the Pi Delts. Another movie, *Mugsy's Girls* (1985), was originally released as *Delta Pi*. *Revenge of the Nerds* (1984) includes a Pi sorority and an Omega Mu house of overweight girls nicknamed the Mus, as in mooing cows. *Rush Week* (1989) includes the "first homosexual fraternity" on campus, Gamma Alpha Epsilon (GAE), which is tormented by the Beta Delta Beta house, whose motto is "Booze, Dope, and Bimbos." *Fraternity Demon* (1992) includes a Sigma Upsilon Xi (SUX) fraternity whose sister sorority is Alpha Sigma Sigma (ASS). The recreational activity of a fraternity in *The Prodigy* (1999) is apparent from its name, Kappa Epsilon Gamma (KEG). In *Sorority Boys* (2002), the Kappa Omicron Kappa (KOK) fraternity torments the sorority house across the street, Delta Omicron Gamma (DOG). A fraternity of nerds in *Van Wilder* (2002) is called Lambda Omega Omega (LOO), bringing to mind both a toilet and the word loser. Another fraternity in the film is named Delta Iota Kappa, the DIKs.

Consistent with some of these acronyms, fraternity men in movies released since the late 1970s often exploit women sexually. In *Revenge of the Nerds* (1984), the geeky members of Lambda Lambda Lambda stage a panty raid on a sorority, set up a live-feed video camera in the house to watch the girls undress, and win the Homecoming Carnival competition by selling plates of whipped cream that conceal photos of the nude girls. Fraternity brothers in *Killer Party* (1986) make sexist comments as three sorority pledges ride by on their bicycles, and later they scare girls out of a hot tub and videotape them as they flee. When local girls who aren't college students are exploited by fraternity members at a "Hell Week Pig Party" in *Pledge Night* (1988), a sorority girl describes them as ignorant townies who probably work in a factory or five-and-dime store. Boys in *Fraternity Demon* (1992) want to attract more sorority girls to their parties and their beds, but they're conflicted between pledging more athletes, who would enhance their house's reputation, and more techies, who would boost its grade point average. The girls describe the brothers as animals, geeks, and jocks and are worried enough about attending a house party that when the boys arrive to pick them up, they insist on driving their own cars so they can leave whenever they want. Fraternities in several films designate an area of the house for sexual conquest; it's called the Sex Room in *Animal House* (1978), the Bordello Room in *Young Warriors* (1983), the Bone Room in *School Daze* (1988), and the Boom Boom Room in *Pledge Night* (1988).

In *The Contender* (2000), Senator Laine Hanson (Joan Allen) is nominated to fill the vacant office of U.S. vice-president, but a rumor that she was involved in a fraternity gangbang as a freshman threatens her appointment. A former member of the fraternity vows the story is true, but Hanson refuses to discuss her personal life, even to deny the story. Later she reveals to the president that as part of her sorority initiation she had to go to a fraternity and have sex with two brothers. She refused to do this, but she did get drunk and go the house, where a boy urged her to perform fellatio. She rejected his suggestion and immediately left the house, but the next day the rumor was all over campus that she had been part of a gangbang. Two fraternity alumni eventually sign affidavits that no such thing happened, clearing the way for approval of Hanson's appointment. Even though the incident did not occur, the film suggests that unwanted sexual activity is normal behavior in Greek-letter organizations: It was a part of the sorority's initiation, fraternity members expected compliance with the tradition, and students on campus readily believed the story of a fraternity gangbang.

Fraternity members in *Sorority Boys* (2002) humiliate girls who are unwilling to have sex with them, lobbing dildos at the sorority house across the street. One brother tells a pledge to increase the number of girls he scores with by lowering the quality of the ones he goes after. Three members who are exiled from the house gain a new perspective when they try to get back in during a party by dressing as women, only to be kicked out after having a net thrown over them. The girls in the house across the street offer them free room and board for the semester if they'll become pledges, because they are in dire need of more members. The boys move in and continue to pass as girls. One of them becomes increasingly infuriated at the demeaning way he's treated by the men on campus. "She" is also the victim of a fraternity tradition in which a girl who has sex with a brother has to walk a gauntlet of mocking men and have her photo taken and hung on the "Wall of Shame" with those of the house members' other conquests. At the end, one "sorority boy" takes off his wig and angrily asks his brothers if they treat women like garbage just to feel like men.

Social scientists who have studied sexual assault on campus have concluded that young men who come to college conditioned to prey on women may be drawn to fraternities that have reputations for such behavior, but that all-male groups such as fraternities and sports teams can foster and reinforce attitudes and behavior conducive to sexual assault. Heavy alcohol consumption, the sexual objectification of women, an emphasis on "scoring," group secrecy, and a shared belief that sexual aggression is normal increase the likelihood of rape by members of these all-male groups, especially when punishment for such behavior is lenient or nonexistent. The heavy use of alcohol in fraternities lowers inhibitions, supports sexual aggression as expected behavior while drunk, and reduces respect for inebriated women.[8] When the social chairman in *Defying Gravity* (1997) fails to provide beer for a party, an annoyed brother warns that frat boys without booze are scary; some would argue that frat boys with booze are even scarier. Inconsistent with the belief that fraternities are conducive to sexual assault are the results of a national survey that found that only one-tenth of female college students who had been sexually assaulted said the attack had occurred in a fraternity house; 60 percent of the victims were assaulted in their own residence, and 30 percent were attacked in other off-campus living quarters.[9]

The definition of masculinity as that which is neither feminine nor homosexual has been linked to homophobia among fraternity members. Often this takes the form of using pejorative terms to question the heterosexual manliness of members who aren't sleeping with enough women. In *Going Greek* (2001), a fraternity member suggests that a new initiate might be gay because he doesn't seem to be interested in girls. Everyone is amazed when the supermodel girlfriend the nerd has been talking about shows up at a party and kisses him passionately. Fraternity members in *Defying Gravity* (1997) discuss the need for damage-control after one of their brothers is the victim of a gay bashing; they worry that if rival houses make a big deal of their having a gay member, it could hurt them in the upcoming rush. When two brothers are arrested for the assault, one says he thought the victim was "just some fag." Other brothers side with the victim and his lover, who is also a member of the fraternity. This is the only college movie that examines what fraternity membership might mean to gay students, despite evidence that many of them relied on these organizations for male camaraderie before the development of campus organizations specifically for gays.[10]

Academic Performance

College movies often portray fraternities and, to a lesser degree, sororities as academically deficient and unsupportive of members who want to do well in their coursework. This image has been especially common since the release of *Animal House* (1978), but it appeared in earlier movies as well. The sorority members in *Take Care of My Little Girl* (1951) are more concerned about not flunking than about getting good grades; one girl says they aren't expected to be Phi Beta Kappas, just to get comfortable grades so they don't have to de-pledge the sorority. A fraternity member in *The Monkey's Uncle* (1965) says his house has the best athletes and the best dances, and it always has one member who is a good student. Another brother remarks, "We figured one brain in the chapter was enough." The Delta fraternity in *Animal House* (1978) has had five consecutive semesters of deficient grades, to which one student has contributed his 0.00 grade point average. Poor academic performance is alluded to in *Defying Gravity* (1997) by a black student who reacts to a racist comment by a white boy by telling her friend that the low grades the fraternity guys get are good for the class curve and help boost their own grades. In *Van Wilder* (2002), the president of a fraternity of nerds wants to throw a party to counteract his house's "stigma" of having the highest GPA on campus.

When fraternity members manage to pass their courses in college movies, they often do so by taking shortcuts and cheating. Fraternities did not invent cheating, but the subculture that emerges from these groups can perpetuate attitudes and techniques that make academic dishonesty more likely. A 1926 survey found that nearly three-fourths of fraternity members, compared to a bare majority of other students, admitted to cheating at least once in college.[11] Research from the early 1950s supports the conclusion that Greeks are more likely than their unaffiliated classmates to cheat.[12] Consistent with this study, the house in *Fraternity Row* (1977), which takes place in the 1950s, is praised for having such great test files that its members don't need to study. In *Final Exam* (1981), a fraternity stages a "terrorist attack" as a diversion to allow a member to cheat on an exam and get the grade he needs so that his parents will keep making payments on his car. After a pledge in the movie breaks into a professor's office to steal an exam, he's commended by an active member as follows: "You might be Gamma material after all." When house members run out of the amphetamines they need to stay awake to study for an exam, one suggests doing it "the old-fashioned way" by stealing an exam.

Positive Images of Greek Life

Few movies portray fraternities and sororities as organizations that serious, tolerant, and well-behaved students would want to join. Even when a sorority supports a charity, does community service, and tries to diversify its membership in *Pumpkin* (2002), its members are still presented as being more interested in winning a sorority-of-the-year contest and improving their image on campus than in doing good deeds. In a similar vein, at the start of *The Prodigy* (1999) a fraternity engaged in community service is doing it only because it's a condition of being on probation for having had an underage girl at a party, though at the end of the film the brotherhood begins a well-intentioned program to tutor inner-city students.

An oft-cited benefit of belonging to a Greek-letter organization is the formation of close friendships that sustain one during the college years and provide useful contacts after graduation. A girl mentions the importance of the beautiful friendships she'll form in a sorority as a major reason for wanting to pledge a house in *Take Care of My Little Girl* (1951). *The Skulls* (2000) focuses on the intense bonding that characterizes a secret fraternal organization and the strengthening of that attachment by alumni who provide undergraduate members with money, gifts, and guaranteed admission to top graduate programs. A fraternity in *Sorority Boys* (2002) holds an annual cruise on which alumni are wined and dined so graduating seniors can make contacts that will land them high-paying jobs. In *Pledge Night* (1988), a young man explains to his hippie mother the importance of fraternities by pointing out that most CEOs and members of Congress once belonged to such organizations. His testimonial loses credibility when he and his fellow pledges are forced to drink smelly cocktails and have bugs set loose on their honey-smeared faces. Their pledgemaster snidely comments that the great institution of the college fraternity shapes the future leaders of the nation.

Elle Woods (Reese Witherspoon, center) and her sorority sisters enjoy themselves on a California campus in *Legally Blonde* (2001, Metro-Goldwyn-Mayer). In the sequel, *Legally Blonde 2: Red, White, and Blonde* (2003, Metro-Goldwyn-Mayer), Elle is a lawyer who uses her sorority network to enlist support for an animal rights march.

Even the bonding of fraternity and sorority members is shown to have a downside in the movies. In *Among Brothers* (2005), three fraternity members burn down a house to conceal the fact that one of them has murdered a female student. At graduation, one of them says to the killer, "Omega Xi, forever." Other films suggest that loyalty among Greeks is tenuous. In *Fraternity Row* (1977), a pledge is blackballed when his father is accused of disloyalty to the government, a charge the brothers fear could tarnish the reputation of the house. Sorority sisters in *Pumpkin* (2002) ostracize a member for the same reason when she falls in love with a disabled boy.

Administrators' Attitudes

Not too surprisingly, the snobbery, hazing, heavy alcohol use, sexism, homophobia, and academic dishonesty of the fraternities and sororities portrayed in the movies often elicit hostile responses from on-screen administrators, typically a dean or president who promises to rid the campus of the disruptive organizations. Students usually fight back and emerge victorious, which is to be expected given the youthful audiences the films are aimed at. In *Animal House* (1978), Dean Wormer (John Vernon) vows to banish the Deltas from campus by the end of the year. When he learns that the house is already on probation, he places it on "double secret probation" and searches for a way to revoke its charter. He tells several members to be off campus by Monday morning and adds that he has informed their draft boards that they're now eligible for military service. The college president in *Time Walker* (1982) immediately suspects a fraternity prank when a mummy is stolen from the school's museum, announcing that he will close every house on campus unless it's returned within twenty-four hours, even though he has no evidence of fraternity involvement in the theft. Members of a fraternity in *PCU* (1994) stage a protest that leads to the dismissal of the school president after she says they qualify for a Sensitivity Awareness Weekend and warns that their house will be repossessed if they don't pay for damage they have caused. In *Old School* (2003), three men who form their own fraternity enrage the dean they taunted when all four were undergraduates together. Eventually the dean is fired for trying to dissolve the fraternity, and its members move into the house he vacates.

Administrators have fewer problems with sororities than fraternities, but in two films a dean confronts a group of sorority sisters. In *Confessions of a Co-ed* (1931), the dean of women interrogates girls when a vanity case with their sorority's name on it is found near a lovers' lane from which a police officer chased a couple, resulting in his being seriously injured. The girls cooperate with the dean out of fear that she might suspend their house charter, take away social privileges, or expel them. The girl who confesses to being in the car is required to leave school, and her male companion is kicked out as well. In contrast to the compliant sorority sisters in this film are the vindictive ones in a movie released more than fifty years later, *Splitz* (1984). A dean announces that one of three sorority houses has to be shut down because land is needed to build a sewage treatment facility. The house to be closed will be determined by a series of athletic competitions, and the girls who expect to lose decide to strike back. They photograph the dean's husband smoking marijuana, inhaling nitrous oxide, and wearing women's clothes. They send the pictures to the dean and tell her they'll keep them from the school's governing board if she lets them make up the rules for the athletic competition. The dean agrees but tells the members of the other two houses that they can cheat.

College movies have been consistently unflattering in their depiction of fraternities and sororities, especially over the past three decades. Whether cinematic representations of Greek life have shaped popular beliefs about these organizations and influenced the attitudes and actions of prospective and current members and college administrators is uncertain, but those who have never belonged to such a group have little to rely on for information about them besides what they see in the movies.

7

THE BIG GAME

Intercollegiate athletic competition developed in the 1850s, with boat racing the first sport to attract a following. Football became popular soon after Rutgers and Princeton played the first organized game in 1869; by the 1880s, games were a weekend ritual that drew crowds to stadiums across the country. Football was promoted as a builder of character and teamwork, and administrators loved the game for inspiring alumni to donate money.[1] Well aware of these benefits, Notre Dame cooperated in the production of *Knute Rockne— All American* (1940), a film that enhanced the school's reputation, and sued when *John Goldfarb, Please Come Home* (1964) seemed to cast aspersions on its football program. More recently, several small colleges have attracted students by developing football programs. Dr. Joanne Boyle, president of Seton Hill University in Greensburg, Pennsylvania, comments:

> I could have started a spiffy new major of study, spent a lot of money on lab equipment and hired a few new high-powered professors. I might have gotten twenty-five more students for that. And I couldn't have counted on that major still being popular in fifteen years.
>
> Instead, I started a football team, brought in hundreds of paying students, added a vibrant piece to our campus life and broadened our recognition factor. And in the long history of American higher education, one thing you can count on is football's longevity. Football is here to stay.[2]

Sports have been an important part of college movies since their inception. One of the four college films released in 1915 featured football (*The College Widow*), and another one dealt with baseball (*The Grandee's Ring*). Nearly one-third of all college movies include varsity sports or recreational athletics as a significant theme. Football is by far the most popular sport in these movies, reflecting its long-time dominance on American campuses. Most movies about football were released between 1925 and 1954, after which the game appeared on the screen less frequently. This was the result of the mass ownership of television, which provided fans with direct access to real games, and a growth in the popularity of professional football. The second most popular sport in college movies is basketball, though it's featured in only one-fourth as many

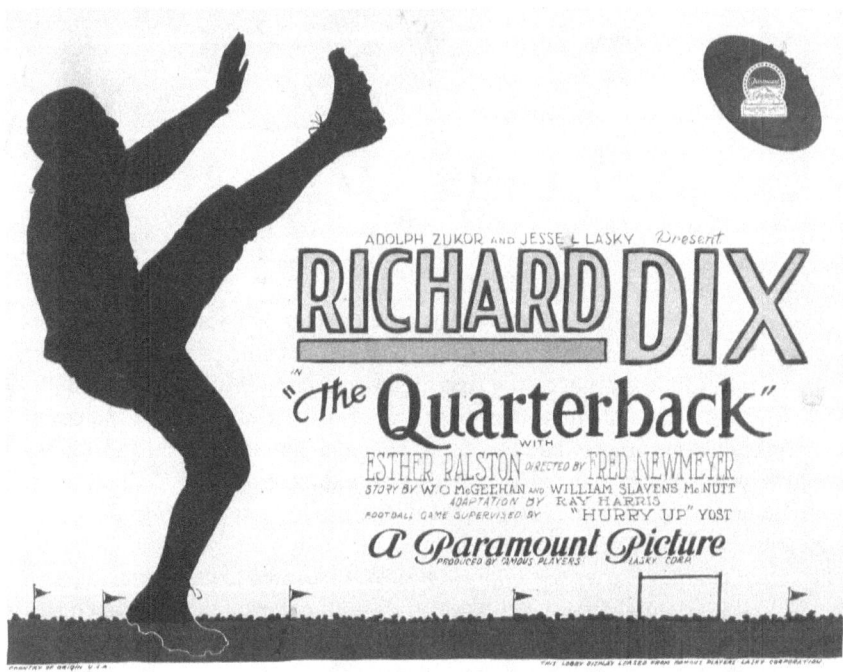

Football had been an important part of American campus life for half a century by the time *The Quarterback* (Paramount) was released in 1926.

movies as football. Following basketball in number of appearances are track, crew, and baseball.

The disproportionate attention given to football on American campuses is alluded to in the movies. In *Jim Thorpe—All American* (1951), the "C" on the letter sweaters of the football players at Carlisle Indian School is significantly larger than the "c" on the track team's sweaters. A dean in *Blackbeard's Ghost* (1968) informs the track coach that his unsuccessful team adds little luster to the school, while the football team has winning seasons that bring in a lot of money. The preeminence of football is made clear in *The Program* (1993) when a tennis player complains to the star quarterback that she has a hard time getting to use the exercise equipment because the football team is always on it, and he replies that there wouldn't be any equipment without the football program to pay for it.

Sports have played a central role in college movies because they allow filmmakers to examine the ways that students balance their commitment to the team with the demands of coursework, weigh the relative importance of winning and sportsmanship, and resolve conflicting loyalties to coaches, teammates, friends, romantic partners, and parents. Making decisions of this sort

Legendary American Indian track and football star Jim Thorpe (Burt Lancaster) learns that the size of the letter on his sweater depends on the sport he plays in *Jim Thorpe—All American* (1951, Warner Brothers). Here Miss Benton (Sarah Selby, left) looks at the letter for track that Margaret Miller (Phyllis Thaxter) has just sewn onto the sweater.

provides dramatic tension that is often relieved by having the student-athlete score the winning points at the end of a big game.

Athletics and Academics

Problems stemming from undergraduates' dual commitment to athletics and academics have shown up in the movies since the 1920s. Nearly every film in which a student-athlete has trouble in the classroom attributes the difficulty to the personal shortcomings of the individual, rather than to the institution of higher learning that has often compromised its academic standards to enroll athletes.

The stereotype of student-athletes as less academically proficient than their non-athlete classmates is consistent with research. A study of thirty highly selective institutions found that athletes recruited by a college coach are much more likely to be admitted than comparable classmates not on a coach's list. The advantage enjoyed by recruited athletes is even greater than the advantages given to members of targeted racial and ethnic minorities and to the children of alumni. As a consequence, recruited athletes enter college with lower SAT scores than other freshmen. The athletes at these elite institutions do graduate at rates similar to their classmates, but those who have been recruited to play have markedly lower grades. This is due less to their low aptitude or poor preparation for college than to their academic underperformance while in college. In other words, athletes' grades are even poorer than would be expected from their SAT scores and demographic characteristics. This academic weakness is attributable to the low priority that student-athletes assign to doing well academically, an attitude with roots in high school but also affected by immersion in a collegiate "culture of sport" that minimizes the importance of scholastic achievement and isolates athletes from the larger campus community. The amount of time spent on sports doesn't account for athletes' weaker-than-expected grades, because classmates involved in equally time-consuming non-athletic extracurricular activities earn grades better than predicted from their SAT scores and demographic characteristics. Moreover, athletes do more poorly than expected in their coursework even during the off-season for their sport and even in years when they don't play.[3]

College movies acknowledge the academic deficiency of student-athletes. When a young fan asks the football coach in *The Spirit of Notre Dame* (1931) if he can get autographs from the team's star players, the coach replies, "I guess so. They can write. They're seniors now." An injured football player in *The Big Game* (1936) tells an opponent that his team should get a rule book and look through it, and the player replies that it wouldn't make any difference because they can't read. A coach in *Freshman Love* (1936) says good crewmen can't be bothered with coursework and is appalled that a professor forced one of his boys to buy a textbook. In *Rise and Shine* (1941), a football star who is trying to stay eligible for the team is stumped during an oral exam when he's asked to name a means of transportation; when he answers "train" to a question about how he keeps in shape, he's awarded a grade of 100. The editor of the campus literary magazine in *The Male Animal* (1942) calls a romantic rival a "handsome, half-witted halfback." *Bonzo Goes to College* (1952) implies that athletes aren't even as smart as chimpanzees. After the football coach complains that the school is too academically demanding and says his team needs less brains and more brawn, a chimpanzee shows up at practice and throws a long pass. The coach decides that the team needs his talents and sends him to take an entrance examination. The chimpanzee is declared a straight-A scholar bright enough to be a professor.

The movies repeatedly raise the possibility that the educational function of colleges might be secondary to their sports programs. An intertitle in *The*

Freshman (1925) reads, "The opening of the Fall Term at Tate University—a large football stadium with a college attached." When a bookish student in *College* (1927) arrives on campus unfashionably dressed but carrying baseball, football, and track uniforms, equipment, and instruction manuals, the dean tells him, "A boy like you can make this athlete-infested college a seat of learning once more." A coach in *Sunny Skies* (1930) remarks, "This college could turn out a whole regiment of Phi Betas, and who'd know about it, but let us turn out just one All-American fullback and the whole country will sit up and take notice." In *Fighting Youth* (1935), a communist agent who has infiltrated a campus remarks, "Somebody has said that a college is only a little red building attached to a stadium filled with two football teams and 70,000 people." College administrators express similar sentiments in *Horse Feathers* (1932), *A Yank at Oxford* (1938), and *Mr. Doodle Kicks Off* (1938).

This tension between athletics and academics shows up in college movies from all eras. In *Campus Confessions* (1938), a wealthy trustee wants to put

A chimpanzee's performance on a college entrance exam and his feats on the football field call into question the academic and athletic abilities of student-athletes in 1952's *Bonzo Goes to College* (Universal International), a sequel to *Bedtime for Bonzo* (1951, Universal International).

more emphasis on education and asks the dean to cancel a big basketball game, claiming the school is paying too much attention to sports. The dean replies that the team's success has boosted students' morale and even improved their academic work. When Professor Hathaway (Don Ameche) questions the eligibility of "Rubber Legs" Ryan (Gordon Jones) for an upcoming football game in *The Feminine Touch* (1941), Dean Hutchinson (Grant Mitchell) says the school shouldn't favor athletic prowess over academics, but he then points out that the trustees do have a strong interest in winning. Hutchinson and Hathaway agree that changing Ryan's grade would be cheating, but when Hathaway suggests that the dean seems to want him to give Ryan a short make-up exam in words of one syllable with no writing required, the dean says they have to be practical. Commenting that even professors have to eat, Hathaway agrees to a retest. When Ryan tries to cut short his exam by claiming he has a headache, a strategy he says was suggested to him by the dean, Hathaway asks the dean, "Which do you consider more important, education or football, the sheepskin or the pigskin?"

Coaches sometimes make their priorities clear. The basketball coach in *Tall Story* (1960) says, "I'd love to work in a college where there wasn't any faculty. They waste so much time on education." A similar attitude is expressed by the football coach in *How I Got Into College* (1989), who tells admissions officers, "It makes me nervous when you boys disappear behind closed doors. I end up with athletic chemists and well-rounded political science majors instead of somebody who can run with the football." The football coach in *The Program* (1993) objects as follows to a professor's claim that "Eastern State University" is an institution of higher learning rather than a football vocational school: "Yeah, but when was the last time 80,000 people showed up to see a kid do a damn chemistry experiment?"

Nationally prominent sports programs at universities like Eastern State are business enterprises. A high-profile team can enhance the size and academic quality of the student body by attracting more applicants, and it can bring in more alumni donations and gate and television revenue. As a result, institutions of higher learning have increasingly used athletics to market themselves. Marshall University and the University of Texas at El Paso, formerly Texas Western College, successfully exploited the publicity surrounding the release of based-on-a-true-story movies, *We Are Marshall* (2006) and *Glory Road* (2006), respectively. Schools also engage in "branding" in the promotional spots they run during football bowl games and other televised sporting events. These commercials usually show a serene campus filled with a clean-cut and diverse student body happily studying in groups or having fun at a game or other school event. The ads evoke both the school's traditions and its vision for the future and emphasize its academic quality, often with photographs of famous alumni.[4]

Administrators, athletic directors, and coaches at schools where sports programs bring in a lot of money have sometimes been accused of keeping student-athletes eligible to play by pressuring professors to treat them with favoritism and by providing tutors and other academic support unavailable to non-athletes. When an Ohio State professor gave two oral exams to football star Maurice Clarett after he walked out of a midterm exam without finishing it, a graduate student claimed the player had been given preferential treatment because of his importance to the team.[5] An instructor at Louisiana State said she was told to ignore what she believed was plagiarized material in football players' papers and give extra credit and hold a special study session to keep them eligible for an upcoming bowl game.[6] Reports have also surfaced of tutors doing players' work for them rather than just helping them with it.

College movies have often showed student-athletes being treated with favoritism. When a football player in *The Band Plays On* (1934) is declared ineligible to play because of his poor performance in a physics course, he asks how he can be expected to excel on the field and be a student at the same time. His professor gives him a special exam, and he passes it and rejoins the team. In *Student Tour* (1934), crew members need to pass their exams to go on a world tour, but they all fail a philosophy test. The niece of the professor suggests that she and her uncle accompany the team on the trip and tutor them along the way, and the dean agrees to this special treatment. When a professor in *She's Working Her Way Through College* (1952) asks several bored football players why they're taking his class, one replies that there's no homework and no one has ever flunked the course, the result of the trustees' pressure on the professor to pass student-athletes. When the basketball coach in *Fast Break* (1979) admits that some of the players he wants to bring in aren't very good students, the president assures him they won't have any problems with the coursework, adding, "You get my meaning." He admits the players without even looking at their high school records. A dean in *Necessary Roughness* (1991) claims that the function of a university is to enlighten and educate and says he won't let athletes compete if their grades are too low, but his rhetoric is contradicted by a football player who says he's never passed anything on his own because his wealthy father always pays for his grades with large donations to the school.

Student-athletes in several movies are offered easy courses and simple exams to keep them eligible to play. When a professor in *The Doctor Takes a Wife* (1940) asks two football players how many bones there are in the human body, one of them says there must be dozens; they both pass. A football star in *Good News* (1930) fails an astronomy exam and won't play in a big game unless he can pass a special exam his professor has been pressured into giving him. While grading the exam, the professor remarks that the student's answers are wrong but it's tough to flunk him, and he gives him a barely passing grade. In the 1947 remake of the film, the football player gets an F in French and tries to fail his makeup exam so he won't have to play in the big game and fulfill his promise to get engaged to a young woman if his team wins, because since making the promise he has fallen in love with his tutor. The professor passes him on the basis of the tutor's assurance he really knows French despite his poor performance on the exam, suggesting that an athlete has a hard time failing even when he tries to. In *One on One* (1977), a basketball player admits that he's not that smart when it comes to books, but he gets by academically by taking a course called "Synergistic Techniques and Prepubescent Kinetic Development," informally known as "How to Coach Peewee Basketball," and by enlisting the aid of a tutor, who says she's never met a jock who could read anything more than a coach's playbook.

Only a few movies feature athletes who are committed to doing well in their coursework. In *College Coach* (1933), Phil (Dick Powell), a football player and dedicated student of chemistry, turns in a blank blue-book because his team has played four straight road games and he's had no time to study. He's surprised to get a D on the test and protests that his passing grade is unfair because some of the non-athletes in his class who studied harder than he did got F's. He quits the team to concentrate on his studies, but later he rejoins to help it win a big game and bring in the revenue needed to save the chemistry laboratory. Another athlete who is a serious student is Steve (John Derek) in *Saturday's Hero* (1951). Studying until two or three in the morning, he falls asleep on his books because he's exhausted from football practice. He responds enthusiastically to instruction by his adviser, Professor Megroth (Alexander Knox), but nonetheless starts to miss classes and fall behind in his coursework. His alumni sponsor, T. C. McCabe (Sidney Blackmer), enlists Steve to help him with a national campaign to bring big-time football to the school, telling him not to worry about the effect it will have on his studies. Steve starts to get C's but promises Megroth that he'll work harder the following year. The professor offers him extra help if he'll return to campus early in the fall, but Steve says he can't do that because he has too many alumni banquets to attend. When Steve suffers a shoulder separation in a game, McCabe says he's nothing without football, because he can't compete academically with the other students and he won't get a decent job if he drops out of school, so he will have to play despite the injury. Steve plays with a shoulder brace and ends up in the hospital. Declaring he no longer loves football, he quits school to take a job and complete his degree at night.

Sports and American Values

In many movies about collegiate sports, underdogs who work hard to overcome extraordinary odds emerge victorious in a dramatic finish to a big game, demonstrating along the way their character, sportsmanship, and loyalty. The culture's reverence for the values that lead to athletic success is suggested by the rewards enjoyed by the winners: crowd adulation, a desirable romantic partner, and a contract to play professional ball.

Athletes in college movies from the 1930s often had to resolve conflicting loyalties to coaches, teammates, romantic partners, and parents. This storyline has not been used much in recent films, though in a scene from *Puddle Cruiser* (1996) that parodies *Spartacus* (1960), all of the members of a rugby team protect one of their own from the police by asserting, "I am Felix Bean." Most of the older films that dealt with loyalty were about football. Even though he's being considered for All-American honors as a running back in *The Spirit of Notre Dame* (1931), Bucky (Lew Ayres) is shifted to blocking back by his coach. His pal Jim (William Bakewell) inherits the more glamorous job of running the ball; he thinks this is unfair to Bucky, but the coach says the switch is best for the team because Jim can't block. When Jim begins to score a lot of touchdowns, he gets conceited from the attention showered on him by the press, alumni boosters, and female students. A resentful Bucky accuses Jim of no longer being a team man, and they get into a fight. Bucky starts to miss his blocks on purpose, and the coach tells him to turn in his uniform because he's letting the team down to get back at Jim. Late in a big game, Jim isn't running well because Bucky isn't playing. Bucky suits up, the coach sends him in, and he blocks effectively, allowing Jim to score the winning touchdown. The two shake hands, recognizing the importance of loyalty to both friends and the team. *Swing That Cheer* (1938) has a similar plot, and again the players' differences are resolved by the blocker accepting his subordinate role and the two players working together to lead their team to victory.

The value of loyalty is made clear in two other football movies from the 1930s. In *Huddle* (1932), Tony (Ramon Novarro) accidentally breaks the leg of his Yale roommate Pidge (John Arledge) in football practice during their freshman year. Tony wants to quit the team, but Pidge convinces him to stick with it. As a junior, Tony is diagnosed with appendicitis and immediate surgery is recommended, but he rejects the advice and suits up for the big Harvard game. Playing in severe pain, he is benched by the coach, but he persuades him to let him go back in. He scores a touchdown, but when he has to be taken out again, his teammates criticize him for quitting. After learning that Tony is in the hospital with a ruptured appendix, Pidge staunchly defends him to the rest of the team. During his senior year, a popular Tony is asked to show everyone his appendix scar, a reminder of his loyalty to the team at a time when he was in excruciating pain.

Putting the good of the team ahead of personal interests is also the message of *The Band Plays On* (1934). Coach Hardy (Preston Foster) takes four destitute youths under his wing, first getting them out of trouble with the law, then teaching them to play football, and finally helping them to get into the college where he works. When Hardy benches Tony (Robert Young) after discovering that he has been associating with a gambler, Tony drops out of school. The other members of the backfield complain that Hardy only cares about them as football players, not as individuals, and they also quit the team. Hardy stops checking to make sure they are keeping up with their studies, seemingly confirming their negative view of him, but when one of them calls Hardy tightfisted, another one says that the coach paid his hospital bill and berates his teammates for turning their backs on the best friend they've ever had, a man who pulled them out of the gutter and made something of them. They rejoin the team, but Hardy gives them little opportunity to play. On the sideline during the season's finale, Tony tells him that they want to win the game for the team and the school, not for themselves. Impressed by their selflessness, Hardy sends them into the game. They score on the last play and the game ends in a tie. The coach congratulates them on a fine game, says he's proud of them, and predicts that after they graduate in a few months they'll succeed at anything they try.

Football is also praised as a builder of character in *Knute Rockne—All American* (1940). One member of the Notre Dame team, George Gipp (Ronald Reagan), praises its legendary coach (Pat O'Brien) for giving his players "something they don't teach in schools, something clean and strong inside, not just courage, but a right way of living that none of us'll ever forget." Rockne emphasizes teamwork, self-sacrifice, sweat, and brains, and he advises his players to keep their grades up, not just play the game, because the public will soon forget even the best of them, and they need to think about the future. A coach in *Rose Bowl* (1936) expresses a different view when he calls a trustee's claim that "college football has no equal in molding men" a lot of malarkey. He says men are molded by their parents, and football is simply something to yell for and be proud of.

The value of sportsmanship shows up in several movies from the 1930s but has rarely been mentioned since. In *Love, Honor, and Behave* (1938), Sally (Barbara O'Neil) has raised her son Ted (Wayne Morris) to play by the rules and be cheerful if he doesn't win. Her husband Dan (Thomas Mitchell) believes people should do everything they can to win. As a junior at Yale, Ted plays an important tennis match against a Harvard player he beat the year before. A spectator describes Ted as the mildest guy on campus and says he never quite wins because he doesn't have enough fight in him. When the judge awards a point to Ted by calling out of bounds a shot made by the Harvard player, Ted argues that the ball was in bounds and his opponent should have been awarded the point. The judge refuses to change his ruling, so Ted deliberately hits his next shot into the crowd in the interest of fair play. The Harvard player wins the match, and Yale loses the meet. Sally is proud of Ted for being a good sport, but Dan is disgusted by his son's willingness to accept defeat.

Sports and Race

The value of racial equality has occasionally been alluded to in movies about collegiate sports. The issue is treated explicitly but gently in *The Jackie Robinson Story* (1950), which stars the first African-American major league baseball player as himself. When a colleague says the only problem in recruiting Jackie to UCLA is that he's a colored boy and some people think too many athletic scholarships are going to colored boys, the football coach replies, "Colored boys are all right with me if they're the right color. I like a good clean American boy with a B average. If that's the kind of boy you're talking about, his colors are blue and gold [UCLA's colors]." After Jackie enrolls and sets school records in several sports, a teammate suggests their opponents are hitting him extra hard because of his race, but the trainer says it's just because he's the best halfback on the field. In *Jim Thorpe—All American* (1951), the hopes of the American Indian football star for a coaching position ride on his performance in a game against a team that includes another leading candidate for the job. When Jim isn't offered the job, he says it's because he's an Indian, but his coach tells him it's actually because the other candidate outplayed him and because Jim allowed a teammate to play despite an injured knee, possibly raising concern among those doing the hiring. The coach does add that if Jim wasn't hired because he's an Indian, that's just one more hurdle for him to clear. The issue of race also arises in *Game Day* (1999), when Harrison (Sean Squire) proclaims that he's the best basketball player on the team but doesn't play as much as he should because he's black and the white coach is a racist. A teammate points out that most of the starting team is black and says Harrison doesn't play more because he's a "dog."

These films downplay the presence of racism in collegiate sports, but the problem is dealt with at length in *Glory Road* (2006), the story of the 1966 national champion basketball team of Texas Western College, which is now called the University of Texas at El Paso. The coach angers alumni boosters, local residents, and other coaches by assembling a team that includes seven African Americans, which at the time was a violation of an unwritten rule to limit the use of black players. The coach decides to make a point by starting five black players in the NCAA tournament, and the team goes on to win the championship with victories over highly favored teams. Its success has been credited with hastening the desegregation of college sports and increasing the number of athletic scholarships awarded to black athletes.

Sports and Gender

Football is a sport well-suited to the movies, because it offers the possibility of a hard-fought battle with a dramatic finish. However, last-second victories had become such a cliché in the movies by the end of the 1930s that few games were truly suspenseful. Most of these games were low-scoring affairs, but the focus of attention was almost always the offensive player whose heroics won the game, rather than the defensive players who prevented the opponent from scoring. The heroes were usually exemplars of traditional masculinity: aggressive, physically skilled, charismatic, and able to perform well under pressure. When the heroes lacked these traits, as in *The Freshman* (1925), *Life Begins in College* (1937), and *Hold That Co-ed* (1938), the anomaly was a source of comedy.

Football not only rewards traditionally masculine behavior, it is also the only major collegiate sport that women don't play. As a result, the heavy emphasis on football in college movies has made the female athlete all but invisible; male athletes appear in fifteen times as many of these films as female ones. Female students in movies about collegiate sports usually appear only as spectators or cheerleaders who are urging male athletes on to victory. Of

Lizzie Olsen (Joan Davis, top left) is a kicker who leads her team to victory with a surprising touchdown run into a fierce headwind in *Hold That Co-ed* (1938, Twentieth Century–Fox). Governor Gabby Harrigan (John Barrymore, with pompom) strongly supports Lizzie's right to be on the football team.

the fifteen college movies that do feature a female athlete, seven were released prior to passage of Title IX of the Education Amendments of 1972, which banned sex discrimination in institutions of higher learning that received federal funds. In three of these older movies—*The Campus Flirt* (1926), *Swim Girl, Swim* (1927), and *The Fair Co-ed* (1927)—women participate in track, swimming, and basketball, respectively, mainly to attract the attention of men. This motivation is less prominent in *Hold That Co-ed* (1938), in which a gubernatorial candidate eager for a "State" football victory adds a talented female kicker to the team after declaring, "Is there any law against girls playing football in this state? If there is, I'll repeal it." Since Title IX became law in 1972, there has been a big increase in participation in collegiate sports by women, but they are still underrepresented relative to their numbers among full-time undergraduates, and their athletic programs continue to be underfunded compared to men's.[7] This unequal treatment is alluded to by a track athlete in *Demolition University* (1997); she complains that she has just a half-scholarship and a job, while male athletes are treated more generously.

Some college movies equate athletic prowess with real manhood by denigrating women and gays. Harold (Harold Lloyd) in *The Freshman* (1925) exhorts his teammates, "Come on, you old women! Are you afraid of mussing your hair? Don't you know how to fight?" To make sure the audience doesn't miss the point that John (Joe E. Brown) in *Local Boy Makes Good* (1931) isn't "a real man," the film presents him as a botany student who worships Luther Burbank, wears glasses, and works in a bookstore. When John gains confidence, he sheds his glasses, an often-used symbol of the studious and athletically inept. After he drops out of a track race for fear of being spiked by a romantic rival, the trainer says, "I don't know whether to kill you or tie a ribbon in your hair." *Freshman Love* (1936) features a slight young man who wears glasses, composes symphonies, can't swim, and is described by his father as "peculiar." In one scene, a trustee who observes the crew coach effeminately demonstrating to the president's daughter how to attract talented oarsmen to the college comments that now he understands why the crew doesn't win. Unhappy that his team failed to score in the first half, the football coach in *Saturday's Hero* (1951) greets his players in the locker room with "Congratulations, girls!" The football coach in *The Swinging Cheerleaders* (1974) makes explicit what some of these earlier films only imply when he tells his players, "You're playing like a bunch of fags."

In some movies, women are an obstacle to men's success in sports. In *The Plastic Age* (1925), Hugh (Donald Keith) is instructed by his track coach to remain virtuous while in college, but at a party he discovers there are two kinds of girls, those who prefer to dance and those who go into a darkened room with a MEN AT WORK sign near the door. Hugh dances with the "hotsy-totsy" Cynthia (Clara Bow), despite a teammate's warning that he should leave the party if he wants to win his race the next day. When he finishes last in the race, the coach says he's out of condition and is a great disappointment. Cynthia breaks up with Hugh after they get into trouble at a tavern, because she wants him to remain the way he is rather than become wild like she is. Hugh is then free to succeed at sports, and he becomes a football star. A romantic rivalry between football teammates hurts their on-field performance in *The College Hero* (1927), *So This Is College* (1929), and *Sunny Skies* (1930). Women also impede male athletes in *Girl o' My Dreams* (1934): After two young men get engaged to their girlfriends the night before a track meet, the distraction causes them to lose their first events. Their fiancées send them notes breaking off their engagements, and the athletes win their second events and their team wins the meet.

Just as studious, unfashionable, and unattractive women in college movies are sometimes made over to fit a feminine ideal, so too are nerdy and athletically inept men often transformed to fit a masculine ideal, enabling them to win the heart of a young woman who was initially attracted to a much stronger and handsomer sports hero. As a second-stringer in *Good News* (1947) complains, "All the girls want football heroes." In *The Freshman* (1925), the bespectacled Harold is ignorant of the rules of football and clumsy on the field, but he wins the love of a young woman, who is being aggressively pursued by a bigger and more talented player, when he miraculously scores the winning touchdown after being sent into the game by a desperate coach whose team has been decimated by injuries. *College* (1927) also features a zero-to-hero transformation. Ronald (Buster Keaton) criticizes sports and praises academic pursuits in his high school graduation speech, but he nonetheless arrives on campus in the fall intent on becoming an athlete. He proves hopeless at the various sports he tries, but at the end he uses the skills required for sprinting, hurdling, broad-jumping, pole-vaulting, and shot-putting to rescue his beloved from the clutches of the school's star athlete.

Athletes and Their Parents

Student-athletes in the movies often play to impress an actual or potential romantic partner, but many of them participate to please their parents or, in some cases, to rebel against them. Having a character wrestle with the decision of whether to play a sport allows a filmmaker to highlight a common problem faced by college students, becoming independent of their parents. In *One Minute to Play* (1926), a man insists that his son attend his alma mater, but the boy wants to go to a different college that has a better football team. The son gets his way, but only after he promises his father not to play on the team. When he breaks his word and excels at the game, his father offers the school an endowment if it will prohibit his son from playing, but eventually he relents and accepts his son's decision. In *Most Precious Thing in Life* (1934), when a young man refuses to go out for the football team despite excelling at the game in prep school, his mother challenges him by saying it would be hard for him to live up to his father's accomplishments anyway. He joins the team, and she says he has his father's speed but lacks his skill, so she teaches him the proper footwork. A wealthy trustee in *Million Dollar Legs* (1939) wants to make his alma mater famous for its basketball team, which his son captains, so he makes big donations to the school to get the dean to support the team. Because his son wants to be liked for who he is rather than for his father's money, he rebels and joins the crew.

Fathers in several films use their sons to make up for their own failures on the football field or to follow in their footsteps and bring more glory to the family name. A boy in *Win That Girl* (1928) is brought up to vindicate losses by his father's and his grandfather's teams to an arch-rival. Though small of stature and modest in athletic ability, he leads his team to victory. Family tradition is also important in *Two Minutes to Play* (1937). A young man explains to the football coach that he hasn't tried out for the team because his father once lost a game for the school by running the wrong way. He has promised his father not to go out for the team, but later he asks to be released from the promise and joins the team with his father's consent. During a game, he becomes dazed and heads toward the wrong goal line, but before he can repeat his father's mistake he recovers his senses and completes a long pass for the winning touchdown. In the biographical *Smith of Minnesota* (1942), the father of Heisman Trophy winner Bruce Smith feels responsible for losing a game to Michigan when he was a student at Minnesota. He vowed that his son would someday beat Michigan, and Bruce manages to avenge his father's defeat. Another former football player pushes his son to play in *That's My Boy* (1951). "Jarring Jack" Jackson (Eddie Mayehoff), whose den is crammed with trophies and photographs commemorating his football exploits, wants his weak and allergy-afflicted son Junior (Jerry Lewis) to emulate him. Jackson pays the college expenses of a potential All-American to get him to teach Junior to play the game. Despite the expert instruction, Junior fumbles, runs the wrong way, and helps an opponent score a touchdown, disgracing his father and the team. After Junior's skills improve and he scores a touchdown, his allergies miraculously disappear and he no longer needs to wear glasses. More importantly, he has earned the respect of his father, who proudly declares, "That's my boy!"

Recruitment and Amateurism

Student-athletes who want to impress their parents or romantic partners must first make the team and then perform well when the opportunity arises. In *Foreign Student* (1994), a French exchange student answers "yes" when asked if he plays football, mistaking the American game for soccer. He joins the team as a place kicker and passes for a touchdown to win a game when the snap for his field goal attempt is mishandled; this wins him acceptance by his classmates. In *Rudy* (1993), a modestly talented young man strives to become one of the few non-scholarship players to make the Notre Dame football team. Unusual because it doesn't present athletic success as a means to win a girl, please a parent, or sign a lucrative professional contract, this movie suggests that with enough determination, anyone can make a big-time college team. The film also conveys a message common to movies from all eras: For collegiate athletes, academic achievement is simply a way to qualify to play the game.

If the quest for glory motivates student-athletes like Rudy, college administrators are inspired by the hope that high-profile sports programs will generate revenue through increased gate receipts and more alumni donations, despite evidence that few programs bring in more money than they cost.[8] Turning to a sports team to bail out a financially strapped institution is a common theme in college movies. Faculty members in *Touchdown* (1931) worry about the ethics of paying their school's football players, but they recognize that the sport can pay for a new laboratory. To keep open a nearly bankrupt university in *$1,000 a Touchdown* (1939), its owner decides to recruit a football team to attract more students, reasoning that students go to college for football, good players attract more girls, and girls attract more boys. In *Trouble Along the Way* (1953), financial problems at "St. Anthony's College" force its rector to hire a football coach who can build a program that will bring in revenue and attract more paying students. When he learns that the newly recruited players have had their academic records doctored, the rector cancels the rest of the season, even though the first game brought in much-needed money. The coach says he isn't ashamed of what he's done and tells the rector his decision to cancel the remaining games has cost thirty to forty students an education they otherwise couldn't afford.

After the title character in *Jim Thorpe—All American* (1951) is stripped of his Olympic medals, has his track records stricken from the books, and is barred from amateur competition for accepting money to play baseball one summer, his coach observes, "We all know that, at best, there is a fine, vague line between amateurism and professionalism." The problem of defining and maintaining amateurism has long played an important role in college movies. In *The Big Game* (1936), a football coach defends a player under investigation by the board of trustees for taking money from a professional gambler by criticizing the president for pretending that football is played out of love and enthusiasm, when it's really a business that buys books and buildings and feeds the endowment fund. He says the college buys talented athletes just like other businesses buy raw materials, and for the same purpose, to make money. In *Saturday's Hero* (1951), a well-off alumnus hires an assistant to pay for the big linemen the school needs to compete with the best football teams in the country, because he's fed up with prep school gentlemen and amateurs and wants real athletes at his alma mater; he comments that the only remaining amateur sport is hopscotch, and he's not so sure about that. His assistant makes the familiar argument that no one deserves the money colleges make from football more than the players, pointing out that people don't work in the mills for free. A football player in *All American* (1953) says he enjoyed the game in high school but it stopped being fun when he had to play for money in college.

Under-the-table payments to athletes are also referenced in *The Absent-Minded Professor* (1961). Professor Ashton (Elliott Reid) chides Professor Brainard (Fred MacMurray) for flunking his school's star basketball player and making him ineligible for a big game. Ashton remarks, "We're much more realistic about things like that at Rutland," to which Brainard replies, "So I hear. I understand you pay your basketball players more than you do your English teachers." Ashton responds, "That's ridiculous. I get twice as much as...I really don't care to discuss it." In a similar vein, a football player in *The Program* (1993) is handed $50 by an alumni booster and commended for the great job he did in the game, prompting a teammate to tell him he'll get $500 or $600 a game when he makes the first team.

Saturday's Heroes (1937) takes a radical stance toward professionalism in collegiate sports. When the college president demands that Val (Van Heflin) quit the team because of his involvement in a ticket-scalping scheme, the star quarterback points out that he made $16 from selling game tickets, while the school brings in a quarter of a million dollars every season from the team's efforts. He warns that if the president doesn't reinstate him, he'll go to the press with a statement signed by all the players that they also sold their tickets. The president gives in, but Val is shunned by his teammates and withdraws from school. He tells President Mitchell (Charles Trowbridge) of another college that he was technically wrong to sell his tickets, but not as wrong as the system that pretends to be amateur but is really professional. He praises Mitchell for espousing the honest position that student-athletes should be rewarded for their services. Mitchell says he wants to make a business of college football, but Val says it already *is* one, with gate receipts exceeding $40 million a year, while unpaid players sacrifice their education to training so alumni can have a good time on weekends. Val and Mitchell believe players should be compensated for their contributions, a proposal that hasn't been seriously entertained in the seven decades since the film was made.

In more recent movies, high school athletes are well aware of what they can demand in exchange for bringing their talents to a collegiate sports program. In *One on One* (1977), Henry (Robby Benson) negotiates a four-year, no-cut scholarship and a new sports car, which the college gives to his father to pass on to him as a "graduation present." At the start of his freshman year, the coach's secretary assigns Henry a paying job that consists of watching the automatic sprinklers at the football stadium turn on and off. Every week, Henry is provided with two tickets that he "sells" for $600 to an alumni sponsor, who

In *Saturday's Heroes* (1937, RKO), star quarterback Val Webster (Van Heflin) strenuously objects to the way that he and his teammates are treated by President Hammond (George Irving). Hammond demands that Val quit the team for scalping his game tickets for $16, but Val fights back, pointing out that the college brings in a quarter of a million dollars every season from the sport.

says it takes a lot of money to keep the players happy. In *The Air Up There* (1994), another basketball recruit tells an assistant coach he wants $50,000, a new car, and a written statement that he'll be on the starting team his freshman year and the school won't recruit another power forward until he's a junior. *Blue Chips* (1994) looks at recruiting violations by the once-successful "Western University" basketball program. The mother of one player tells Coach Bell (Nick Nolte) that for her son to enroll at Western she'll need references for a new job and a new house. He asks if she's aware this would violate NCAA rules, and she replies that a foul isn't a foul until the referee blows the whistle. The father of another "blue chip" recruit tells Bell he wants a new tractor, claiming other schools offered him one. His son tells the coach that as one of the few white blue-chippers he deserves extra consideration, and he wants the same thing from Western that other schools have offered, $30,000 in cash. Bell later shocks a packed press conference by saying the alumni association pays for the best players money can buy and the program isn't about winning or education or even basketball, it's about money, and he bought into it big time and now despises himself, so he is quitting.

The recruiting of football players is satirized in *Johnny Be Good* (1988). Star quarterback Johnny (Anthony Michael Hall) is urged by his coach to enroll at "Piermont University" because its chancellor has promised the coach a five-year contract, a weekly television show, and a country club membership if he can convince Johnny to go there. Johnny visits the campus of "Ol' Tex" and is seduced by the coach's wife on the football field as the coach and his colleagues watch from the stands. At "UCC," Johnny is told the best steroids are available and someone is paid to provide urine samples when the players are tested. When his mother questions UCC's academic standards, Johnny tells her the school can get her a bigger house.

Even before the movies showed male athletes being offered money and gifts to enroll at a college or to play on a team, women were used as enticements. In films released between 1915 and 1940 these women were often referred to as "college widows," older married or single women, but sometimes students, who lived on or near a campus and dated, and by implication had sex with, undergraduates. The very first feature-length college film is *The College Widow* (1915), a story remade several times. In the original version, Jane (Ethel Clayton), the daughter of the school president, is called "the college widow" because she says goodbye to another graduating fiancé every year, as close to describing her as promiscuous as permitted by standards of the time. The football coach convinces Jane to "charm" one student into joining the team. In the 1927 remake with the same title, the president is told he'll have to resign if he can't find better football players, so his daughter Jane (Dolores Costello) uses her wiles to recruit other schools' star players at a vacation resort. One of them falls in love with her, but when he learns that she's been free with her affections, he persuades the others to quit the team. In the end, Jane persuades them all to rejoin the squad, and her father's job seems secure. The same plot is used in *Maybe It's Love* (1930) and *Freshman Love* (1936), though in the latter film the sport is changed from football to crew. Women also lure male athletes to a college or to a team in *Mr. Doodle Kicks Off* (1938), *$1,000 a Touchdown* (1939), and *Million Dollar Legs* (1939). This theme rarely appears in college movies between 1941 and 1987, but since then, heavily recruited athletes have been fawned over by women during campus visits in several films, including *Johnny Be Good* (1988), *The Program* (1993), and *He Got Game* (1998).

Gambling on Sports

In the movies, student-athletes are lured to college by women, money, and gifts. Once there, they face other corrupting influences: professional gamblers, alcohol, and drugs. Between 1919, when the Eighteenth Amendment prohibit-

The college president's daughter Jane Witherspoon (Dolores Costello) flirts with a football player to persuade him to transfer to her father's school in this 1927 version of *The College Widow* (Warner Brothers).

ing the manufacture, distribution, and sale of alcohol beverages was ratified, and 1947, many college movies located the threat of gambling and drinking in "roadhouses," a term covering speakeasies, bars, and seedy nightclubs where students would get drunk, fight, destroy property, lose money, and meet gangsters and disreputable women. A stark contrast to the cloistered "ivory tower," the roadhouse confronted young people with the evils of the "real world." After 1947, the roadhouse as a den of iniquity rarely appeared in college movies, because the influx of veterans onto the nation's campuses following World War II undermined the belief that college students were innocents who could be corrupted by what went on in the local tavern.

Professional gamblers in movies made between 1925 and 1952 got student-athletes into trouble that led to their suspension from the team or expulsion from school, usually just before a big game. Sometimes the gangsters kidnapped a player before a game on which they had bet heavily so as to increase their chance of winning. By the end of the 1930s, it was a cliché for a star athlete to be exonerated of criminal charges or rescued from his captors during the closing minutes of a big game and then be rushed to the field just in time to score the winning points. The storyline is used, with minor variations, in *College Days* (1926), *Rolled Stockings* (1927), and *College Love* (1929), and it is parodied in *Bonzo Goes to College* (1952).

Several movies released between 1918 and 1946 deal with gambling on crew races. The earliest is *Brown of Harvard* (1918), in which a gangster tries to get an oarsman who owes him money disqualified from a race so he can win a bet. In *The Winning Stroke* (1919), a professional gambler and a Yale student conspire to make it seem that a member of the crew has agreed to throw the big race with Harvard. The oarsman is suspended, but after the matter is straightened out, he helps win the race, is named captain, and takes the dean's niece away from the student who tried to frame him. A professional gambler in *All-American Sweetheart* (1937) places a bet against a crew that has lost three oarsmen due to academic problems. When a member of the crew goes to the gambler's club to borrow money to help out a friend, he's arrested for taking a bribe to lose the race, but he rows the crew to victory despite a serious injury and receives an apology after it becomes clear that he didn't take a bribe. In *Sweetheart of Sigma Chi* (1946), the owner of a roadhouse tells two gangsters that the local college is favored to win an upcoming race, so the gangsters plot to fix the race and bet $10,000 on the opponent. One member of the crew punches a gangster when he offers him a bribe to throw the race. A gangster drills a hole in the shell so it will sink, but an oarsman plugs the hole and his crew wins the race. Not only do crew members in these films preserve their innocence in the face of the corrupting influence of gamblers' money, they also make heroic efforts to win their races and cause the gamblers to lose their bets.

Even more common in college movies than gambling on crew races is gambling on football games. In *Braveheart* (1925), an American Indian is accused of selling signals and plays, when it was actually a white teammate who gave the information to a gambler to pay off a debt. Braveheart is expelled from school when the guilty player's denial of guilt is accepted over his own. Jim (Robert Young) in *Saturday's Millions* (1933) thinks that everyone likes him only for his football feats, not for who he really is, and for solace he turns to a woman he meets at a roadhouse. He refuses her request that he not play in a game because the club's owner, her husband, has bet on the opposing team. The owner threatens to reveal Jim's affair with his wife unless he cooperates. They fight and Jim's hand is injured. In an unusual conclusion, Jim drops a pass at the end of the game and his team loses, but his teammates and coach congratulate him on a great game and say they'd rather lose with him than win without him. A star quarterback in *The Big Game* (1936) justifies taking money from a professional gambler by saying that without it he couldn't pay for college. A teammate tells the gambler when the quarterback injures his knee at practice, and the gambler uses the information to win a lot of money. In *While*

Thousands Cheer (1940), Kenny (played by football star Kenny Washington) is offered $25,000 to miss a game on which a gambler has bet $100,000. He refuses, is blackmailed, and agrees to skip the game, but later decides to play and leads his team to victory. The gambler has Kenny kidnapped before the next game, but the star is rescued and rushed to the stadium just in time to help his team win again.

One of the few college movies to deal with gambling and football since the end of World War II is *The Swinging Cheerleaders* (1974). Alumni booster Putnam (George Wallace) tells Coach Turner (Jack Denton) they can win a lot of money by betting on the team. He gives Turner $1,000 to manipulate the margin of victory, which the coach does by taking his best players out of the game to keep the score down. Putnam tells Turner to lose a game his team is heavily favored to win so they can make a killing. Putnam tells Buck (Ron Hajek), the team's star player, that his company provided the money for Buck's scholarship and now he has a chance to show his gratitude by throwing the

Black college students were a rarity on the screen when *While Thousands Cheer* (Million Dollar Productions) was released in 1940. Starring real-life football star Kenny Washington as Kenny Harrington (in uniform, right), the film used a storyline recycled from the 1930s.

game. When Buck refuses, Putnam has the campus police beat him up, force-feed him alcohol, and leave him naked with a woman in a mountain cabin. In the tradition of college movies from the 1930s, Buck is rescued, delivered to the stadium in the fourth quarter, and has his team on the road to victory by the end of the movie.

Collegiate basketball is also corrupted by professional gamblers in the movies. A player in *The Big Fix* (1947) is blackmailed into manipulating the margin of victory to keep secret his sister's involvement in a car accident. A police lieutenant tells him how to control the score, supposedly to entrap the gangsters, but the lieutenant himself is the head of the gambling syndicate. A point-shaving scandal at the University of Kentucky during the 1948–1950 seasons, which led to the conviction of five players and the censuring of the coach, was the apparent inspiration for *The Basketball Fix* (1951). While working as a lifeguard at a country club to earn money to pay for college, Johnny (Marshall Thompson) meets Mike (William Bishop), a bookmaker. As a freshman, Johnny leads the league in scoring. When Mike hands him $100, saying he's earned it, Johnny turns it down. Mike says he (Johnny) knows where to come if he's ever short of money. Johnny later tells Mike he needs cash for the holidays, and the gambler says he can pick up $500 by deliberately missing an occasional basket, though not too obviously. Mike says he isn't asking Johnny to throw a game, just to keep the score closer so he can win his bets against the point spread. Johnny refuses, but after Mike tells him that one of his teammates has been taking money to shave points and he didn't even notice, Johnny begins missing shots and turning the ball over. When he wants out of the scheme and starts to score more than ever, Mike tells him he's in too deep to quit. Johnny scores a lot in the first half of the championship game, but he starts to miss on purpose in the second half, afraid that Mike's men have kidnapped his girlfriend to force him to cooperate. Johnny's team wins, but he is arrested and led away in handcuffs, unlike the player in *The Big Fix*, who is commended for his role in bringing professional gamblers to justice.

Point-shaving and intentionally losing show up in other films about collegiate basketball. In *Tall Story* (1960), Ray (Anthony Perkins) is instructed by a voice on the dispatch radio in the cab he drives to look for $1,500 in the glove compartment and is told he'll get an additional $2,500 if he lets a visiting Russian team win an upcoming game. He decides to fail a test so he'll be ineligible to play, but his professor gives him a makeup exam and he easily passes it in the locker room as the game is going on. He dashes onto the floor and scores several baskets, including a buzzer-beater that wins the game. In *Harvard Man* (2001), a Holy Cross student bets $250,000 of her own money on a Harvard-Dartmouth basketball game, lying to her boyfriend that her gangster father has placed the bet, and wants him to shave points so Harvard wins by less than seven points. The point-shaving idea gets lost in the movie, and for the girl to win her bet Harvard seemingly has to lose the game, which it does.

Drugs, Alcohol, and Sports

In addition to being corrupted by gamblers, the integrity of collegiate sports is threatened by the use of performance-enhancing substances, though college movies treated this problem as a source of humor until the late 1970s. In *The Gladiator* (1938), a studious non-athlete whose father and grandfather were sports heroes is urged by a young woman to try out for the football team. He proves inept until fed a special formula developed by a professor. He then joins the team and scores a winning touchdown, taking care to avoid injuring his opponents with his phenomenal strength. In *Let's Go Collegiate* (1941), an oarsman gets seasick during a crew race and eats a mothball to give him the energy to win. Another chemical shortcut to success appears in *Hold That Line* (1952), in which a student uses a mixture he concocts in a laboratory to become a powerful track and football star.

More recently, "pep pills" are used by a basketball player in *One on One* (1977), and steroids are the performance-enhancers of choice in *Johnny Be*

Hugo Kipp (Joe E. Brown) becomes a standout at football after being pumped up by a special formula concocted by a professor in *The Gladiator* (1938, Columbia).

Good (1988), *Necessary Roughness* (1991), and *The Program* (1993). In the last film, Steve (Andrew Bryniarski), a steroid-using defensive end, crashes his head through several car windows to celebrate making the starting team. When he tries to rape a diminutive student at a fraternity party, two teammates have to pull him off her. The girl's father doesn't want the assault reported in the press, because it would hurt the team, but Steve is suspended for three games and his coach tells him to stop using steroids. Steve replies that he needs them, because he doesn't have exceptional natural ability. He throws out his drug paraphernalia, but after failing to make a critical goal-line play, he starts using steroids again.

Despite its reputation for producing wholesome entertainment for America's youth, Walt Disney Pictures released seven movies between 1961 and 1997 that seem to condone cheating by college students; four involve chemical shortcuts to winning athletic contests. The final film in the Dexter Reilly trilogy, *The Strongest Man in the World* (1975), finds humor, but nothing to condemn, in the use of a performance-enhancing concoction to win a wrestling meet. *The Absent-Minded Professor* (1961), its sequel *Son of Flubber* (1963), and *Flubber* (1997), a remake of the first film, involve the use of miracle substances developed by a chemistry professor to win games against bigger, more talented teams. In the first and third movies, Flubber (flying rubber) is affixed to basketball players' sneakers so they can bounce over their opponents and score at will. Flubbergas is used in *Son of Flubber* to inflate football players' padding so they can bounce over or repel their opponents. These films even offer justifications for using these substances to win. In *Son of Flubber*, the puny "Medfield College of Technology" team is said to need "a secret weapon" to compete with the bigger "Rutland University" team for the national championship. When Rutland's coach complains that something is crooked, the referee responds, "Okay, here's the rule book. You think there's something wrong. You find it." Of course, there's no specific rule banning Flubbergas, but clearly something isn't quite right about using it.

A few movies look at athletes' abuse of alcohol, which invariably hurts their performance. Tom (William Haines) in *Brown of Harvard* (1926) gets drunk the night before a Harvard-Yale crew race, thinking he won't be rowing, but at the last minute he has to step in for an oarsman who has injured his hand. A hung-over Tom falters at the end of the race and Yale wins. He's shunned on campus, and during the summer he tells his father he's not going back to school because he cost the crew a victory by getting drunk and being out of shape. Later he redeems himself. After a quarterback in *The Program* (1993) gets into a barroom fight, his coach tells him he had to agree to send him to a rehab program to get the police to drop the charges of assault and driving while intoxicated. The player is surprised that his actions have consequences.

The film that looks most closely at alcohol abuse by a student-athlete is

Last Time Out (1994). After losing the final game of the season, wide receiver Danny (Christian Conrad) says he feels suspended in time during the off-season, because football is what he is and what he does. He drinks from a flask alone in the locker room, and at home his mother finds alcohol hidden in his closet. After learning of Danny's drinking problem, his father Joe (John Beck) enrolls as a student the following fall to keep an eye on him. When he finds out that his father is going to join his team, Danny drinks ten beers. Joe tells him he's a drunk and is jeopardizing his education and his future in professional ball. Danny denies having a drinking problem and nearly gets into a fight with Joe. After the coach benches him, Danny admits Joe was right and he could lose everything. Joe says he hasn't lost anything yet and at the end of the movie throws Danny a winning touchdown pass. Despite its facile conclusion, the movie does a nice job of examining a problem that is certainly more common than suggested by the infrequency with which it appears on the screen.

College movies raise important questions about the relationship of athletics to academics, the way players are recruited, and the corruption of sports by gamblers and performance-enhancers. Older films focus almost exclusively on the athletes' years in college, but newer ones deal with the recruitment of high school stars and with players' dreams of playing professional ball after college. Recent movies also focus more on the hours that student-athletes spend training and practicing and the pressures they face to cheat in their coursework or use chemical shortcuts. Other extracurricular activities also draw undergraduates away from their studies, but the culture of sport common on many campuses exacerbates the problem by failing to emphasize the value of getting grades any better than needed to remain eligible to play.

8

THE ACTIVIST

The lives of undergraduates extend beyond the dormitory, the lecture hall, and the library. Students do volunteer work in the community, work on campus newspapers and magazines, participate in musical groups and theatrical productions, run the student government, and engage in political activity. In these activities, they put to practical use what they have learned in the classroom, enrich the campus environment, explore career opportunities, and improve the world around them. Extracurricular activities can ease the transition from adolescence to adulthood by offering students both independence and supervision.[1]

By the time the first college movie was released in 1915, administrators were already persuaded of the need for organized campus activities such as sports, fraternities and sororities, newspapers, magazines, clubs, theater, and student government. Activities of this sort grew in popularity between the 1920s and the early 1940s as administrators increasingly saw them as a way to establish control over campus life and at the same time make the school more attractive to applicants and donors. Trustees, presidents, and deans also saw the extracurriculum as useful for developing the character and social skills that could balance academic pursuits and produce well-rounded graduates. Extracurricular activities can strengthen a sense of community and build allegiance to the school, but they can also divide a campus by isolating students from those who have different interests.[2]

Campus Organizations

The most common extracurricular activities in college movies, other than Greek-letter organizations and sports teams, are working on a campus newspaper or magazine, putting on a dramatic or musical show, and singing or playing in a band. Usually these activities get little screen time and are peripheral to the main story.

Working on a campus newspaper is an activity that shows up as often in recent movies as it did in those from the 1930s and 1940s. In *Freshman Year* (1938), a student gets into trouble for writing an editorial accusing a professor of being behind the times because he's been using the same exams for twenty years. The student supports his charges before a disciplinary board and is let off with an apology to the professor, who then changes his ways. A professor in *Dancing Co-ed* (1939) is not amused when his class is interrupted by students soliciting new subscriptions for the campus newspaper. Patty (Lana Turner), a professional dancer who has been sent to the college to be "discovered" in a nationwide search for a new movie star, becomes an assistant reporter so she can monitor its investigation of the allegation that the contest is fixed. The bespectacled editor is uncomfortable around women, and his stuffy assistant always wears a jacket and tie and says he dates only occasionally. When Patty confesses to the assistant that she's been planted on campus for the dance contest, he calls her a liar and a cheat but says he loves her anyway.

College newspaper reporters are sometimes portrayed as ambitious, even unscrupulous. In *Snafu* (1945), a journalism student intent on getting an exclusive story about a fifteen-year-old soldier (a scoop she hopes to sell to a national wire service) agrees with a woman who says that what she'd really like is a nice murder or suicide to write about. Connie (Wanda McKay), a journalism major and editor of the campus newspaper in *Kilroy Was Here* (1947), wants to save her job as the school's publicist and attract more donations by drawing attention to the college. She devises a scheme to publicize a returning veteran as the model for a cartoon character that showed up everywhere during World War II. In *Mr. Belvedere Goes to College* (1949), Ellen (Shirley Temple) is an ambitious reporter who photographs middle-aged freshman Lynn Belvedere (Clifton Webb) being disciplined by a committee of sophomores. In her article she writes that Belvedere believes boys are better students than girls, that wearing beanies is ridiculous, and that athletes are unfairly subsidized by the school. Belvedere complains that Ellen's gossipy article has hurt his reputation, and he rejects her proposal for an interview that would earn her a much needed $500 from a national news weekly. Later he consents to the interview, and his picture appears on the cover of *Life* magazine.

More recently, a journalism student in *The Swinging Cheerleaders* (1974) investigates cheerleading for a term paper after a newspaper editor describes it as the most exploitative and demeaning activity on campus. She's chosen to be on the cheerleading squad and does her research undercover, but she's ostracized by the other girls when the editor gets angry at her and posts a draft of her paper on a bulletin board. In *A Small Circle of Friends* (1980), a student smuggles a periodical out of the library, explaining that he couldn't check it out but needs it for an article he's writing about a cafeteria worker whose son is fighting in Vietnam. When the editor of the campus newspaper says no one

Randy "Scoop" Pruitt (Yvonne Craig), a journalism major and campus newspaper reporter, greets French professor Helene Gauthier (Nicole Maurey) and middle-aged undergraduate Harvey Howard (Bing Crosby) as they return to campus in the fall in *High Time* (1960, Twentieth Century–Fox).

cares about the story, the student and a friend break into the office at night and slip inserts of the story into the papers that are to be delivered the next day. In the morning, students all over campus are reading and talking about it. A reporter in *Primal Rage* (1988) gets a less favorable response from students who are incensed that an article he wrote accuses them of engaging in prostitution to lure star athletes to the school. Perhaps the most negative portrayal of a campus newspaper appears in *Class of Nuke 'Em High Part II: Subhumanoid Meltdown* (1991), in which an editor tells a reporter to bring her some dirt, because her readers want gossip and lies and rumors, not truth. Another devious reporter gets office workers to reveal confidential information about the title character in *Van Wilder* (2002). Her articles draw so much attention to Van that everyone on campus wants him to throw a party for them, allowing him to earn money for his tuition.

Another extracurricular activity that shows up in college movies, especially between the 1930s and the 1950s, is the student musical or dramatic production. In *Varsity Show* (1937), the continued existence of the campus "Quadrangle Club" depends on the success of its new musical review. The club's old-fashioned faculty adviser approves only of classical singing and dancing and won't let the students include the "vulgar" acts they've been rehearsing, so for help they turn to an alumnus, down-on-his-luck Broadway producer Chuck Daly (Dick Powell). When the dean tells the students the show is a college activity and must remain under the control of the club's faculty adviser, the students march in protest and boycott their classes. Chuck lectures the faculty, "Kids come to school for something else besides sticking their noses in a lot of books," and he argues that it's important to let them run the show. The faculty adviser refuses to let an outsider dictate school policy. Rather than cause the students to be expelled, Chuck leaves campus for New York, but the students follow him there. They stage a sit-in demonstration in a theater until they're given the right to rehearse there. When they mount their show on Broadway, it's a huge success.

Drumline (2002) also features a student musical performance that is more like a professional production than an amateur one. Many members of the "Atlanta A & T University" band have won scholarships for their musical talent, and the band is an important part of the school's identity. Student-musicians get up early for tryouts and practice sessions that stress teamwork and military-style training. They avidly compete for positions in the band, with lower-tier musicians challenging those at the higher levels and replacing them if they outperform them. This band has more in common with big-time sports programs than it does with other extracurricular activities.

Student dramatic productions also appear in a few movies. In *That Hagen Girl* (1947), Mary (Shirley Temple) tries out for the drama club's production of *Romeo and Juliet* after she is encouraged to do so by a faculty member. She wins the role of Juliet, but a disappointed rival has her influential family force the dean to get the role reassigned to her. After that girl gets drunk at a tavern, Mary steps in for her and wins accolades for her performance. In *She's Working Her Way Through College* (1952), a professor's theater arts class votes to stage a musical rather than a Shakespearean play, because the previous year only sixty people attended its production of *Romeo and Juliet*, and the students hope to boost their professor's reputation by drawing a bigger crowd with a musical. More recently, *The Delicate Art of the Rifle* (1996) includes a "Panhellenic Fashion Show" in which sorority members model clothing while badly acting out scenes from Shakespeare's plays.

An extracurricular activity that rarely shows up in college movies is the student club aimed at enhancing appreciation of an academic discipline.[3] A Philosophy and Self-Knowledge Club that committed mass suicide by jumping off a roof together is alluded to briefly in *The Delicate Art of the Rifle*, and *Harold and Kumar Go to White Castle* (2004) includes a scene of an East

Mary Hagen (Shirley Temple, standing, right) is told by Julia Kane (Lois Maxwell, seated) that she has been chosen to play Juliet in *Romeo and Juliet* in *That Hagen Girl* (1947, Warner Brothers). Christine Delaney (Penny Edwards, standing) is disappointed not to have gotten the role, but her wealthy parents convince the dean to give her the part. She later gets drunk in a tavern, and Mary performs in her place to great acclaim.

Asian Students' Club meeting, but the only club that gets any sustained attention is the Philosophy Club in *End of the Harvest* (1995). After a student gives an unconvincing presentation on the existence of God to the club, two of his friends offer to help put the group's "atheists" and "intellectuals" in their place. Scott (Brad Heller) has found a paper in the library that claims the Bible contains numerological clues about when the world will end, and he convinces the president of the Philosophy Club to let him make a presentation on the subject. Club members launch an *ad hominem* attack on Scott, which consists of revealing that he has been arrested for drunken driving, quit a fraternity, and dated nine girls over the past year. Afraid that his behavior will undermine the credibility of his presentation, Scott sends Matt (David A. R. White) to tell the club he wasn't prepared to speak. Matt is goaded into discussing his own beliefs and presenting the theory of when the world will end, and he overcomes the members' skepticism and convinces several of them to commit themselves to Christianity.

Student government is an extracurricular activity that rarely appears in college movies. One instance in which it does is *Sorority Girl* (1957), in which Rita (Barboura Morris) is running for student council president on a platform of eliminating racial discrimination by the university and democratizing its fraternity system. No one else on campus seems to care about these issues, but because Rita does, she is vulnerable to blackmail by Sabra (Susan Cabot), who threatens to undermine Rita's campaign by exposing her father's misdeeds unless she agrees not to report Sabra's abuse of a pledge.

No reliable measure exists of the extent of student participation in campus organizations, but anecdotal evidence suggests that *a capella* groups and student clubs have grown in number since the mid–1990s. Nonetheless, college movies today pay no more attention to this aspect of undergraduate life than they did in the past.

Collective Protest

Large numbers of American college students engaged in protest demonstrations during the 1930s and the Vietnam War era (1965–1973), but otherwise they have been less politically active than their counterparts in foreign countries. In general, activists in the United States have been more successful in shaping the way their colleges are run and the curricula they offer than in changing national and international policies.

College movies occasionally show undergraduates organizing to change campus life. Students in *The Fair Co-ed* (1927) protest a school policy of no cars on campus. After a professor in *The Male Animal* (1942) risks his job by reading his class a letter by a socialist, carefully explaining that he's teaching composition rather than advocating the author's ideas, a trustee tells him he's out of a job. The student editor of the campus literary magazine writes a fiery editorial calling the trustees "fascists," and students rally to support the professor for his inspiring defense of free speech. He keeps his job. Students in *Dear Brigitte* (1965) carry signs and march to the home of a professor to demand that poetry be brought back into the curriculum.

Several films look at students' efforts to change gender relations on campus. In *Girls Demand Excitement* (1931), Peter (John Wayne) is fired from his job as a gardener after he insults his employer's daughter Joan (Virginia Cherrill). Peter and Joan meet again on campus, where he's leading a movement to make the school all-male again. Joan leads the women who want to keep the school coeducational, proposing a *Lysistrata*-like plan in which they will withhold kissing and petting privileges until the men renounce their plan. Peter refuses to buckle under the pressure, arguing that the presence of women on campus has ruined the athletic program. The women challenge the men to a basketball game, and Joan tells them to distract the men with their sex appeal. At the end, the school remains coeducational. More than sixty years later, sexual politics is still an issue on campus in *PCU* (1994). A young man complains about political correctness, saying the "womynists" insist on being called women rather than girls, with one of them objecting to being called a freshman by saying, "Freshperson, please." In *A Reason to Believe* (1995), a woman tells her fellow feminists that to mainstream their message about sexual harassment they need to become more physically attractive and reach out to the sorority girls. Two members of the group reply that those people will never understand the problem, but the first woman argues that they need to expand their membership beyond the homosexual club and the women's studies program.

Political activism aimed at changing national and global policies shows up several times in college movies from the Great Depression. In *Bachelor of Arts* (1934), a boy falls in love with a girl he finds standing over him after a brawl at an antiwar speech. *Fighting Youth* (1935) focuses on communist activity on campus. When Carol (Ann Sheridan) secretly meets with Markoff (Alden Chase), a Russian agent posing as a law student, he tells her a committee of radicals has chosen her to be the next president of the Student League of Freedom. After the SLF decides to attack collegiate football for its exploitation of student-athletes, Carol flirts with Larry (Charles Farrell), an All-American, and persuades him to come to an SLF meeting, where he criticizes the school's football program. Larry fumbles twice in the next game, and Markoff starts a rumor that he lost the game on purpose. The coach suspends Larry, who then quits the team. A federal agent who has infiltrated the SLF reveals that he and other agents have been working on campuses across the country to stop enemy aliens from subverting the government. A dean describes campus radicals as young people full of ideas and says the college is supposed to foster ideas, so he can't interfere with them if they follow the rules. The coach initially refuses to let Larry return to the team because of his radical views, but then he relents and sends him into a game that they win by one point.

Communist activity on campus also shows up in *Pigskin Parade* (1936), in which a radical student distributes pamphlets attacking capitalism and announces he was expelled from a college back east after spending two months in jail for throwing a brick through a bank window. A more recent film, *The Way We Were* (1973), looks back at student activism in the 1930s. Katie (Barbra Streisand) speaks at a rally against Franco and in favor of the Soviet Union's efforts to stop fascism in Spain. Students both boo and applaud the president of the Young Communist League as she calls for world peace and asks them to take a pledge refusing support for the U.S. government in any war it conducts. Pranksters raise a sign behind her that reads, "Any Peace but Katie's Piece," and she calls the crowd fascists when they jeer at her. An apolitical

The Way We Were (1973, Columbia) deals in part with campus activism during the 1930s. Here Young Communist League president Katie Morosky (Barbra Streisand) addresses a crowd of students as some of them mock her behind her back.

classmate later suggests she could have defused the students' hostility by laughing when the sign was raised.

Soak the Rich (1936) mixes romance with campus radicalism. Students protest a dean's refusal to let a professor teach a controversial economics course in which he proposes higher taxes for the wealthy as a way to pull the country out of the Depression. The activists hose the dean's office, and when their leader, Buzz (John Howard), finds Belinda (Mary Taylor) there, he calls her the world's dopiest heiress and says the university belongs to the intellectuals. She asks him what is so intellectual about squirting people. After Buzz is injured in a confrontation with the police, Belinda visits him in the hospital, causing him to worry about how his friends will react to his associating with the daughter of a wealthy man. She tells him she wants to be a radical, but he dismisses her as a rich girl looking for a thrill. She repudiates her family and donates her allowance and jewelry to Buzz's group, but he's skeptical of her conversion and tells her not to fall in love with him. He says love stultifies the mind and makes people useless, describes marriage as the "guillotine of the soul," and claims that Russians don't kiss. After they kiss later in the movie, he calls himself a hypocrite for kissing his individuality goodbye and he throws her out of the group, again calling her a society girl looking for excitement. Despondent over their breakup, he loses interest in an upcoming protest march. At the end he declares his love for her but says his ideals are intact, and they plan to marry and work together for the radical cause.

Political activism was largely absent from college movies between the early 1940s and the early 1960s. One of its few appearances is in the biographical *The Iron Major* (1943), in which Dartmouth undergraduate Frank Cavanaugh (Pat O'Brien) speaks at an 1896 rally in support of William Jennings Bryan for president. His comments inflame student supporters of William McKinley, and they attack him and his friends.

Several films released between 1963 and 1968 deal with student protest in the blandest possible way, trivializing the issues and suggesting that political activism is just a passing phase in the transition from adolescence to adulthood. In *Take Her, She's Mine* (1963), Mollie (Sandra Dee) protests against nuclear weapons, the Berlin Wall, segregation, and fluoridation. Her father Frank (James Stewart) says she's arrived at the "social consciousness or the don't-wash-your-hair stage" and mistakenly believes that her political activities will leave her no time for romance. When she takes part in a sit-in protesting a library's ban on Henry Miller's books, Frank worries that her involvement with "cheap, shabby causes" will keep her from attending class and studying, but he nonetheless shows up at the library and argues that the mayor should at least listen to the protesters' arguments. In *C'mon, Let's Live a Little* (1967), campus activist Rego (John Ireland, Jr.) and the dean's son Tim (Mark Evans) stage a political rally. The dean tells the students that they want a more open discussion of problems, but he isn't sure what problems they want to talk about. Rego is booed by the students and says he's leaving campus, suggesting that he's an "outside agitator" rather than an enrolled student.[4] The film ends with Tim pleading for differences to be resolved in a civilized manner rather than by turning to mass meetings and violence. In *The Impossible Years* (1968), the police break up a campus demonstration in support of student power and free love. Students rock a patrol car, and several are arrested. The movie proposes that political activism is a problem of adolescent development best treated by psychiatrists rather than a thoughtful response to the world's problems.

Student activism in *The Impossible Years*, *C'mon, Let's Live a Little*, and *Take Her, She's Mine* bears little resemblance to actual events of the time. The formation of Students for a Democratic Society at the University of Michigan in the early 1960s gave rise to the New Left or the Movement. In 1964, activists in Berkeley's Free Speech Movement vociferously argued that the university was curbing freedom of expression, offering an irrelevant curriculum, and serving the military. FSM activists disrupted the school, elicited a strong police response, and radicalized a large number of liberals and moderates. In 1968, Columbia University students demonstrated to limit the school's impact on the nearby black community, empower students, and change teaching practices. In contrast to the FSM, the Columbia model of student activism was characterized by the destruction of university property, the use of police force, and strong disciplinary measures by the university. Harsh reactions by the police and the university increased student activism by reinforcing the protesters' commitment to their cause.[5] Another seminal event during this period was the "police riot" at the 1968 Democratic National Convention in Chicago. Although it did not occur on a college campus, many of the demonstrators who were shown being beaten on national television were students.

U.S. involvement in the Vietnam conflict began to escalate in 1965, and the number of campus demonstrations against the war grew after 1967. These demonstrations were characterized by the destruction of property and confrontation with the police, the result of the protesters' frustration with the increased scale of the war and their perception that the government was ignoring their demands for change. Antiwar protests peaked in 1970, the year that four students were killed by Ohio National Guardsmen at Kent State University.

Six movies about political activism were released in 1970 alone, though *Zabriskie Point* is about a former student, *The Revolutionary* and *Getting Straight* deal with graduate students, and *R.P.M.* focuses on a professor who is pressed into duty as a college president during a student protest. One year earlier, *The Activist* (1969) became the first film to look seriously at student opposition to the war. Mike (Michael Smith) meets Lee (Leslie Gilbrun) at a demonstration, she's attracted to his dedication to the cause, and they fall in love and move in together. After the police attack Mike and his group at a sit-in at the Berkeley induction center, Lee and a professor encourage him to quit the Movement and re-enroll in the university. He rejects the advice, leaves Lee, and continues his political activities.

Zabriskie Point opens with a meeting of student radicals discussing whether to burn down the building housing ROTC, a program that trains undergraduates to become military officers. One student wants to shift the group's attention from the war to the problem of racial oppression. Ex-student Mark (Mark Frechette) says he is willing to die but not of boredom, and he walks out of the meeting, later commenting that he needs to act and is tired of kids talking about violence while the cops do it. He goes to a demonstration at which the police use tear gas and clubs as bloodied protesters chant, "Power to the People."

Students in *Getting Straight* (1970) discuss the Vietnam War, the need for a black studies department, and the legalization of marijuana. One complains that there are only 400 committed activists among the 15,000 students at the school. When someone proposes demonstrating for student self-rule, long-time radical Harry (Elliott Gould) says the campus is a safe environment and

When Harry (Elliott Gould) questions his girlfriend Jan (Candice Bergen) about her commitment to the causes for which she marches in *Getting Straight* (1970, Columbia), he reflects the demeaning attitude toward activist women also seen in *Soak the Rich* (1936, Hecht-MacArthur Productions-Paramount).

they should protest in the real world where it counts, maybe at a munitions factory. Later, reflecting the sexism about which some Movement women complained, Harry tells his girlfriend as she marches with a sign that for her protesting is just a turn-on; she indignantly replies that she cares about the issues. The police show up at an antiwar demonstration in riot gear, having pocketed their identification badges, and they attack the protesters with night sticks, tear gas, and hoses. The school president agrees to make a few minor concessions to the students, but Harry tells him it's too late for petty reforms and warns that offering them will turn the protesters into full-scale revolutionaries who want to burn down the university. The president says he won't turn the school over to a misguided mob, and Harry replies that suppression breeds violence and the school has to change to survive. During Harry's oral exam for his master's degree, a riot starts and students rush the building. He says he hasn't passed the exam anyway and doesn't belong in school, and he heaves a brick through a window and joins the protesters.

In *R.P.M.*, which stands for revolutions per minute, sociology professor Paco Perez (Anthony Quinn) is appointed university president at the insistence of student protesters who have taken over the administration building. He convinces the trustees to accede to some of the protesters' demands but has to tell the students that three of their demands cannot be met. In an address to the non-protesting students, he criticizes those occupying the building for refusing to acknowledge that faculty members know more than freshmen, and asserts that civilization requires people to recognize authority and admit that not everyone is equal. He calls for less confrontation and more cooperation and says the basic question is whether the students still want a university. The assembly yells in support of Perez. Rossiter (Gary Lockwood), the leader of the sit-in, accuses Perez of demagoguery, and Perez replies that most of the students on campus reject Rossiter's methods. Rossiter admits that even if all of his group's demands had been met, there would have had more. When Perez

R.P.M. (1970, Columbia) is one of several movies from its era to use a computer to symbolize the impersonal and oppressive character of the modern university. Here students occupying an administration building precipitate police action by throwing computer tapes out the windows and threatening to destroy the university's $2 million computer.

learns that the protesters plan to destroy the university's $2 million computer, which contains essential records, he sends the police to the building. Rossiter tells the protesters how to cope with tear gas, saying it was all he learned at Berkeley. When the protesters begin to throw computer tapes out the windows, the police launch tear gas canisters and storm the building. Fleeing students are clubbed as Perez stands helplessly in the midst of the turmoil he couldn't prevent.

Based on a book about the 1968 takeover of five buildings at Columbia, *The Strawberry Statement* (1970) was relocated to the San Francisco area because neither the mayor of New York nor the university would allow filming on campus. Students in the movie protest their university's plan to replace a neighborhood playground and recreation center with an ROTC building. When they take over the president's office, they discover papers that reveal the administration intends to hold a piece of land until a utility company is ready to build a new facility there; they also learn that the company's chairman is a university trustee. Simon (Bruce Davison), who is at first politically uninvolved, is attracted to student activist Linda (Kim Darby) at a rally at which defense contractors and ROTC are assailed. She criticizes him for rowing crew, describing it as a game. A fellow oarsman calls the protesters "pukes" and "commie liberals," but later he's radicalized when the police break his leg during a demonstration. At the end of the film, a demonstration in the gym attracts national television coverage, and the school president sends in the National Guard and the police when the students refuse to leave. As the protesters sit in circles chanting "Give Peace a Chance," the police use tear gas, beat them, and make arrests.

Another demonstration against the Vietnam War opens *Drive, He Said* (1971). After the lights go out during a basketball game, student activists stage a mock-military operation on the court. The police break it up, the school president announces that he's open to talking with anyone, and the lights are turned back on and the game continues. One protester reports for a physical exam at the induction center, where he tries to show he's unfit for duty by deliberately misreading an eye chart, kissing a doctor on the forehead, and behaving violently. He later has a mental breakdown and is led away in a straitjacket.

Several movies made after the United States disengaged from the Vietnam War in 1973 look back at this era. In *A Small Circle of Friends* (1980), which is set at Harvard during the height of the war, one student enlists her friends to hang from the outside of a building her huge antiwar painting, "The American Way of Life," which shows people standing on a pile of skulls. Photographs of soldiers killed in the war are displayed on a fence as another student reads their names. A group of anxious students watches televised "Vietnam bingo," the selection of ping pong balls with birthdays written on them that will determine the order in which men will be drafted. A young woman comments, "Only men would come up with a draft lottery using balls."

When Leo's (Brad Davis) birthday is drawn third, he says he doesn't want to die. He's ordered to report for a physical exam, but he uses an altered medical record to keep from being drafted. When he visits a farm where a former roommate is living with other antiwar activists to try to convince him to leave the group, a homemade bomb accidentally explodes and kills Leo and his friend. Another film from the 1980s, *'68* (1988), focuses on the relationship between Alana (Miran Kwun), a non-student member of the Peace and Freedom Party, and Peter (Eric Larson), a Berkeley student-journalist, who at first supports the war as an honest effort to bring prosperity and democracy to Vietnam. Alana argues that professors lie about the political process and students accept everything they're told, and Peter grows more critical of the war. After he's expelled from school, he and Alana find a middle ground by working together on Senator Robert Kennedy's presidential campaign. In *1969*, another movie from 1988, two roommates and their visiting relatives get caught up in a demonstration that culminates in a vicious police beating of the protesters.

Campus demonstrations abated after four Kent State students were shot to death in 1970, three years before the United States ended its involvement in the war. As campuses again became peaceful, filmmakers turned away from the subject of political activism, though several movies have dealt with the issue of race relations. The only college movie to deal extensively with student involvement in the civil rights movement (1954–1968) is *Heart of Dixie* (1988), which takes place in Alabama in the 1950s. Associated Press reporter Hoyt (Treat Williams) tells sorority girl Maggie (Ally Sheedy) that an article she has written on race relations for her journalism class is about an important problem, but she needs to learn more about it firsthand. They go to an Elvis Presley concert at which black fans are segregated in the balcony, and they see a group of white men beat up a black man who has come down to the floor for a better view. Police officers pull the black man away but then beat him some more. Maggie tries to stop the attack while Hoyt takes photographs. She criticizes him for not helping the man, but he says his pictures will show the world what happened. The editor of the campus newspaper tells Maggie he can't run her story on race relations because an earlier one she did caused problems, but he agrees to present her story to the publications board for further consideration. A dean on the board tells Maggie that hers has been a sane and eloquent voice that needs to be heard, and he applauds her sensitivity on the question of racial inequality, but the college depends on the wisdom of its regents and the pocketbooks of its alumni, and he regrets that the volatile political atmosphere in the state makes it impossible to publish her story. He threatens to expel her if the article is published. When it is, she leaves school rather than apologize.

Unlike *Heart of Dixie*, which takes place in the past and is told from the perspective of a white student, several other films focus on the present-day experiences of black students. *School Daze* (1988) opens at an all-black college with Dap (Laurence Fishburne) berating his fellow students for lagging behind predominantly white schools in demanding divestment from South Africa. A fraternity president worries that Dap's revolutionary politics will hurt both the college and their brothers in South Africa. The student council president intervenes in their argument and says he won't tolerate violence among the factions on campus. Even though Dap is threatened with expulsion because of his political activities, he continues to urge his friends to fight apartheid, but they say there are times to be quiet and this is one of them. The movie ends with Dap ringing a bell and warning everyone to "Wake up!" *Divided We Stand* (2000) begins with a member of the Black Student Coalition telling incoming freshmen that over the next four years they will win out, lose out, or sell out. The BSC protests discrimination by a recently fired professor and works to restore a scholarship program for minorities, but its efforts are undermined when a member gets into a fight with a white student in the library and the group's president is accused of rape.

Another kind of political activism makes a brief appearance in *Fast Food Nation* (2006). A high school student joins the three undergraduate members of the campus Environmental Policy Discussion Group to protest the desecration of their Colorado community by a meatpacking plant that supplies a McDonald's-like restaurant chain. Andrew (Aaron Himelstein) suggests a letter-writing campaign, but Paco (Lou Taylor Pucci) mocks the proposal as a lame tactic in light of the enormous influence the company has with state politicians. Arguing that the group needs to takes more risks like Greenpeace members do, Paco supports the high school student's suggestion that they cut the fence penning in the cattle that are destined for the slaughterhouse. Andrew fears that doing this will cause the federal government to use the Patriot Act against them, claiming it regards environmental activists as terrorists more threatening than right-wing militias. Paco replies, "Right now, I can't think of anything more patriotic than violating the Patriot Act." Andrew reluctantly goes along with the rest of the group and they cut the fence, but the cattle, symbolic of the American fast-food buying public, refuse to budge from the field, too stupid to realize there are better things to eat than the synthetic grain they are fed by the meatpackers.

Community Activism

Political activists are usually but a small percentage of the student body. During the Vietnam War, only one in every four undergraduates reported ever protesting against it, and as many as 85 percent of campuses were quiescent.[6] Movies released around 1970 exaggerated the extent of campus political activity, because violence and the intergenerational conflict implicit in students' confrontations with the authorities are dramatically appealing. By contrast, undergraduates who quietly try to effect change by volunteering at a battered women's shelter or attending a trustees' meeting are less attractive subjects for filmmakers. The result is that college movies both create and reinforce the misconception that today's students are less politically involved than their counterparts during the Vietnam War era.

Few movies show undergraduates doing community service work, despite the fact that two-fifths of them engage in activities such as neighborhood improvement, church service, helping children, tutoring, fund raising, and volunteering in health-care facilities, nursing homes, homeless shelters, and soup kitchens.[7] Many students also take trips during breaks from classes to volunteer in another part of the country, most recently in the Gulf Coast area devastated by Hurricane Katrina in 2005.

One of the few movies to deal with civic engagement by college students is *Top Man* (1943). When a junior college student learns there aren't enough workers in the local plant to build airplanes as fast as they're needed for the

Alan Newell (Sidney Poitier) is a college student who does volunteer work for a suicide hotline in *The Slender Thread* (1965, Paramount). Here he discusses with his supervisor Dr. Joe Coburn (Telly Savalas) how to handle a call from a despondent woman who has taken an overdose of pills.

war effort, he suggests to his fellow students that they help out. Volunteers are bused to the plant, production rises dramatically, and the students are commended for helping to solve the labor shortage. In *Smart Politics* (1948), another group of junior college students plans a dance and variety show to raise money to build a recreational center that will honor local war heroes and help to reduce delinquency. *The Slender Thread* (1965) opens with a student leaving campus for his weekly shift as a volunteer on a suicide hotline. He expects to have enough quiet time to study for an exam, but he gets involved in a long phone call with a woman who has taken an overdose of barbiturates. In *College Kickboxers* (1990), a black student runs a karate academy for poor kids in an off-campus building that's slated for demolition. His white roommate wins a martial arts tournament and donates his $25,000 prize money to keep the academy open.

Today's college students "work within social structures to create the same kind of change the students of the '60s tried to effect with demonstrations."[8] Their efforts are directed at a wide range of problems, more often campus or local ones rather than national or global ones. Their activities include volunteering at daycare centers and social service agencies, working for the equal treatment of gay and lesbian students, striking for better pay for college custodians and food workers, and urging their schools to divest from companies with ties to oppressive regimes. If today's student activists lack a single galvanizing issue like the Vietnam War, which would enhance the visibility of their efforts, their reformist approach to a broad range of problems may eventually produce a more fundamental transformation of the society than did student demonstrations of the past.

College movies pay relatively little attention to students' efforts to change the world, with the exception of several made around 1970. Even in those movies, the activists are as likely to be graduate students, college dropouts, and administrators as they are to be undergraduates. The few undergraduate activists who do show up in these films often appear in groups of protesters rather than as sharply defined individuals. Movies from the Vietnam War era and some from the 1930s sometimes raise political issues in a thoughtful way, though they typically leaven their stories with romance and often focus on violent confrontations. The quiet work students do to improve the world around them rarely makes it the screen.

9

THOSE WERE THE DAYS

The college years end most happily when students graduate with friends and family congratulating them and wishing them well for the future. Others drop out along the way to work or marry, and some are expelled for poor grades or misconduct. Several movies include departures prior to finishing a degree, and graduation exercises show up as well, though less often as the culmination of years of study than as a device to open a film that follows the graduates into young adulthood. Rarely do the movies allude to the most common reasons for leaving college before graduating: inadequate academic preparation, insufficient financial resources, and the belief that a diploma won't necessarily result in a better job.[1]

Leaving College Voluntarily

Undergraduates in earlier movies sometimes quit college to get married, but this is uncommon in movies made since the mid–1960s. This change reflects the rise in the average age at which people first get married. Students have also been less likely to get married in recent years because of easier access to abortion and women's greater commitment to completing a degree and starting a career.

The assumption in films prior to the mid–1960s was that undergraduates who got married were effectively ending their education, because their parents would stop paying for college on the assumption that their children would take full-time jobs to support themselves. A girl in *The Band Plays On* (1934) tells her boyfriend that nine of every ten college students who get married never complete their degrees. Marriage has this effect in *Love, Honor, and Behave* (1938), in which a Yale student marries his childhood sweetheart and, as a result, can't finish his senior year and go on to medical school as his mother had planned for him since he was ten. *Cynthia* (1947) begins with a woman reminiscing about her freshman year seventeen years earlier when she met her husband. They got married as undergraduates and, after she became

The college years end on a happy note but the future holds uncertainty for these new Georgetown University graduates in *St. Elmo's Fire* (1985, Columbia), which runs the opening credits over this scene and then shows the friends adjusting to life after college.

pregnant, settled down in a small town instead of attending graduate school as they had planned. In *The Young Lovers* (1964), when a "scholastic bum" and his girlfriend decide to get married, they plan for her to finish her degree but for him to quit school and sell used cars for her father. Another movie in which a student leaves school to get married is *Rich and Famous* (1981), which opens in 1959 with two Smith College students sneaking out of their dorm at night so one of them can elope; her friend wishes her a wonderful trip and a wonderful life.

Undergraduates voluntarily leave college before graduating for reasons other than marriage. In *All I Want* (2002), a freshman who is bullied by his roommate quits school on his very first day to pursue his goal of becoming a writer. In *Been Down So Long It Looks Like Up to Me* (1971), an alienated young man drops out of college but returns when he doesn't find what he was looking for, which is never clearly defined. He sold drugs during the hiatus but refuses to work for his supplier once he returns to campus.

Involuntary Withdrawal

Many departures from college are involuntary. In the past, students could be taken out of school by their families for mental health problems, but today's privacy laws restrict parents' access to information about these situations if their children are over the age of eighteen. These problems are now quite extensive; one survey found that 45 percent of college students have felt so depressed they've had trouble functioning and 15 percent have had symptoms that fit the clinical definition of depression.[2] One of the few films to deal with this issue is *The Bell Jar* (1979). After Esther (Marilyn Hassett) is sexually assaulted and suffers a mental breakdown while doing a summer internship at a woman's magazine in New York, she moves home rather than return to college for her senior year. She undergoes electroshock therapy and tries to commit suicide before being institutionalized in what one patient calls an "Ivy League loony bin." In *Foreign Student* (1994), which takes place in Virginia in 1955, a freshman from Boston who fakes a Southern accent and uses a false name is taken out of school by her parents, who describe her as seriously ill.

Other college educations are ended prematurely by alcohol abuse. In *College Humor* (1933), the football coach refuses to let Mondrake (Richard Arlen) play after he is charged with drunk and disorderly behavior, released from jail, and shows up in the locker room inebriated. The dean expels the student, telling him there's no room for drunken rowdies at the university. Mondrake is later found drunk on a football field on a rainy night, waxing nostalgic about his glory days but angry at his expulsion. At the end, he cheers his former team to victory from the stands.

Students are also expelled for breaking the law, frequently while drunk. A football star in *St. Louis Woman* (1934) is kicked out of school for drinking and for accidentally punching a dean in a ruckus in a nightclub that is off-limits to students. In *All American* (1953), another football player is expelled for getting into a barroom fight, but he is improbably reinstated when the barmaid convinces the dean he was just trying to help another student. The title character in *Van Wilder* (2002) faces expulsion for having underage drinkers at a party he organized. He tells an appeals board he isn't ready for life on the outside yet, gets good grades when he goes to class, and needs only eighteen more units to complete his degree in Leisure Studies. He's reinstated after he convinces the panel to punish him by forcing him to graduate.

Other expulsions result from property crimes that are not associated with alcohol abuse. A dean in *Sis Hopkins* (1941) tells a freshman to leave school because he mistakenly believes she has stolen a mink coat; she is readmitted after the misunderstanding is cleared up. A football player is kicked out of school in *Saturday's Hero* (1951) for stealing $20 from the chapel donation box to give to a girl so she can escape a bad situation at home. His punishment is portrayed as unduly harsh because he wasn't important to the team, whereas another player who stole but was critical to the team's success was not expelled. In *Puddle Cruiser* (1996), two students who are caught breaking into the cafeteria to gorge on food are threatened with suspension, but the judiciary board instead requires them to do 500 hours of community service.

Undergraduates in several films are expelled or threatened with expulsion for using the campus newspaper in a way offensive to the administration. A student in the classic adventure film *Northwest Passage* (1940) is thrown out of Harvard for his cartoon lampooning the school president. In *Dancing Co-ed* (1939), the president orders all copies of the campus newspaper confiscated and summons two student-journalists to his office, where he chastises them for their vulgar photographs and humorous captions, especially the picture of him drinking from a bottle of what he claims is an old cough remedy. He tells them they've been deliberately disloyal to the school and will have to withdraw, but then he relents and says that instead they'll have to give up their school activities until he can meet with their parents. Two students in *The Love-Ins* (1967) are dismissed by the chancellor for refusing to stop publication of their underground newspaper. A professor tells the chancellor the school has no jurisdiction over students' off-campus activities, but the chancellor says that underground papers have been the cause of campus disturbances all over the country and he won't let that happen at his school. The professor resigns in protest and is cheered by students who praise him for defending their right to free speech.

Sexual escapades are another reason for the expulsion of students in the movies. *She Loves Me Not* (1934) revolves around the risk of expulsion for Princeton students who are hiding a runaway stripper in their all-male dorm. In a subplot of the remake of this film, *How to Be Very, Very Popular* (1955), fourth-year freshman Toby Marshall (Orson Bean) has been thrown out of school. President Tweed (Charles Coburn) is looking for Toby, because his absence from the graduation ceremony will jeopardize a large donation promised by Toby's father. Tweed tells Mr. Marshall that his son's college career has been unique and he hasn't had to speak to him about his behavior for months, failing to mention that this is because Toby has been expelled. Tweed assures Marshall that his son hasn't gotten into any trouble with the girls, but Marshall is disappointed because he wants his son to have girlfriends. When he learns that Toby was actually thrown out for drinking and organizing a panty raid, he's proud of him and thanks Tweed for making him a man. Expulsion for sexual misconduct also shows up in *Hamburger—The Motion Picture* (1986). The movie begins with a dorm mother catching a boy making love to a girl in a shower stall. He's required to undergo counseling and tells his female therapist that all he does at college is have sex and get thrown out for "lewd and nude conduct." Finding him irresistible, she takes off her glasses, lets down her hair, and bares her breasts just as the dean walks into the office. In *Deconstructing Harry* (1997), Woody Allen plays a novelist who is attending a ceremony in his honor at the college that expelled him years earlier for trying to give an enema to the dean's wife.

Expulsion from college is usually the result of poor grades or academic dishonesty, but these reasons for being thrown out of school don't show up in the movies very often, though the threat of this happening is frequently mentioned. In *Splendor in the Grass* (1961), Bud (Warren Beatty), who is flunking his courses at Yale, tells his father and the dean that he'd rather be ranching than studying. The dean says college isn't for everyone and advises Bud to leave school, but Bud's father offers to take him to New York for the weekend and return him to school ready to study. The stock market crashes, Bud's father commits suicide after losing his fortune, and Bud apparently leaves Yale for good.

Graduation

Unlike Bud, students in other movies are reluctant to leave college. In *The Seniors* (1978), four men who know their parents soon won't be paying for their good times procure a research grant to support themselves and hire sex partners. Unwillingness to leave college also shows up in *The Muppets Take Manhattan* (1984), when one of the creatures responds as follows to the suggestion that their theatrical troupe take its senior variety show to Broadway after graduation: "If we don't do it, then we just say goodbye to each other."

Recognition that life after college will be different underlies the following statement by a young man in *A Reason to Believe* (1995): "I think people know they have to stop doing drugs when they get out of school, especially with testing and everything now. I'm quitting two months before graduation. And I don't think anybody's going to get too far using shit, fuck, and bitch in every sentence. I think people grow out of it. Hope I do." A similar resolution is made by the title character in *April Is My Religion* (2001), who responds as follows to a question about whether potential employers might be concerned about her drug use: "After this semester, I'm going clean." A Harvard graduate in *A Small Circle of Friends* (1980) is initially unwilling to make these kinds of changes after finishing college, so he spends some time traveling, getting drunk, and lounging on the beach before realizing he needs to get on with his life. In recent years, more college graduates are reportedly taking a "timeout" before continuing their education or committing to a career.[3]

One consequence of graduation rarely dealt with in the movies is its impact on students' parents, who have to adjust to their children leaving home for good. In *All That Heaven Allows* (1955), college students Ned (William Reynolds) and Kay (Gloria Talbott) worry that their wealthy widowed mother Cary's

(Jane Wyman) romance with handyman Ron (Rock Hudson) will adversely affect their family's social position and put their home in jeopardy. Cary reluctantly breaks off the relationship, but as Ned and Kay near graduation, they announce they'll be settling down elsewhere. Ned tells his mother she can sell the house because it will be his last Christmas at home, since he will either be drafted, attend graduate school, or take a job. Kay tells Cary she's engaged and will be living far from home after she marries. Realizing she has to think of her own future, Cary reconciles with Ron.

Three versions of *Daddy Long Legs* (1919, 1931, 1955) make it clear how important it is to graduating seniors to have their parents or guardians present at commencement exercises. In each version, the orphaned young woman is disappointed when her benefactor doesn't come to her graduation to share her pride in getting her diploma. Her unhappiness is accentuated by having to watch her classmates getting hugs and congratulations from their parents. *New Best Friend* (2002) suggests that even though parents are proud of their children at graduation, they are blissfully unaware of what they've really been up to for the past four years. This idea is supported by a scene in *The Upside of Anger* (2005) in which a girl surprises everyone by correctly guessing that her older sister, who has just gotten her diploma, is about to tell the family that she's going to marry her boyfriend because she's pregnant.

Some college movies reveal a cynical attitude toward graduation. After a public address announcer in *The All American* (1932) comments at the end of a football hero's last game that he could be elected governor today but will be lucky to find a job tomorrow, the player quits school before completing his degree, a decision that leads to gambling, indebtedness, and unemployment. A Harvard student in *Spring Madness* (1938) plans to finish his coursework but skip commencement, saying, "I don't see any reason for tricking myself out in a black nightshirt or cardboard hat to celebrate four practically wasted years." A friend says, "After all, Sam, we worked for a diploma," but Sam (Lew Ayres) replies, "Not I. Never." A senior in *Learning Curves* (2003) watches his graduation ceremony from a distance rather than march in the procession, commenting that a diploma is just a piece of paper and "College shouldn't be about mapping out the rest of your life. It's where you figure out you don't need to." He observes that it took him four years and $200,000 of his father's money to learn that.

Students who deliver commencement addresses in the movies reminisce about their undergraduate days and offer clichéd words of wisdom to their classmates. In the 1931 version of *Daddy Long Legs*, a valedictorian says that after graduation they will all go their separate ways but will always remain united by the memory of what they've been through together. She describes college as a gift, a time to reach out for enlightenment and beauty, and says it was precious to her because she knows how cruel life can be. After a woman is honored at her graduation ceremony in *Elopement* (1951), she reminds the audience that commencement means beginning and says that getting her award is like being given a victory cup before the tournament's even started. In *High Time* (1960), a fiftyish man who has returned to college after a successful business career gives a valedictory speech in which he quotes George Bernard Shaw's statement that youth is wasted on the young. He says he came to college to find his youth but instead found something far better, his life, and he praises the school for the warmth and friendship it offers and for being an "exalting world of thought, science, and feeling." *The Group* (1966) begins with the Class of 1933 valedictory speech at an all-women's school. A senior speaks of women's role in society and claims the goals of a college education are personal fulfillment and social service. The movie follows several of the graduates into adulthood and ends ironically with a voice-over of the earlier speech, contrasting its idealism with the reality of the women's lives following college. In *Back to School* (1986), Thornton Melon (Rodney Dangerfield) tells graduating seniors to move back with their parents and let them worry about things, warning, "It's a jungle out there. You gotta look out for number one. But don't step in number two." In her speech in *Reality Bites* (1994), Lelaina (Winona Ryder) asks, "What are we going to do now? How can we repair all the damage we inherited? Fellow graduates, the answer is simple...The answer is...This answer is, I don't know." The graduation exercises in this film and others such as *St. Elmo's Fire* (1985) and *Herbie Fully Loaded* (2005) function as a device for beginning a story about young adults making their way in the world immediately after college.

The Years After College

Graduates often rely on their classmates long after they have left college. In *The Sport Parade* (1932), Dartmouth football teammates Johnny (William Gargan) and Sandy (Joel McCrea) plan to work together on a newspaper after graduation, but Sandy signs up with a gambler who promises to promote his career in professional football. When this doesn't work out, Sandy has an unproductive interview with a Dartmouth alumnus; on the way out, he overhears a man comment that football players should realize college only lasts four years. Johnny offers the unemployed Sandy a job in the sports department of the newspaper where he's been working since graduation, and the two collaborate on a popular series of columns in which each takes a different perspective on the same sporting event. *Forty Little Mothers* (1940) begins at a reunion with alumni wondering about the absence of their smartest classmate. Gilly (Eddie Cantor), an unemployed professor who is too ashamed to attend the reunion, is arrested trying to steal milk to feed an abandoned baby he's caring for. The judge turns out to be a college classmate, and when he recognizes Gilly, he loans him money and finds him a teaching job.

Lelaina Pierce (Winona Ryder) delivers a graduation speech expressing her confusion about the future to begin *Reality Bites* (1994, Universal), which focuses on the lives of a group of friends after they leave college.

The favors done by classmates and other alumni have unexpected consequences in several films. In *College Rhythm* (1934), Larry (Lanny Ross), who plays the piccolo, sings in the glee club, and is a member of Phi Beta Kappa, tells campus football hero Francis J. Finnegan (Jack Oakie) that he came to college to study his books, but Finnegan came to study his press clippings. He tells Finnegan, who once beat him for freshman class president, that he doesn't have what it takes to stay on top. After graduating, Finnegan is down on his luck and has to take a menial position in the department store owned by Larry's father. Larry also works there, but the modern retailing methods he learned in college are bringing in few customers and the store is losing money, so he resigns. The store then does a booming business after Larry's father reopens it with a college theme, replete with cheerleaders, dancers, a band, a glee club, and a newly promoted Finnegan wearing a football uniform. This film's suggestion that academic success doesn't necessarily translate into a rewarding career is consistent with evidence that athletes enjoy greater financial success after graduation than non-athletes. This has been attributed to the

College Rhythm (1934, Paramount) suggests that athletes who are mediocre students, such as ukulele-strumming Francis J. Finnegan (Jack Oakie), enjoy greater financial success after college than their academically more talented classmates. Gloria van Dayham (Mary Brian) seems to be enjoying Finnegan's antics.

kinds of careers that athletes are attracted to; the alumni networks that provide them with entry into well-paid jobs; and a culture of sport that teaches and rewards teamwork, competitiveness, goal-directedness, discipline, self-confidence, leadership, time management, and decision-making under pressure.[4]

One movie in which help from an alumnus in getting a job doesn't pay off is *The Sin of Harold Diddlebock* (1947), also known as *Mad Wednesday*. The film begins with a sequence from the end of *The Freshman* (1925), in which water-boy Harold (Harold Lloyd) miraculously scores a winning touchdown. In the locker room after the game, an old grad hands him a business card and tells him to contact him about a job in his advertising firm after he finishes school. An enthusiastic Harold begins at the lowest level in the company, but his career stagnates and twenty-two years later he is fired and given a watch and a small sum of money. By this time, the man who gave him the job doesn't even remember what sport Harold played.

The Sin of Harold Diddlebock and *College Rhythm* are but two of many movies that question the value of higher education rather than treat it as essential to a successful career and a satisfying life. In the Depression era film *Pigskin Parade* (1936), the Yacht Club Boys sing about having been in college for fourteen years because there's no place to go if they leave. They ask why they should graduate when millions are out of work, pointing out they don't need a college degree to help their fathers lose money in their factories. Songs in *Varsity Show* (1937) and *She's Working Her Way Through College* (1952) also raise doubts about the value of going to college to learn things that will never be of any practical use. An army officer in *Beyond Glory* (1948) talks about the possibility of enrolling in college after he leaves the military, commenting that he's aware of the difference between integral and differential calculus and knows that knowledge is supposed to come in handy, but the tone of his voice makes it clear that he doubts this is true.

More recent films also ask what a college degree is worth. *The Graduate* (1967) begins at a party honoring Benjamin (Dustin Hoffman) for graduating from college. He wants to be left alone to ponder his uncertain future, but eventually he joins the party, where he's bewildered by the terse career advice offered by a family friend: "I just want to say one word to you...just one word...*plastics*. There's a great future in plastics." When Benjamin's father asks him what his four years of hard work were for, his son answers, "You got me." Mr. Patimkin (Jack Klugman) in *Goodbye, Columbus* (1969) criticizes his son to his daughter's boyfriend Neil (Richard Benjamin) as follows: "College kid? Four years of college and he can't even load a truck." Neil replies, "Well, they don't teach too much about truck loading anymore in college." Patimkin responds, "And what do they teach in college? About books? A lot you can learn from books. Let me tell you something, in the real world you need a little *gonif* [thief] in you." In *The Seniors* (1978), a student who is contemplating what to do after graduation observes that while he'll have his degree in business administration, his business professor has gone bankrupt. In a similar vein, a young woman in *The One and Only* (1978) asks, "So I have this degree in sociology and, um, well, what'll I do with it?" Her boyfriend advises, "Open a sociology store." A middle-aged woman in *Change the Frame* (1995) is even more cynical about the value of her diploma, saying there are "only so many times you can use it to wipe your ass."

A few movies look at the long-term repercussions of events that occurred in college. In *The League of Frightened Gentlemen* (1937), ten students cripple a freshman during a hazing incident. Years later, two of them are murdered and the others get threatening notes, but it turns out that while their hazing victim has sent the notes, someone else is committing the murders. *The Brute Man* (1946) begins with two murders by the grotesque "Creeper." When a police officer discovers an old photograph of three college students, he learns the quick-tempered Hal (Rondo Hatton), who is the murderer, was captain of

Benjamin Braddock (Dustin Hoffman, looking down) joins a party celebrating his recent graduation from college in *The Graduate* (1967, Avco Embassy). He will soon be bewildered when a family friend advises him to consider a career in plastics.

the football team but a weak student. He and Clifford (Tom Neal) both loved Virginia (Jan Wiley), and to get revenge against Hal for "scoring" off the field with Virginia, Clifford gave him incorrect answers to a chemistry quiz. When Hal failed the quiz, the professor made him stay after class to work on a difficult problem in the laboratory. Clifford taunted Hal by walking by the lab with Virginia, and the enraged Hal threw the compound he was working on to the floor, starting a fire that left him severely injured and disfigured, the motive for his revenge murders years later. Another film that deals with the long-term consequences of undergraduate romance is *These Wilder Years* (1956). A business tycoon begins a search for the son he fathered twenty years earlier by going to his college's alumni office, where he's given the records of his former girlfriend. He learns that she failed to graduate because of her pregnancy, completed a degree some years later, but has since died. Her resentful sister refuses to give him any information about his son, but he tracks him down anyway.

Several movies look at the disappointed expectations of college graduates. In *Hero for a Day* (1939), Frank Higgins (Charley Grapewin), an embittered alumnus who was once a football legend, works as a night watchman on a construction site. He says most people see colleges as quiet, polite places where no one cares about making a living and believe a diploma is a blank check, but he claims the world isn't like that. As an undergraduate he was voted most likely to succeed, turned down an assistant coaching job, and became a success in business, but that ended with the Great Depression. He says no one really cares who wins a football game and what really matters is what comes after college. *Yesterday's Heroes* (1940) also looks at the life of a collegiate football player after he leaves school. Alone in his hotel room with his rent overdue, Duke (Robert Sterling) relives his glory days by leafing through a scrapbook of newspaper clippings. The film flashes back to his undergraduate years, when he was pressured to join the team despite wanting to concentrate on his studies. As a senior, he was ready to quit the team to enter medical school early, but his coach got the offer of early admission rescinded. After Duke's fumble in the conference championship game cost his team a victory, he walked off the field in silence and quit school. Back in the present, Duke takes his college roommate's advice to stop being one of "yesterday's heroes" and go back to his college girlfriend. Life after college for the football hero is also the theme of *Everybody's All-American* (1988). At his team's twenty-fifth reunion, former All-American Gavin Grey (Dennis Quaid), once worshipped by everyone on campus, is introduced to a decidedly indifferent crowd before a homecoming game. At a banquet the members of his team recount their past exploits and watch films of their old games, but their efforts to conjure up the past are depressing. Gavin decides there's more to life than scoring touchdowns and realizes he played because he loved the game, rather than for the glory.

Disappointed expectations are also the theme of *Carnal Knowledge* (1971). The first part of the film is infused with the innocent enthusiasm of two Amherst students, but in the second part one has become a middle-aged hippie with a stultifying marriage and a girlfriend half his age, and the other is making a lot of money but is unhappy that he can't sustain a satisfying relationship with a woman. Disillusionment comes more quickly to Jake (Eric Stoltz) in *Naked in New York* (1993). Taking the advice not to remain in his college town after he graduates, he moves to New York to pursue a career as a playwright. He is frustrated by his lack of success and says it's hard to discover that the play he once thought was so great really isn't. His unhappiness is exacerbated by a classmate who comments that Jake "must be on Broadway by now." Jake answers, "No, no, not...not yet," and asks how he is doing. The classmate replies, "Great. I was in Oxford when one of the little plays I wrote got done by the BBC." Jakes mutters, "Well, if you'll excuse me, I have to go over here and slit my wrists."

Memories of College Days

A child in *Hero for a Day* (1946) comments that people who go to college stay "sort of goofy" about it for the rest of their lives. This observation is consistent with the recent increase in the number of retired people choosing to live near the campus where they went to school decades earlier in the hope of refreshing "old memories of a seemingly carefree time when they met classmates and were just beginning to think seriously about their careers."[5]

Nostalgia for the college years is encouraged by class reunions, homecoming weekends, and other visits to campus. Two old grads in *Saturday's Millions* (1933) renew their acquaintance on homecoming weekend, wrestling like boys when they meet and reminiscing about their time together in college. As Yale alumni return to campus by train for a tribute to classmate Cole Porter in *Night and Day* (1946), Monty Woolley is asked if the university has changed. He replies, "The ivy may be a little thicker on the buildings, the cracks in the walls may be a little deeper...and a few more names have been carved on the Yale fence, but underneath it's no different, the same spirit, the same tradition." He later tells an audience they still feel as much a part of Yale as when they were freshmen. When alumni get together to plan their twenty-fifth reunion in *H. M. Pulham, Esq.* (1941), a former All-American football player asks if they don't all agree that "the happiest time we ever spent were those four years back at Harvard." In *Goodbye, My Fancy* (1951), a renowned politician returns to campus to receive an honorary degree from the college that expelled her years earlier for staying out all night with a professor. She is in awe of her old dorm room and emotional about the memories conjured up by her visit, commenting that it's like seeing herself at eighteen again, eager, expectant, and a little frightened.

We Went to College (1936) deals in its entirety with alumni returning to campus for homecoming weekend. One asks as they get off the train if they ever looked like the undergraduates waiting in the station, and one of the students asks a friend if they're ever going to look like the arriving alumni. The old grads dress in silly costumes for a parade and drink heavily at a football game, with two of them disrupting the game by running onto the field. The wife of a professor at the college and her heartthrob from their college days get drunk together, and she nearly makes a fool of herself when she mistakenly comes to believe that he's going to leave his wife for her. A long-ago romance between a professor's wife and a former football hero is also revived on homecoming weekend in *The Male Animal* (1942). Dartmouth's *Winter Carnival* (1939) becomes the occasion for a professor to renew his acquaintance with a former Carnival queen he courted six years earlier as an undergraduate.

Classmates sometime reunite at places other than their alma maters. In the slasher movie *Mother's Day* (1980), three women hold a tenth-anniversary

Alumni who return to campus for a homecoming weekend make fools of themselves when they try to recapture their lost youth in *We Went to College* (1936, Metro-Goldwyn-Mayer).

get-together in a wooded area of New Jersey; their "mystery weekend" results in a vicious attack by the degenerate sons of a sadistic old woman. In *The Big Chill* (1983), University of Michigan classmates gather for the funeral of a friend who has committed suicide. One contrasts the revolutionary politics of their undergraduate days with their current financial well-being, another says she was at her best with her friends in college, and a third remarks that at least they expected something of each other then. One man jokes that getting away from the group was the best thing that ever happened to him, because, "I mean, how much sex, fun, friendship, can one man take?" The cynical friends miss the idealism of a time when they thought they could change the world and spend their time together reminiscing about protest demonstrations, smoking marijuana, and trying to rekindle past romances. One observes that "a long time ago we knew each other for a short period," adding that it was "easy back then. No one ever had a cushier berth than we did. It's not surprising our friendship could survive that. It's only out here in the world that it gets tough." A similar story is told in *Everything Relative* (1996), in which seven women gather at a bris and reminisce about their undergraduate days as feminists and members of a street theater group.

Alumni's memories of their college days are affected both by their experiences as students and by their current life circumstances. An unemployed graduate might look back at college differently than a successful lawyer, and a person who is divorced from a college sweetheart might view the undergraduate years less nostalgically than a happily married person. Memories of college days fade and become distorted over time, but they're also shaped by the way undergraduate life is presented in the movies. Watching a film in which a student is humiliated during a fraternity initiation can bring back unpleasant memories, and watching one in which young people fall in love can evoke happy thoughts of a long-ago romance. Because the movies can shape memories, the question of how accurately they portray college life becomes an important one for understanding how people remember the past. Their memories can affect decisions such as where they'll send their children to college and how much money they'll donate to their alma mater.

Alumni who look to the movies for information about how students get into college will be puzzled. Older generations didn't face the highly competitive admissions process depicted in movies made since the mid–1980s. Even younger graduates may be surprised at the intense pressure to get into college often seen in contemporary films, because the vast majority of them didn't go to, or even apply to, the nationally prominent schools disproportionately featured in these movies. The importance of doing well on the SAT exam is also exaggerated in recent movies, because admissions officers consider it as only one of many factors in deciding whom to accept.

Anyone who relies on the movies for an idea of what college is all about will be surprised to learn how difficult it is to pay for an education. This issue rarely arises in the movies, and when it does, students and their parents usually find a way to pay, often by having the student win an athletic scholarship or take a part-time job. Neither is a feasible way for most students to pay all their college expenses, and the movies give little attention to the sources of money that finance most educations: parental contributions, need-based financial aid, and loans. Even with funds from these sources, Americans find it increasingly difficult to pay for college, and many lower-income students who start college fail to complete a degree because of financial hardship.

Freshmen in older films are often reluctant to leave family and friends for college, but in recent ones they are more likely to be eager for their independence and apt to treat parents who accompany them to campus as an embarrassment. The freshman orientation programs that many alumni vividly remember are absent from college movies, but the confusion of registration and the first few days of class are well represented. Older alumni will find reminders in early college movies of freshman hazing and events aimed at creating class loyalty, but these practices largely disappeared from the movies after World War II. Recent graduates will find these practices quaint and alien to their own experiences as freshmen.

When alumni reminisce about their college days, the first things that come to mind are probably not the lectures they heard, the papers they wrote, and the exams they took. Movies from all eras reinforce this inattention to the academic side of college life, emphasizing instead the fun enjoyed by young people still free of adult responsibilities. However, a close look at college films reveals that academic matters are sometimes dealt with seriously, even if they are rarely the dominant theme in the movie. These movies can bring back to alumni memories of the problems they had in choosing courses and settling on a major. Many graduates will find that the frequent depiction of undergraduates as academic slackers willing to cheat or negotiate for a grade clashes with the kinds of students they and their classmates were.

Most alumni remember their professors from lectures and advising sessions, and while scenes of this sort are not absent from the movies, neither are they very common. When students are shown in the classroom, they are more often bored than engaged, and their professors are frequently portrayed as apathetic or harshly critical. Faculty mentoring outside the classroom shows up in few films, but romantic and sexual relationships between students and professors show up in many. Graduates will be surprised at the amount of attention the movies pay to what was likely a rare occurrence during their undergraduate years, especially in the form it often takes on the screen: sexual intimacy initiated by a seductive female student who is attracted to an older instructor rather than trying to improve her grade in his course.

More common in the movies than student-faculty intimacy are romantic and sexual relationships between students, an emphasis that reflects the experiences of most alumni. Students in the movies find romance in the registration line, at fraternity parties, and at off-campus vacation spots. Since the late 1960s, undergraduates in the movies have pursued sex more than romance, as the husband-hunting common in movies made before the mid–1960s has been replaced by the hooking-up often seen in today's films. Older alumni may find the intimate relationships in today's movies quite different from their own experiences, though they could also think that older films present an unrealistic picture of what romance was like when they were in college. Recent college graduates are likely to see the depiction of romance in earlier movies as old-fashioned, but they might also think that contemporary films exaggerate their generation's obsession with sex and lack of interest in a lasting relationship.

At no time have more than one-third of the nation's undergraduates belonged to fraternities and sororities, but Greek-letter organizations have nonetheless dominated student life on many campuses. As a result, even alumni who were not fraternity or sorority members may find that the frequent appearance of these organizations in the movies reflects their own memories of campus social life. Students who did belong to fraternities and sororities may react negatively to post–*Animal House* (1978) portrayals of Greeks as boorish, inebriated, sex-obsessed, and academically deficient. Few positive images of fraternities and sororities show up in the movies, and the way they are depicted clashes with the fond memories many alumni have of their college years.

Even though most undergraduates do not play on high-profile varsity teams, sports is one of the most common themes in college movies. However, because many students attend games, films about collegiate sports can evoke pleasant memories even in alumni who never played on a team. The movies' emphasis on football above all other sports fits with many alumni's recollections of their undergraduate years, because the game has been the dominant sport on most campuses since well before the first college movie appeared in 1915. One incorrect impression fostered by the movies is that women rarely participate in collegiate athletics. Few female student-athletes show up on the screen, but their participation in sports has a long history and has increased significantly since 1972.

Extracurricular activities play a larger role in the lives of most undergraduates than the movies acknowledge, so alumni of all generations may be surprised at the infrequent appearance of students who are working on the campus newspaper, deliberating in a student government meeting, rehearsing for a musical or dramatic production, or planning a social event. Political and community activism is also rare in the movies, with the exception of some made during the Great Depression and the Vietnam War era.

College movies are produced to be profit-making forms of entertainment, and to expect them to document undergraduate life accurately and in depth is unreasonable. However, these films might be more entertaining, and hence more profitable, if they did reflect the experiences of real students. Over the years, the movies have presented some aspects of campus life well, but they have also distorted it in many ways.

Chapter Notes

Introduction

1. James Monaco, *How to Read a Film: Movies, Media, Multimedia*, 3rd ed. New York: Oxford University Press, 2000, p. 247.
2. Helen Lefkowitz Horowitz, *Campus Life: Undergraduate Cultures from the End of the Eighteenth Century to the Present*. Chicago: University of Chicago Press, 1987; Christopher J. Lucas, *American Higher Education: A History*, 2nd ed. New York: Palgrave Macmillan, 2006.
3. Mary Andom, "Traditional-Age College Students Are Not Adults in Most Parents' Eyes, or Their Own, Study Finds," *The Chronicle of Higher Education*, December 6, 2007.
4. Arthur W. Chickering and Linda Reisser, *Education and Identity*, 2nd ed. San Francisco: Jossey-Bass, 1993.
5. Horowitz, op. cit.
6. Of the ninety-two films I did not see, nine are listed by the Internet Movie Database as "lost films" and at least six others are probably lost, because the AFI was unable to locate them for viewing when preparing its catalog. Of the remaining seventy-seven, forty-eight were released before 1928. Film historians estimate that perhaps 80 percent of films from the silent era no longer exist. Only five of the twenty-nine "talkies" I was unable to watch were released after 1948. I discuss in limited ways some of the movies I was unable to see by using the plot summaries in the *AFI Catalog* and the Internet Movie Database.

Chapter 1

1. These four clusters of reasons for deciding to go to college are based on survey evidence from John H. Pryor et al., *The American Freshman: Forty Year Trends*. Los Angeles: Higher Education Research Institute, University of California, Los Angeles, 2007, pp. 62–63.
2. Anthony P. Carnevale, "Discounting Education's Value," *The Chronicle of Higher Education*, September 22, 2006; Gary S. Becker and Kevin M. Murphy, "The Upside of Income Inequality," *The American* #1 (May-June 2007), pp. 20–23.
3. Tamar Lewin, "At Colleges, Women Are Leaving Men in the Dust," *The New York Times*, July 9, 2006, pp. 1, 18.
4. Ernest L. Boyer, *College: The Undergraduate Experience in America: The Carnegie Foundation for the Advancement of Teaching*. New York: Harper and Row, 1987, p. 17.
5. There is some evidence that student-athletes do make more money after graduating than their non-athlete classmates, despite the athletes' weaker academic records in high school and college. James L. Shulman and William G. Bowen, *The Game of Life: College Sports and Educational Values*. Princeton, NJ: Princeton University Press, 2001; William G. Bowen and Sarah A. Levin, *Reclaiming the Game: College Sports and Educational Values*. Princeton, NJ: Princeton University Press, 2003.
6. Justin Pope, "Once Confined to 'Hot Spots,' Admissions Anxiety Spreads." Online at http://encarta.msn.com/encnet/departments/college/ (accessed on November 26, 2006).
7. James Fallows, "The Early-Decision Racket," *Atlantic Monthly* #288 (September 2001), pp. 37–40, 42.
8. An anecdotal account of favoritism in

the admission of students to highly selective institutions on the basis of large donations, celebrity, legacy status, and skill at upper-class sports such as polo and sailing is Daniel Golden's *The Price of Admission: How America's Ruling Class Buys Its Way Into Elite Colleges—and Who Gets Left Outside the Gate*. New York: Crown, 2006. Preferential treatment of legacies and athletes is also challenged in Jerome Karabel's *The Chosen: The Hidden History of Admission and Exclusion at Harvard, Yale, and Princeton*. Boston: Houghton Mifflin, 2005.

9 Karabel, op. cit.

10. Jacques Steinberg. *The Gate-Keepers: Inside the Admissions Process of a Premier College*. New York: Viking, 2002.

11. In 2006, 67 percent of all freshmen were at the school that was their first choice, 23 percent attended their second choice, and another 6 percent were at their third choice. Pryor et al., op. cit., p. 65.

12. The 2006 report by the Commission on the Future of Higher Education noted that the 38 percent increase in average tuition between 1999 and 2004 dwarfed the 13 percent growth in median family income over that time, and recommended a search for new ways to control the cost of college. Sam Dillon, "Federal Panel Hammers Out Report on Recommendations to Shape Up Higher Education," *The New York Times*, August 11, 2006, p. A12.

13. Sara Lipka, "Freshmen Increasingly Discuss Politics, Worry about Money, Survey Finds," *The Chronicle of Higher Education*, January 19, 2007.

14. Jeffrey J. Williams, "A New Indentured Class," *The Chronicle of Higher Education*, June 30, 2006, pp. B6–B7.

15. *The Chronicle of Higher Education, Almanac Issue 2007–8*, August 31, 2007, p. 17.

16. Sean Kean, "Report Blames College Practices for Limited Access of Minority and Low-Income Students," *The Chronicle of Higher Education*, September 1, 2006.

Chapter 2

1. Amy Rainey, "Survey Provides Further Evidence of High Parental Involvement with College Students," *The Chronicle of Higher Education*, March 31, 2006.

2. Wendy S. White, "Students, Parents, Colleges: Drawing the Lines," *The Chronicle of Higher Education*, December 16, 2005, p. B16; Sara Lipka, "State Legislators as Co-Pilots," *The Chronicle of Higher Education*, December 16, 2005, p. A22.

3. Hank Nuwer, *Wrongs of Passage: Fraternities, Sororities, Hazing, and Binge Drinking*. Bloomington: Indiana University Press, 2001.

4. Nearly 90 percent of freshmen entering college in 2006 went to a school more than ten miles from their permanent home, and 46 percent went to a school more than 100 miles away. Nearly four-fifths of the freshmen planned to live in a college dormitory, and only 14 percent planned to live with family members. John H. Pryor et al., *The American Freshman: Forty Year Trends*. Los Angeles: Higher Education Research Institute, University of California, Los Angeles, 2007, pp. 65, 71.

5. This is consistent with evidence that extreme problems with a roommate often result in poor academic performance. James R. Davis, *Going to College: The Study of Students and the Student Experience*. Boulder, CO: Westview, 1977.

6. Davis, op cit.

7. Harold T. Shapiro, "Cognition, Character, and Culture in Undergraduate Education: Rhetoric and Reality," in Ronald G. Ehrenberg, ed., *The American University: National Treasure or Endangered Species?* Ithaca, NY: Cornell University Press, 1997, pp. 58–99.

Chapter 3

1. The most common reason cited by college freshmen for going to college is to learn about things that interest them; nearly as many mention getting a general education and gaining an appreciation of ideas. John H. Pryor et al., *The American Freshman: Forty Year Trends*. Los Angeles: Higher Education Research Institute, University of California, Los Angeles, 2007, pp. 62–63. The most important factor in choosing a school is its academic reputation; this is especially true for students with the best high school grades and the highest SAT scores. Eric Hoover, "Academic Quality Influences Where High-Achieving Students Enroll, Survey Finds," *The Chronicle of Higher Education*, April 10, 2006.

2. Harold T. Shapiro, "Cognition, Character, and Culture in Undergraduate Education: Rhetoric and Reality," in Ronald G. Ehrenberg, ed., *The American University: National Treasure or Endangered Species?* Ithaca, NY: Cornell University Press, 1997, p. 80.

3. Helen Lefkowitz Horowitz, *Campus Life: Undergraduate Cultures from the End of the Eighteenth Century to the Present.* Chicago: University of Chicago Press, 1987, p. 12.

4. Ibid., p. 140.

5. Survey by Donald McCabe of students at ninety-six colleges and universities, conducted between 2002 and 2006, cited in Jonathan D. Glater, "Colleges Chase as Cheats Shift to Higher Tech," *The New York Times*, May 18, 2006, pp. A1, A24.

6. Horowitz, op. cit.; David Callahan, *The Cheating Culture: Why More Americans Are Doing Wrong to Get Ahead.* Orlando, FL: Harcourt, 2004.

7. Glater, op. cit.

8. Michael J. Bugeja, "Distractions in the Wireless Classroom," *The Chronicle of Higher Education*, January 26, 2007, pp. C1, C4

9. Charles McGrath, "At $9.95 a Page, You Were Expecting Poetry?" *The New York Times*, September 10, 2006, sec. 4, pp. 1, 14; Charles McGrath, "Term Paper Project, Part II," *The New York Times*, September 17, 2006, sec. 4, p. 5.

Chapter 4

1. Helen Lefkowitz Horowitz, *Campus Life: Undergraduate Cultures from the End of the Eighteenth Century to the Present.* Chicago: University of Chicago Press, 1987, p. 25.

2. Robert Cooley Angell, *The Campus: A Study of Contemporary Undergraduate Life in the American University.* New York: D. Appleton, 1928, p. 44.

3. Billie Wright Dziech and Linda Weiner, *The Lecherous Professor: Sexual Harassment on Campus.* Boston: Beacon Press, 1984; Billie Wright Dziech, "The Abuse of Power in Intimate Relationships," *The Chronicle of Higher Education*, March 20, 1998; Ann J. Lane, "Gender, Power, and Sexuality: First, Do No Harm," *The Chronicle of Higher Education*, May 5, 2006.

4. Barry M. Dank and Joseph S. Fulda, "Forbidden Love: Student-Professor Romances," *Sexuality and Culture* #1 (1997), pp. 107–30; Paul R. Abramson, *Romance in the Ivory Tower: The Rights and Liberty of Conscience.* Cambridge, MA: MIT Press, 2007.

Chapter 5

1. Bill Marsh, "The Innocent Birth of the Spring Bacchanal," *The New York Times*, March 19, 2006, sec. 4, p. 3.

2. Lynn Peril, *College Girls: Bluestockings, Sex Kittens, and Coeds, Then and Now.* New York: Norton, 2006, pp. 92–95.

3. Nena and George O'Neill, *Open Marriage: A New Life Style for Couples.* New York: M. Evans, 1972.

4. For an extended discussion of this movie and the novel it is based on, see Peril, op. cit., pp. 303–08.

5. Patrick Dilley, *Queer Man on Campus: A History of Non-Heterosexual College Men, 1945–2000.* New York: RoutledgeFalmer, 2002.

Chapter 6

1. Helen Lefkowitz Horowitz, *Campus Life: Undergraduate Cultures from the End of the Eighteenth Century to the Present.* Chicago: University of Chicago Press, 1987.

2. Henry Wechsler et al., "Trends in College Binge Drinking During a Period of Increased Prevention Efforts: Findings from 4 Harvard School of Public Health College Alcohol Study Surveys: 1993–2001," *Journal of American College Health* #50 (March 2002), pp. 203–17; Jeffrey S. DeSimone, "Fraternity Membership and Drinking Behavior." National Bureau of Economic Research Working Paper No. W13262, July 2007. Online at http://papers.ssrn.com/sol3/papers.cfm?abstract_id=1000364 (accessed on January 2, 2008).

3. Jeffrey R. Cashin, Cheryl A. Presley, and Philip W. Meilman, "Alcohol Use in the Greek System: Follow the Leader?" *Journal of Studies on Alcohol* #59 (January 1998), pp. 63–70.

4. Cited in Andrew J. Edelstein and Kevin McDonough, *The Seventies: From Hot Pants to Hot Tubs.* New York: Dutton, 1990, p. 61.

5. In 2007, the DePauw University chapter of Delta Zeta sorority made news when

its national organization deactivated twenty-three of its thirty-five members in an effort to change the house's reputation as a "dog house" of socially awkward, brainy, and overweight girls. The only girls kicked out were overweight or minorities, but half of the remaining members quit in protest. The university banished the sorority from campus for its demeaning treatment of the students. Sam Dillon, "Evictions at Sorority Raise Issue of Bias," *The New York Times*, February 25, 2007, p. 13; Sam Dillon, "After Evicting Members, Sorority Is Itself Evicted," *The New York Times*, March 13, 2007, p. A13.

6. Hank Nuwer, *Wrongs of Passage: Fraternities, Sororities, Hazing, and Binge Drinking.* Bloomington: Indiana University Press, 2001, p. 31.

7. Elvis Mitchell, "Revisiting Faber College (Toga, Toga, Toga)," *The New York Times*, August 25, 2003, pp. C1, C5.

8. Martin D. Schwartz and Walter S. DeKesered, *Sexual Assault on the College Campus: The Role of Male Peer Support.* Thousand Oaks, CA: Sage, 1997.

9. Bonnie S. Fisher, Francis T. Cullen, and Michael G. Turner, *The Sexual Victimization of College Women.* Washington, D.C.: U.S. Department of Justice, December 2000.

10. Patrick Dilley, *Queer Man on Campus: A History of Non-Heterosexual College Men, 1945–2000.* New York: Routledge-Falmer, 2002.

11. Daniel Katz and Floyd Henry Allport, *Students' Attitudes: A Report of the Syracuse University Reaction Study.* Syracuse, NY: Craftsman Press, 1931.

12. Rose K. Goldsen et al., *What College Students Think.* Princeton, NJ: D. Van Nostrand, 1960.

Chapter 7

1. Christopher J. Lucas, *American Higher Education: A History,* 2nd ed. New York: Palgrave Macmillan, 2006.

2. Cited in Bill Pennington, "Small Colleges, Short of Men, Embrace Football," *The New York Times*, July 10, 2006, p. A1.

3. James L. Shulman and William G. Bowen, *The Game of Life: College Sports and Educational Values.* Princeton, NJ: Princeton University Press, 2001; William G. Bowen and Sarah A. Levin. *Reclaiming the Game: College Sports and Educational Values.* Princeton, NJ: Princeton University Press, 2003.

4. Barbara F. Tobolowsky and John W. Lowery, "Commercializing College: An Analysis of College Representations During Bowl Games," *International Journal of Educational Advancement* #6 (May 2006), pp. 232–42.

5. Mike Freeman, "When Values Collide: Clarett Got Unusual Aid in Ohio State Class," *The New York Times*, July 13, 2003, sec. 8, pp. 1, 4.

6. Stephen Burd, "Louisiana State U. Settles Lawsuit by Instructor Who Said She Was Pressured to Raise Athletes' Grades," *The Chronicle of Higher Education*, September 19, 2005.

7. Welch Suggs, "Gender Quotas? Not in College Sports," *The Chronicle of Higher Education*, July 1, 2005, pp. A24–A26.

8. Andrew Zimbalist, *Unpaid Professionals: Commercialism and Conflict in Big-Time College Sports.* Princeton, NJ: Princeton University Press, 1999; Shulman and Bowen, op. cit.; Robert H. Frank, *Challenging the Myth: A Review of the Links Among College Athletic Success, Student Quality, and Donations.* Report for the Knight Foundation Commission on Intercollegiate Athletics, May 2004. Online at http://www.knightcommission.org/about/frank_report/ (accessed on January 2, 2008).

Chapter 8

1. Rudolph W. Weingartner, *Undergraduate Education: Goals and Means.* New York: American Council on Education and Macmillan, 1992.

2. Helen Lefkowitz Horowitz, *Campus Life: Undergraduate Cultures from the End of the Eighteenth Century to the Present.* Chicago: University of Chicago Press, 1987; Philip G. Altbach, "Students," in Arthur Levine, ed., *Higher Learning in America, 1980–2000.* Baltimore, MD: Johns Hopkins University Press, 1993, pp. 212–21; Christopher J. Lucas, *American Higher Education: A History,* 2nd ed. New York: Palgrave Macmillan, 2006.

3. Linda K. Wertheimer, "Join the Club: Colleges See Surge in New Student Groups," *The Boston Globe*, October 27, 2007, pp. A1, A6.

4. During the 1960s and early 1970s, there was much discussion of "outside agitators," non-student radicals who were thought to move from campus to campus fomenting unrest. This idea, which is also referenced in *The Graduate* (1967) and *The Computer Wore Tennis Shoes* (1969), was a way of calling into question the commitment of student protesters and undermining the legitimacy of their arguments.

5. *The Report of the President's Commission on Campus Unrest.* Washington, D.C.: U.S. Government Printing Office, 1970.

6. Jenna Russell, "Campuses with a Cause," *The Boston Globe*, April 18, 2005, pp. B1, B4.

7. *The Chronicle of Higher Education, Almanac Issue 2007–8,* August 31, 2007, p. 17.

8. Rob Rhoads, cited in Russell, op cit., p. B4.

Chapter 9

1. David Leonhardt, "The College Dropout Boom," *The New York Times*, May 24, 2005, pp. A1, A18–A19.

2. Mary Duenwald, "The Dorms May Be Great, but How's the Counseling?" *The New York Times,* October 26, 2004, pp. 1, 6.

3. Alan Finder, "For Some College Graduates, a Fanciful Detour (or Two) before Their Careers Begin," *The New York Times*, October 23, 2005, p. 23.

4. James L. Shulman and William G. Bowen, *The Game of Life: College Sports and Educational Values.* Princeton, NJ: Princeton University Press, 2001; Penelope Trunk, "Athletes Know How Game Is Played," *The Boston Globe*, July 9, 2006, pp. G1, G7.

5. Tatsha Robertson, "Seniors Opting to Retire with a Touch of Class," *The Boston Globe*, October 17, 2005, pp. A1, A16.

FILMOGRAPHY

The following movies were used in the writing of this book. A single asterisk means I was unable to view the film. A double asterisk means I did not see the film and it is presumed no longer to exist.

Abandon (2002)
The Absent-Minded Professor (1961)
Accepted (2006)
The Accused (1949)
The Activist (1969)*
The Affairs of Dobie Gillis (1953)
After Midnight (1989)
The Age of Consent (1932)
The Air Up There (1994)
The All American (1932)
All American (1953)
All-American Co-ed (1941)
All-American Sweetheart (1937)**
All I Want (Try Seventeen) (2002)
All of Me (1934)
All That Heaven Allows (1955)
All the Fine Young Cannibals (1960)
All the Right Moves (1983)
All Women Have Secrets (1939)
The Allnighter (1987)
American Chai (2001)
American Desi (2001)
American Graffiti (1973)
American Pie (1999)

American Pie 2 (2001)
Among Brothers (2005)
Ancient Evil: Scream of the Mummy (2000)
Andy Hardy's Blonde Trouble (1944)
Andy Hardy's Double Life (1942)
Animal Behavior (1989)
Animal House (National Lampoon's Animal House) (1978)
Apartment for Peggy (1948)
April Fool's Day (1986)
April Is My Religion (2001)
Art School Confidential (2006)
Ashamed of Parents (1921)*
Assault of the Party Nerds 2: The Heavy Petting Detective (1995)
Baby, It's You (1983)
Bachelor Flat (1962)
Bachelor of Arts (1934)*
Back to School (1986)
The Band Plays On (1934)
The Basketball Fix (1951)
Bathing Beauty (1944)
Beach Party (1963)

Beat Street (1984)
A Beautiful Mind (2001)
Been Down So Long It Looks Like Up to Me (1971)
The Bell Jar (1979)
Betrayed (1916)*
Better Luck Tomorrow (2003)
Betty Co-ed (1946)**
Beware (1946)
Beyond Glory (1948)
Big Business Girl (1931)
The Big Chill (1983)
The Big Fix (1947)
The Big Game (1936)
Big Man on Campus (1989)
Black and White (1999)
Black Christmas (2006)
Blackbeard's Ghost (1968)
Blind Alley (1939)
Blondie Goes to College (1942)
Blood Sisters (1987)
The Blot (1921)
Blue Chips (1994)
The Bob Mathias Story (1954)
Boggy Creek 2 (...and the Legend Continues) (1985)

Bonzo Goes to College (1952)
Born on the Fourth of July (1989)
Bowery at Midnight (1942)
Boys and Girls (2000)
Braveheart (1925)
Breaking Away (1979)
Brown of Harvard (1918)*
Brown of Harvard (1926)
The Brute Man (1946)
The Burden of Race (1921)*
Camp Fear (1991)
Campus Confessions (1938)
The Campus Flirt (1926)*
Campus Honeymoon (1948)
Campus Knights (1929)
Campus Man (1987)
Campus Rhythm (1943)
Campus Sleuth (1948)
Can It Be Love (1992)
Candyman (1992)
Cannibal Women in the Avocado Jungle of Death (1989)
Carnal Knowledge (1971)
Chain Reaction (1996)
A Change of Seasons (1980)
Change the Frame (1995)
The Cheer Leader (1928)*
Cheer Up and Smile (1930)*
Cinderella Jones (1946)
A Cinderella Story (2004)
The Circuit (2001)
Class of '44 (1973)
Class of Nuke 'Em High Part II: Subhumanoid Meltdown (1991)
C'mon, Let's Live a Little (1967)
College (1927)
The College Boob (1926)*
College Coach (1933)
College Confidential (1960)
The College Coquette (1929)*
College Days (1926)*
The College Hero (1927)

College Holiday (1936)
College Humor (1933)
College Kickboxers (1990)
College Love (1929)*
College Lovers (1930)**
The College Orphan (1915)*
College Rhythm (1934)
College Scandal (1935)
College Swing (1938)
The College Widow (1915)**
The College Widow (1927)*
Collegiate (1926)*
Come Back, Little Sheba (1952)
Coming Soon (1999)
The Computer Wore Tennis Shoes (1969)
Confessions of a Co-ed (1931)
Confidentially Connie (1953)
The Contender (2000)
The Courage of the Common Place (1917)*
Cover Me Babe (1970)
The Craving (1916)*
Crazylegs (1953)
Crossover (2006)
The Curve (1998)
Cynthia (1947)
D.O.A. (1988)
Daddy Long Legs (1919)
Daddy Long Legs (1931)
Daddy Long Legs (1955)
Dancing Co-ed (1939)
Dangerous Curves (1987)
Daughters of Today (1924)*
The Day It Came to Earth (1979)
Dead Man on Campus (1998)
Deadly Obsession (1989)
Dear Brigitte (1965)
Dearie (1927)*
Death Tunnel (2005)
The Debut (2000)
Deconstructing Harry (1997)
Defying Gravity (1997)
The Delicate Art of the Rifle (1996)

Demolition University (1997)
Didn't You Hear... (1983)
Dirty Harry (1971)
Dirty Tricks (1981)
Divided We Stand (2000)
Dr. Alien (1988)
Doctor Detroit (1983)
The Doctor Takes a Wife (1940)
The Doorway (2000)
The Dorm That Dripped Blood (1982)
Down to You (2000)
The Dream Machine (1990)
Dream Trap (1990)
Dreamboat (1952)
Drive, He Said (1971)
The Drop Kick (1927)
Drumline (2002)
Dude, Where's the Party (2004)
The Duke Steps Out (1929)*
The Dunwich Horror (1970)
Eadie Was a Lady (1945)
Eden's Curve (2003)
Edge of Seventeen (2000)
The Eiger Sanction (1975)
8 Heads in a Duffel Bag (1997)
Elopement (1951)
End of the Harvest (1995)
End of the Road (1970)
Everybody's All-American (1988)
Everything Relative (1996)
Evolution (2001)
Extortion (1938)
The Fair Co-ed (1927)*
False Women (1921)*
Fandango (1985)
Fast Break (1979)
Fast Food Nation (2006)
Fatal Pulse (1998)
Father Was a Fullback (1949)
The Fear (1995)
The Feminine Touch (1941)
Fifty Pills (2006)
Fighting Youth (1935)
Final Exam (1981)

First Daughter (2004)
First Love (1977)
5 Against the House (1955)
The Floating College (1928)**
Flubber (1997)
Foolin' Around (1980)
For the Love of Mike (1927)*
For Those Who Think Young (1964)
Foreign Student (1994)
Forty Little Mothers (1940)
The Forward Pass (1929)**
The Fountainhead (1949)
Four Friends (1981)
Fraternity Demon (1992)
Fraternity Row (1977)
Fraternity Vacation (1985)
Fresh Horses (1988)
The Freshie (1922)*
The Freshman (1925)
The Freshman (1990)
Freshman Love (1936)
Freshman Year (1938)
Freshmen (1999)
Future-Kill (1985)
The Gambler (1976)
Game Day (1999)
Geraldine (1954)
Get Yourself a College Girl (1964)
Getting In (1994)
Getting Straight (1970)
Ghoulies 3: Ghoulies Go to College (1991)
Girl Crazy (1943)
The Girl in White (1952)
The Girl Next Door (2004)
Girl o' My Dreams (1934)
The Girl Who Couldn't Grow Up (1917)*
Girls Demand Excitement (1931)*
Girls Nite Out (1984)
The Girls on the Beach (1965)
The Girls' Room (2000)
The Gladiator (1938)
Glory Road (2006)
Going Greek (2001)
Good News (1930)
Good News (1947)

The Good Shepherd (2006)
Good Will Hunting (1997)
Goodbye, Columbus (1969)
Goodbye, My Fancy (1951)
Gossip (2000)
The Graduate (1967)
The Grandee's Ring (1915)*
The Great Alone (1922)*
Gridiron Flash (1934)
The Group (1966)
H. M. Pulham, Esq. (1941)
Hamburger—The Motion Picture (1986)
Happiness (1917)*
Happy Together (1989)
Harold and Kumar Go to White Castle (2004)
The Harrad Experiment (1973)
Harvard, Here I Come (1941)
Harvard Man (2001)
The Haunting of Hell House (1999)
The Hazing (The Campus Corpse) (1977)
The Hazing (2004)
He Got Game (1998)
Heart of Dixie (1989)
The Heart of Ezra Greer (1917)*
The Heartbreak Kid (1972)
Hell Night (1981)
Her First Romance (The Right Man) (1940)
Her Secret (1933)*
Herbie Fully Loaded (2005)
Here Come the Co-eds (1945)
Here I Am a Stranger (1939)
Hero for a Day (1939)
Hi, Neighbor (1942)
Hide-Out (1930)**
High Time (1960)
Higher Learning (1995)
Hold 'Em Yale (1928)*
Hold 'Em Yale (1935)
Hold That Co-ed (1938)
Hold That Line (1952)
Horse Feathers (1932)
Hot Stuff (1929)*

The House on Sorority Row (1983)
House Party 2 (1991)
How Do I Love Thee? (1970)
How High (2001)
How I Got into College (1989)
How to Be Very, Very Popular (1955)
Howdy Broadway (1929)
Huddle (1932)
The Human Stain (2003)
I Met My Love Again (1938)
I Shot Andy Warhol (1996)
I Still Know What You Did Last Summer (1998)
I Think I Do (1997)
Ice Princess (2005)
If Ever I See You Again (1978)
I'll Be Home for Christmas (1998)
Imaginary Crimes (1994)
The Impossible Years (1968)
In Good Company (2004)
In the Cut (2003)
Inexchange (2006)
The Initiation (1984)
Interface (1984)
The Iron Major (1943)
It Happens Every Spring (1949)
It's My Turn (1980)
Jack London (1943)
Jack Spurlock, Prodigal (1918)*
The Jackie Robinson Story (1950)
Jim Thorpe—All American (1951)
John Goldfarb, Please Come Home (1965)
Johnny Be Good (1988)
Joy in the Morning (1965)
Joy Ride (2001)
The Kick-Off (1926)*
Kicking and Screaming (1995)
Killer Me (2001)
Killer Party (1986)
Kilroy Was Here (1947)
King Frat (1979)

Kinsey (2004)
A Kiss Before Dying (1956)
A Kiss Before Dying (1991)
Knute Rockne—All American (1940)
The Land of the College Prophets (2005)
The Last Game (1980)
The Last Kiss (2006)
Last Time Out (1994)
The Last Year (2002)
The League of Frightened Gentlemen (1937)*
Learning Curves (2003)
Legally Blonde (2000)
Let's Go Collegiate (1941)
Li Ting Lang (1920)*
Lianna (1983)
Life 101 (1995)
Life Begins in College (1937)
The Little Brother of the Rich (1919)*
Little Sister (1992)
Live Wires (1921)*
Local Boy Makes Good (1931)
Loser (2000)
Louisiana (1947)
Love and Basketball (2000)
Love, Honor, and Behave (1938)
Love in a Goldfish Bowl (1961)*
The Love-Ins (1967)
Love Laughs at Andy Hardy (1947)
Love Story (1970)
Love the Hard Way (2001)
Lovelife (1997)
The Magic Garden of Stanley Sweetheart (1970)*
Make a Million (1935)
Maker of Men (1931)
Making the Varsity (1928)*
The Male Animal (1942)
Malice (1993)
Man of the House (2005)
Marjorie Morningstar (1958)

Mark of the Witch (1970)
A Matter of Degrees (1990)
Maybe It's Love (Eleven Men and a Girl) (1930)
Meatcleaver Massacre (Hollywood Meat Cleaver Massacre) (1977)
Midnight Madness (1980)
Million Dollar Legs (1939)
Mind Games (1996)
The Mirror Has Two Faces (1996)
The Misadventures of Margaret (1998)
The Misadventures of Merlin Jones (1964)
Mr. Belvedere Goes to College (1949)
Mr. Doodle Kicks Off (1938)
Mr. Music (1950)
Mona Lisa Smile (2003)
The Monkey's Uncle (1965)
Most Precious Thing in Life (1934)
Mother Is a Freshman (1949)
Mother's Day (1980)
Mugsy's Girls (Delta Pi) (1985)
The Muppets Take Manhattan (1984)
Murder on the Campus (1933)
My Big Fat Greek Wedding (2002)
My Lucky Star (1938)
Naked in New York (1993)
National Lampoon Presents Dorm Daze (2003)
Necessary Roughness (1991)
New Best Friend (2002)
New York Minute (2004)
Night and Day (1946)
Night into Morning (1951)
Night of the Creeps (1986)
Night School (1981)

Nine Girls (1944)
1969 (1988)
Nobody's Fool (1921)*
Nobody's Perfect (1989)
Northwest Passage (1940)
Now You See Him, Now You Don't (1972)
The Nutty Professor (1963)
The Nutty Professor (1996)
Nutty Professor II: The Klumps (2000)
Oh, Boy! (1919)*
Old Man Rhythm (1935)
Old School (2003)
Oleanna (1994)
The Olympic Hero (1928)*
The One and Only (1978)
100 Girls (2000)
One Minute to Play (1926)*
One on One (1977)
$1,000 a Touchdown (1939)
One True Thing (1998)
Only 38 (1923)**
Orange County (2002)
Ordinary Sinner (2003)
Our Hearts Were Growing Up (1946)
Outta Time (2002)
Over the Goal (1937)
Overnight Delivery (1998)
Palm Springs Weekend (1963)
Pardon My Stripes (1942)
The Party Animal (1984)
PCU (1994)
Peggy (1950)
Penelope (1966)
The Perfect Score (2004)
Pieces (1983)
Pigskin Parade (1936)
The Pinch Hitter (1917)*
The Pinch Hitter (1925)*
Plain Jane (1916)*
The Plastic Age (1925)
Pledge Night (1988)
The Poor Nut (1927)*
Prefontaine (1997)
Preppies (1982)
The Pride of the Yankees (1942)
Primal Rage (1988)
The Prince and Me (2004)

The Private Public (2000)
The Prodigy (1999)
The Program (1993)
The Prowler (1981)
Prozac Nation (2001)
Psychic (1992)
Psychomania (Violent Midnight) (1964)
Puddle Cruiser (1996)
Pumpkin (2002)
The Quarterback (1926)*
The Quarterback (1940)
Quiz Show (1994)
R.P.M. (1970)
Rackety Rax (1932)*
Raiders of the Lost Ark (1981)
A Raisin in the Sun (1961)
Readin', 'Ritin', 'Rithmetic (1926)*
Real Genius (1985)
Reality Bites (1994)
A Reason to Believe (1995)
Red Letters (2000)
Red Lips (1928)*
Redemption (1917)*
Return of the Living Dead: Rave to the Grave (2005)
Return to Campus (1975)*
Revenge of the Nerds (1984)
Revenge of the Nerds II: Nerds in Paradise (1987)
The Revolutionary (1970)
Rich and Famous (1981)
Rise and Shine (1941)
Risky Business (1983)
Road Kill (1999)
Road Rage (A Friday Night Date) (2000)
Road Trip (2000)
Rodentz (Altered Species) (2001)
Rolled Stockings (1927)**
Rosalie (1937)
Rose Bowl (1936)
The Rose Bowl Story (1952)
Rose of the South (1916)*
Roughly Speaking (1945)
Rudy (1993)
The Rules of Attraction (2002)

Rush Week (1989)
St. Elmo's Fire (1985)
St. Louis Woman (Missouri Nightingale) (1934)
Sarge Goes to College (1947)
Saturday's Hero (1951)
Saturday's Heroes (1937)
Saturday's Millions (1933)
Scalps (1983)
Scandal Sheet (1940)
Scary Movie 2 (2001)
School Daze (1988)
School Ties (1992)
Scream 2 (1997)
Second Chorus (1941)
Secrets of a Co-ed (1942)
Secrets of a Sorority Girl (1945)**
Senior Prom (1958)
The Seniors (1978)
Senseless (1998)
September 30, 1955 (1977)
70,000 Witnesses (1932)
Sex Kittens Go to College (1960)
The Shape of Things (2003)
She Loves Me Not (1934)
She Wrote the Book (1946)
She's All That (1999)
She's Working Her Way Through College (1952)
A Shot in the Dark (1935)
Shriek of the Mutilated (1974)
Shrieker (1997)
Silent Madness (1984)
The Silent Scream (1980)
The Silent Witness (1917)*
The Sin of Harold Diddlebock (Mad Wednesday) (1947)
Sing Neighbor Sing (1944)*
Sis Hopkins (1941)
The Sixth Man (1997)
'68 (1988)
Ski Party (1965)
The Skulls (2000)
Slackers (2002)
The Slender Thread (1965)

A Small Circle of Friends (1980)
Small Town Girl (1936)
Smart Politics (1948)
Smith of Minnesota (1942)*
Snafu (1945)
The Snob (1921)*
So Big (1953)
So This Is College (1929)
Soak the Rich (1936)
Social Error (1935)
Someone to Remember (1943)
Son in Law (1993)
Son of Flubber (1963)
The Sophomore (1929)*
Sorority Babes in the Slimeball Bowl-O-Rama (1988)
Sorority Boys (2002)
Sorority Girl (1957)
Sorority House (1939)
Sorority House Massacre (1987)
Sorority House Massacre II (1990)
Sorority House Party (Rock and Roll Fantasy) (1992)
Soul Survivors (2001)
Spencer's Mountain (1963)
Spider-Man 2 (2004)
The Spirit of Notre Dame (1931)
The Spirit of Stanford (1942)*
Splatter University (1984)
Splendor in the Grass (1961)
Splitz (1984)
The Sport Parade (1932)
Spring Break (1983)
Spring Madness (1938)
The Squid and the Whale (2005)
The Stand-In (1999)
Start Cheering (1938)
Stay (2005)
Stealing Harvard (2002)
The Sterile Cuckoo (1969)
Strange Illusion (1945)
The Strawberry Statement (1970)

The Strength of the Weak (1916)*
Stricken (1998)
Strictly in the Groove (1942)
Strike Me Pink (1936)
The Strongest Man in the World (1975)
The Student Body (1976)
Student Tour (1934)
Summer Catch (2001)
Summertree (1971)
Sunny Skies (1930)
Superdad (1974)
The Sure Thing (1985)
Surviving Desire (1991)
Sweater Girl (1942)
Sweet Lavender (1920)**
The Sweetheart of Sigma Chi (1933)
Sweetheart of Sigma Chi (1946)*
Sweetheart of the Campus (1941)
Swim Girl, Swim (1927)*
Swing That Cheer (1938)
A Swingin' Affair (1963)
The Swinging Cheerleaders (1974)
Tag: The Assassination Game (1982)
Take Care of My Little Girl (1951)
Take Her, She's Mine (1963)
Tall Story (1960)
Tammy Tell Me True (1961)
Teacher's Pet (1958)
Teacher's Pet (Devil in the Flesh 2) (2000)
Teen Wolf Too (1987)
10 Things I Hate About You (1999)
Terror Train (1980)
That Hagen Girl (1947)
That's My Boy (1932)*
That's My Boy (1951)
These Glamour Girls (1939)
These Wilder Years (1956)
They Won't Forget (1937)

They're Playing with Fire (1984)
13 Conversations About One Thing (2001)
This Reckless Age (1932)
This Side of Heaven (1934)
Those Were the Days (At Good Old Siwash) (1940)
The Thousand Dollar Husband (1916)*
3 in the Attic (1968)
Threesome (1994)
The Time, the Place, and the Girl (1929)**
Time Walker (1982)
Timeline (2003)
Too Many Girls (1940)
Top Man (1943)
Touchdown (1931)
Train Ride (2000)
Trick Dribble (2001)
Triple Threat (1948)*
Trouble Along the Way (1953)
The Trouble with Women (1947)
Tucson (1949)**
20,000 Men a Year (1939)
Two Minutes to Go (1921)*
Two Minutes to Play (1936)
Under the Yum Yum Tree (1963)
Unmarried (1939)
The Unnamable (1988)
The Unnamable II: The Statement of Randolph Carter (1993)
Up in the Cellar (1970)
Up the Creek (1984)
The Upside of Anger (2005)
Urban Legend (1998)
Urban Legends: Final Cut (2000)
Vamp (1986)
Van Wilder (2002)
Varsity (1928)**
Varsity Blues (1999)
Varsity Show (1937)
Vivacious Lady (1938)

Voodoo (1995)
Voodoo Academy (2000)
The Waterboy (1998)
We Are Marshall (2006)
The Way We Were (1973)
We Don't Live Here Anymore (2004)
We Went to College (1936)
Weird Woman (1944)
Welcome to the Dollhouse (1995)
Wheat and Tares: A Story of Two Boys Who Tackle Life on Diverging Lines (1915)*
When the Boys Meet the Girls (1965)
Where the Boys Are (1960)
Where the Boys Are '84 (1984)
While Thousands Cheer (1940)**
White Flannels (1927)*
Wild Is My Love (1963)*
Wild on the Beach (1965)
The Wild Party (1929)
Wild, Wild Winter (1966)
Win That Girl (1928)*
The Winning Stroke (1919)*
Winter Carnival (1939)
Witch Academy (1993)
Witches' Brew (1980)
With Honors (1994)
Without Limits (1998)
Wonder Boys (2000)
Words and Music (1929)*
The World's Greatest Athlete (1973)
XX/XY (2002)
A Yank at Oxford (1938)
Yes Sir, That's My Baby (1949)
Yesterday's Heroes (1940)
You Can't Ration Love (1944)
Young Ideas (1943)
The Young Lovers (1964)
Young Warriors (1983)
Youth on Parade (1942)
Zabriskie Point (1970)
Zis Boom Bah (1941)

BIBLIOGRAPHY

Abramson, Paul R. *Romance in the Ivory Tower: The Rights and Liberty of Conscience.* Cambridge, MA: MIT Press, 2007.

Altbach, Philip G. "Students," in Arthur Levine, ed., *Higher Learning in America, 1980–2000.* Baltimore, MD: Johns Hopkins University Press, 1993, pp. 212–21.

American Film Institute. *The American Film Institute Catalog of Motion Pictures Produced in the United States.* Berkeley: University of California Press, 1971–1999.

Andom, Mary. "Traditional-Age College Students Are Not Adults in Most Parents' Eyes, or Their Own, Study Finds," *The Chronicle of Higher Education*, December 6, 2007.

Angell, Robert Cooley. *The Campus: A Study of Contemporary Undergraduate Life in the American University.* New York: D. Appleton, 1928.

Becker, Gary S., and Kevin M. Murphy. "The Upside of Income Inequality," *The American* #1 (May-June 2007), pp. 20–23.

Bowen, William G., and Sarah A. Levin. *Reclaiming the Game: College Sports and Educational Values.* Princeton, NJ: Princeton University Press, 2003.

Boyer, Ernest L. *College: The Undergraduate Experience in America: The Carnegie Foundation for the Advancement of Teaching.* New York: Harper and Row, 1987.

Bugeja, Michael J. "Distractions in the Wireless Classroom," *The Chronicle of Higher Education*, January 26, 2007, pp. C1, C4.

Burd, Stephen. "Louisiana State U. Settles Lawsuit by Instructor Who Said She Was Pressured to Raise Athletes' Grades," *The Chronicle of Higher Education*, September 19, 2005.

Callahan, David. *The Cheating Culture: Why More Americans Are Doing Wrong to Get Ahead.* Orlando, FL: Harcourt, 2004.

Carnevale, Anthony P. "Discounting Education's Value," *The Chronicle of Higher Education*, September 22, 2006.

Cashin, Jeffrey R., Cheryl A. Presley, and Philip W. Meilman, "Alcohol Use in the Greek System: Follow the Leader?" *Journal of Studies on Alcohol* #59 (January 1998), pp. 63–70.

Chickering, Arthur W., and Linda Reisser. *Education and Identity*, 2nd ed. San Francisco: Jossey-Bass, 1993.

The Chronicle of Higher Education. Almanac Issue 2007–8, August 31, 2007.

Dank, Barry M., and Joseph S. Fulda, "Forbidden Love: Student-Professor Romances," *Sexuality and Culture* #1 (1997), pp. 107–30.

Davis, James R. *Going to College: The Study of Students and the Student Experience.* Boulder, CO: Westview, 1977.

DeSimone, Jeffrey S. "Fraternity Membership and Drinking Behavior." National Bureau of Economic Research Working Paper No. W13262, July 2007. Online at http://papers.ssrn.com/sol3/papers.cfm?abstract_id=1000364 (accessed on January 2, 2008).

Dilley, Patrick. *Queer Man on Campus: A History of Non-Heterosexual College Men, 1945–2000.* New York: Routledge-Falmer, 2002.

Dillon, Sam. "After Evicting Members,

Sorority Is Itself Evicted," *The New York Times*, March 13, 2007, p. A13.

———. "Evictions at Sorority Raise Issue of Bias," *The New York Times*, February 25, 2007, p. 13.

———. "Federal Panel Hammers Out Report on Recommendations to Shape Up Higher Education," *The New York Times*, August 11, 2006, p. A12.

Duenwald, Mary. "The Dorms May Be Great, but How's the Counseling?" *The New York Times*, October 26, 2004, pp. 1, 6.

Dziech, Billie Wright. "The Abuse of Power in Intimate Relationships," *The Chronicle of Higher Education*, March 20, 1998.

———, and Linda Weiner. *The Lecherous Professor: Sexual Harassment on Campus*. Boston: Beacon Press, 1984.

Edelstein, Andrew J., and Kevin McDonough. *The Seventies: From Hot Pants to Hot Tubs*. New York: Dutton, 1990.

Fallows, James. "The Early-Decision Racket," *Atlantic Monthly* #288 (September 2001), pp. 37–40, 42.

Finder, Alan. "For Some College Graduates, a Fanciful Detour (or Two) Before Their Careers Begin," *The New York Times*, October 23, 2005, p. 23.

Fisher, Bonnie S., Francis T. Cullen, and Michael G. Turner. *The Sexual Victimization of College Women*. Washington, D.C.: U.S. Department of Justice, December 2000.

Frank, Robert H. *Challenging the Myth: A Review of the Links among College Athletic Success, Student Quality, and Donations*. Report for the Knight Foundation Commission on Intercollegiate Athletics, May 2004. Online at http://www.knightcommission.org/about/frank_report/ (accessed on January 2, 2008).

Freeman, Mike. "When Values Collide: Clarett Got Unusual Aid in Ohio State Class," *The New York Times*, July 13, 2003, sec. 8, pp. 1, 4.

Glater, Jonathan D. "Colleges Chase as Cheats Shift to Higher Tech," *The New York Times*, May 18, 2006, pp. A1, A24.

Golden, Daniel. *The Price of Admission: How America's Ruling Class Buys Its Way into Elite Colleges—and Who Gets Left Outside the Gate*. New York: Crown, 2006.

Goldsen, Rose K., et al., *What College Students Think*. Princeton, NJ: D. Van Nostrand, 1960.

Hinton, David B. *Celluloid Ivy: Higher Education in the Movies, 1960–1990*. Metuchen, NJ: Scarecrow Press, 1994.

Hoover, Eric. "Academic Quality Influences Where High-Achieving Students Enroll, Survey Finds," *The Chronicle of Higher Education*, April 10, 2006.

Horowitz, Helen Lefkowitz. *Campus Life: Undergraduate Cultures from the End of the Eighteenth Century to the Present*. Chicago: University of Chicago Press, 1987.

The Internet Movie Database. Online at http://www.imdb.com/.

Karabel, Jerome. *The Chosen: The Hidden History of Admission and Exclusion at Harvard, Yale, and Princeton*. Boston: Houghton Mifflin, 2005.

Katz, Daniel, and Floyd Henry Allport. *Students' Attitudes: A Report of the Syracuse University Reaction Study*. Syracuse, NY: Craftsman Press, 1931.

Kean, Sean. "Report Blames College Practices for Limited Access of Minority and Low-Income Students," *The Chronicle of Higher Education*, September 1, 2006.

Lane, Ann J. "Gender, Power, and Sexuality: First, Do No Harm," *The Chronicle of Higher Education*, May 5, 2006.

Leonhardt, David. "The College Dropout Boom," *The New York Times*, May 24, 2005, pp. A1, A18–A19.

Lewin, Tamar. "At Colleges, Women Are Leaving Men in the Dust," *The New York Times*, July 9, 2006, pp. 1, 18.

Lipka, Sara. "Freshmen Increasingly Discuss Politics, Worry about Money, Survey Finds," *The Chronicle of Higher Education*, January 19, 2007.

———. "State Legislators as Co-Pilots," *The Chronicle of Higher Education*, December 16, 2005, p. A22.

Lucas, Christopher J. *American Higher Education: A History*, 2nd ed. New York: Palgrave Macmillan, 2006.

McGrath, Charles. "At $9.95 a Page, You Were Expecting Poetry?" *The New York Times*, September 10, 2006, sec. 4, pp. 1, 14.

———. "Term Paper Project, Part II," *The New York Times*, September 17, 2006, sec. 4, p. 5.

Marsh, Bill. "The Innocent Birth of the Spring Bacchanal," *The New York Times*, March 19, 2006, sec. 4, p. 3.

Mitchell, Elvis. "Revisiting Faber College (Toga, Toga, Toga)," *The New York Times*, August 25, 2003, pp. C1, C5.

Monaco, James. *How to Read a Film: Movies, Media, Multimedia*, 3rd ed. New York: Oxford University Press, 2000.

Nuwer, Hank. *Wrongs of Passage: Fraternities, Sororities, Hazing, and Binge Drinking*. Bloomington: Indiana University Press, 2001.

O'Neill, Nena and George. *Open Marriage: A New Life Style for Couples*. New York: M. Evans, 1972.

Pennington, Bill. "Small Colleges, Short of Men, Embrace Football," *The New York Times*, July 10, 2006, p. A1.

Peril, Lynn. *College Girls: Bluestockings, Sex Kittens, and Coeds, Then and Now*. New York: Norton, 2006.

Pope, Justin. "Once Confined to 'Hot Spots,' Admissions Anxiety Spreads." Online at http://encarta.msn.com/encnet/departments/college/ (accessed on November 26, 2006).

Pryor, John H. *The American Freshman: Forty Year Trends*. Los Angeles: Higher Education Research Institute, University of California, Los Angeles, 2007.

Rainey, Amy. "Survey Provides Further Evidence of High Parental Involvement with College Students," *The Chronicle of Higher Education*, March 31, 2006.

The Report of the President's Commission on Campus Unrest. Washington, D.C.: U.S. Government Printing Office, 1970.

Robertson, Tatsha. "Seniors Opting to Retire with a Touch of Class," *The Boston Globe*, October 17, 2005, pp. A1, A16.

Russell, Jenna. "Campuses with a Cause," *The Boston Globe*, April 18, 2005, pp. B1, B4.

Schwartz, Martin D., and Walter S. DeKeseredy. *Sexual Assault on the College Campus: The Role of Male Peer Support*. Thousand Oaks, CA: Sage, 1997.

Shapiro, Harold T. "Cognition, Character, and Culture in Undergraduate Education: Rhetoric and Reality," in Ronald G. Ehrenberg, ed., *The American University: National Treasure or Endangered Species?* Ithaca, NY: Cornell University Press, 1997, pp. 58–99.

Shulman, James L., and William G. Bowen. *The Game of Life: College Sports and Educational Values*. Princeton, NJ: Princeton University Press, 2001.

Steinberg, Jacques. *The Gate-Keepers: Inside the Admissions Process of a Premier College*. New York: Viking, 2002.

Suggs, Welch. "Gender Quotas? Not in College Sports," *The Chronicle of Higher Education*, July 1, 2005, pp. A24–A26.

Tobolowsky, Barbara F., and John W. Lowery. "Commercializing College: An Analysis of College Representations During Bowl Games," *International Journal of Educational Advancement* #6 (May 2006), pp. 232–42.

Trunk, Penelope. "Athletes Know How Game Is Played," *The Boston Globe*, July 9, 2006, pp. G1, G7.

Umphlett, Wiley Lee. *The Movies Go to College: Hollywood and the World of the College Life Film*. Rutherford, NJ: Farleigh Dickinson University Press, 1984.

Wechsler, Henry, et al., "Trends in College Binge Drinking During a Period of Increased Prevention Efforts: Findings from 4 Harvard School of Public Health College Alcohol Study Surveys: 1993–2001," *Journal of American College Health* #50 (March 2002), pp. 203–17.

Weingartner, Rudolph W. *Undergraduate Education: Goals and Means*. New York: American Council on Education and Macmillan, 1992.

Wertheimer, Linda K. "Join the Club: Colleges See Surge in New Student Groups," *The Boston Globe*, October 27, 2007, pp. A1, A6.

White, Wendy S. "Students, Parents, Colleges: Drawing the Lines," *The Chronicle of Higher Education*, December 16, 2005, p. B16.

Williams, Jeffrey J. "A New Indentured Class," *The Chronicle of Higher Education*, June 30, 2006, pp. B6–B7.

Zimbalist, Andrew. *Unpaid Professionals: Commercialism and Conflict in Big-Time College Sports*. Princeton, NJ: Princeton University Press, 1999.

INDEX

The Absent-Minded Professor (1961) 68, 159, 167
Academic dishonesty 64–71, 138–39, 190
Academic work 3, 5, 53–71, 77–82, 138–39, 145–50, 168, 201
Accepted (2006) 13, 26
The Accused (1949) 93
ACT (American College Testing Program) 25, 27, 28
Activism *see* Community activism; Political activism
The Activist (1969) 178
Administrators, college 2, 5, 12, 25–26, 35–36, 40–41, 63, 123, 140–42, 148–49, 158–61, 169, 180–81, 182, 189
Admissions, college *see* College admissions
Adolescence 6–8
Advisers 36, 77–82, 150, 201
The Affairs of Dobie Gillis (1953) 9, 30, 41, 56, 62, 69, 74, 95, 96
African Americans 33–34, 81–82, 110, 119, 120, 127, 153, 164, 182–83
The Age of Consent (1932) 77, 102, 105, 106
The Air Up There (1994) 160
Alcohol use 12, 122–23, 137, 140, 161–62, 166–68, 188, 190
The All American (1932) 191
All American (1953) 124, 159, 188
All-American Sweetheart (1937) 31, 163
All I Want (Try Seventeen) (2002) 46, 187
All of Me (1934) 89
All That Heaven Allows (1955) 61, 190
All the Fine Young Cannibals (1960) 106
All the Right Moves (1983) 17
All Women Have Secrets (1939) 78, 106
Alumni 2, 139, 192–202
Amateurism and sports 157–61
American Chai (2001) 20, 58, 120
American Desi (2001) 20, 49, 58
American Film Institute 1, 8
American Graffiti (1973) 22
American Pie (1999) 21
American Pie 2 (2001) 37, 43, 108

Amherst College 95, 96
Among Brothers (2005) 92, 140
Andy Hardy's Blonde Trouble (1944) 35, 39, 41, 59, 85
Andy Hardy's Double Life (1942) 35, 43
Angell, Robert Cooley 72
Animal House (1978) 1, 5, 12, 43, 63, 108, 122, 123, 129, 131, 135, 136, 138, 141, 202
Antiwar movement *see* Vietnam War era
Apartment for Peggy (1948) 51, 59, 78, 106
April Is My Religion (2001) 190
Arrival on campus 38–43, 95
Art School Confidential (2006) 81
Ashamed of Parents (1921) 117
Athletics *see* Sports

Baby, It's You (1983) 14, 38, 42
Bachelor Flat (1962) 87
Bachelor of Arts (1934) 175
Back to School (1986) 42, 87, 192
The Band Plays On (1934) 16, 105, 149, 151, 186
Baseball *see* Sports
Basketball *see* Sports
The Basketball Fix (1951) 165
Bathing Beauty (1944) 22, 73
Bedtime for Bonzo (1951) 147
Been Down So Long It Looks Like Up to Me (1971) 124, 125, 187
The Bell Jar (1979) 59, 113, 188
Betrayed (1916) 119
Better Luck Tomorrow (2003) 26
Beyond Glory (1948) 195
The Big Chill (1983) 199
The Big Fix (1947) 51, 165
The Big Game (1936) 146, 158, 163
Binge-drinking 122
Bisexuals *see* Gays, lesbians, and bisexuals
Blackbeard's Ghost (1968) 68, 144
Blacks 33–34, 81–82, 110, 119, 120, 127, 153, 164, 182–83
Blondie Goes to College (1942) 51
Blood Sisters (1987) 135

The Blot (1921) 72
Blue Chips (1994) 160
Bonzo Goes to College (1952) 146, 147, 163
Books, cost of 30
Boyle, Joanne 143
Boys and Girls (2000) 57, 95
Braveheart (1925) 16, 119, 163
Breaking Away (1979) 116
Brown of Harvard (1926) 36, 39, 47, 106, 163, 167
Brown University 18, 26, 27, 29, 97
The Brute Man (1946) 195
Buckley Amendment 38
The Burden of Race (1921) 120

California Institute of Technology 80
Camp Fear (1991) 73
Campus Confessions (1938) 45, 147
The Campus Flirt (1926) 21, 155
Campus Honeymoon (1948) 51
Campus Man (1987) 69, 73, 80
Campus Rhythm (1943) 23, 133
Campus student organizations 169–74
Can It Be Love (1992) 97
Cannibal Women in the Avocado Jungle of Death (1989) 61
Carlisle Indian School 17, 144
Carnal Knowledge (1971) 31, 95, 96, 107, 197
Carrington, Matthew 129
Catalog of Motion Pictures Produced in the United States (American Film Institute) 1, 8
Celluloid Ivy: Higher Education in the Movies, 1960–1990 (Hinton) 1
A Change of Seasons (1980) 89, 90
Change the Frame (1995) 195
Character-building and sports 143, 150, 152
Cheating 64–71, 138–39, 167
Chico State University (CA) 129
Chinese-Americans 119, 120, 127, 128
Cinderella Jones (1946) 18, 49
A Cinderella Story (2004) 21
City College of New York 111
Civil rights movement 182
Clarett, Maurice 149
Class of '44 (1973) 13, 66, 74, 131, 132
Class of Nuke 'Em High Part II: Subhumanoid Meltdown (1991) 171
Classes 55–58, 72–77, 96–97, 201
Clubs 172–74
C'mon, Let's Live a Little (1967) 177
Colgate University 97
Collective protest 7–8, 12, 169, 174–83, 202
College (1927) 22, 147, 156
College admissions 5, 7, 25–30, 200; *see also* ACT; College education, reasons for pursuing; Paying for college; SAT; *U.S. News and World Report*
College Coach (1933) 150

College Confidential (1960) 11
College Days (1926) 163
College education, reasons for pursuing 3, 13–24, 195
College expenses 30–34, 200
The College Hero (1927) 11, 46, 156
College Humor (1933) 44, 188
College Kickboxers (1990) 49, 185
College, leaving 186–92
College Love (1929) 163
College movies 1–2, 202; brief history 9–12; definition 8–9; impact on attitudes and behavior 2, 5–6, 123, 141–42; social reality and 3–6
College of the Holy Cross 165
College Rhythm (1934) 193–94, 195
College Swing (1938) 67
The College Widow (1915) 9, 143, 161
The College Widow (1927) 161, 162
College widows 161
College years 6–7
College, years after 192–202
Collegiate (1926) 66, 117
Collegiate subculture 6–8, 54
Columbia University 16, 97, 178, 181
Come Back, Little Sheba (1952) 104, 108
Coming Soon (1999) 5, 26, 29
Commencement addresses 191–92, 193
Communism on campus 175–77
Community activism 139, 183–85, 202
The Computer Wore Tennis Shoes (1969) 61, 62, 68, 207
Confessions of a Co-ed (1931) 11, 40, 104, 141
Confidentially Connie (1953) 76
The Contender (2000) 136
Cornell University 1, 18, 29
Courses, registering for 40–41, 55–58, 201
Crew *see* Sports
Cross-dressing 44, 111–12
Culture of sport 146, 168, 194
The Curve (1998) 66
Cynthia (1947) 105, 186

Daddy Long Legs (1919) 18, 49, 50, 191
Daddy Long Legs (1931) 18, 58, 191
Daddy Long Legs (1955) 18, 49, 50, 59, 191
Dancing Co-ed (1939) 170, 189
Dartmouth College 1, 165, 177, 192, 198
Daughters of Today (1924) 108
The Day It Came to Earth (1979) 63, 135
Dead Man on Campus (1998) 37, 46, 66
Dear Brigitte (1965) 174
The Debut (2000) 20
Deconstructing Harry (1997) 189
Defying Gravity (1997) 114, 137, 138
The Delicate Art of the Rifle (1996) 172
Demolition University (1997) 155
Didn't You Hear... (1983) 73, 107, 132
Dirty Harry (1971) 61
Dirty Tricks (1981) 89

Disney Pictures, Walt (Walt Disney Productions) 61, 62, 68, 167
Divided We Stand (2000) 82, 110, 183
D.O.A. (1988) 75, 89
Dr. Alien (1988) 57, 91
The Doctor Takes a Wife (1940) 149
Dodd College 75
The Doorway (2000) 52
The Dorm That Dripped Blood (1982) 64
Dormitories 46–52, 122
Down to You (2000) 58
Drag 44, 111–12
Dramatic productions 169, 172, 173, 174, 202
The Dream Machine (1990) 130, 132
Dream Trap (1990) 110, 132
Dreamboat (1952) 61, 74
Drive, He Said (1971) 181
The Drop Kick (1927) 38
Drugs 107, 124, 166–68, 187, 190
Drumline (2002) 21, 58, 107, 172
Duke University 20

Eadie Was a Lady (1945) 32, 69
Eden's Curve (2003) 93
Edge of Seventeen (2000) 9
The Eiger Sanction (1975) 89
Elopement (1951) 86, 191
End of the Harvest (1995) 173
End of the Road (1970) 73
Environmental movement 183
Every Girl Should Be Married (1948) 12
Everybody's All-American (1988) 101, 197
Everything Relative (1996) 199
Evolution (2001) 64
Expulsion 186, 188–90
Extortion (1938) 66
Extracurricular activities 169–74, 202

Faculty-student intimacy 82–94, 201
The Fair Co-ed (1927) 39, 155, 174
False Women (1921) 22
Family Educational Rights and Privacy Act of 1964 (FERPA) 38
Fandango (1985) 132
Fast Break (1979) 111, 149
Fast Food Nation (2006) 183
The Feminine Touch (1941) 148
Fighting Youth (1935) 147, 175
Filipino-American students 20, 129
Final Exam (1981) 63, 89, 124, 131, 139
First Daughter (2004) 36, 47
First Love (1977) 31, 32, 57
Flubber (1997) 68, 167
Followers (2000) 127
Foolin' Around (1980) 30
Football *see* Sports
For Those Who Think Young (1964) 118
Foreign Student (1994) 157, 188
Ft. Lauderdale (FL) 97, 107
Forty Little Mothers (1940) 192

The Fountainhead (1949) 9
Four Friends (1981) 118
Fraternities *see* Greek-letter organizations
Fraternity Demon (1992) 136
Fraternity Row (1977) 102, 128, 134, 139, 140
Fraternity Vacation (1985) 97
Free Speech Movement 177
Fresh Horses (1988) 57, 117
The Freshman (1925) 6, 35, 38, 42, 108, 109, 116, 146–47, 154, 155, 156, 194
The Freshman (1990) 27, 30, 36, 47
Freshman Love (1936) 146, 155, 161
Freshman Year (1938) 43, 44, 73, 127, 170
Freshmen 35–52, 95–96, 122, 123
Freshmen (1999) 20, 34, 73, 81, 110, 120, 127

Gambling on sports 161–65, 168, 192
Game Day (1999) 153
Gays, lesbians, and bisexuals 11, 36, 93, 111–15, 121, 155
Gender 43–44, 153–56, 174–75, 202
George Washington University 114
Georgetown University 82
Get Yourself a College Girl (1964) 107
Getting into College *see* College admissions
Getting Straight (1970) 88, 178–79
G.I. Bill (Servicemen's Readjustment Act of 1944) 51, 59
Gipp, George 152
Girl Crazy (1943) 23
The Girl in White (1952) 18, 59
The Girl Next Door (2004) 31, 33
Girl o' My Dreams (1934) 16, 156
The Girl Who Couldn't Grow Up (1917) 21
Girls Demand Excitement (1931) 174
The Girls' Room (2000) 65, 115
The Gladiator (1938) 166
Glory Road (2006) 148, 153
Going Greek (2001) 109, 122, 125, 131, 133, 138
Good News (1930) 9, 99, 106, 149
Good News (1947) 9, 31, 54, 100, 149, 156
The Good Shepherd (2006) 128
Good Will Hunting (1997) 80, 117
Goodbye, Columbus (1969) 116, 123, 195
Goodbye, My Fancy (1951) 86, 198
Gossip (2000) 93
Government, student 169, 174, 183, 202
Grades 53, 64–71, 76, 82–84, 89, 91–92, 136, 138, 145–50, 165, 190
The Graduate (1967) 195, 196, 207
Graduation 186, 190–92
The Grandee's Ring (1915) 143
Greek-letter organizations (fraternities and sororities) 1, 2, 5, 52, 97, 100, 101, 102–4, 109, 114, 122–42, 167, 169, 174, 201–2
The Group (1966) 113, 192

Hamburger—The Motion Picture (1986) 19, 189

Happy Together (1989) 48, 66, 76, 112
Harold and Kumar Go to White Castle (2004) 172
The Harrad Experiment (1973) 49, 105
Harvard Crew (1897) 9
Harvard, Here I Come (1941) 14, 15
Harvard Man (2001) 20, 27, 93, 165
Harvard University 3, 14, 15, 17, 18, 20, 21, 26, 27, 28, 31, 36, 37, 38, 61, 66, 82, 97, 119, 129, 151, 152, 163, 165, 167, 181, 189, 190, 191, 198
Hazing 43–46, 129–35, 200
The Hazing (The Campus Corpse) (1977) 133
He Got Game (1998) 161
Heart of Dixie (1989) 101, 110, 182
The Heart of Ezra Greer (1917) 117
Hell Night (1981) 135
Her First Romance (The Right Man) (1940) 60, 132
Herbie Fully Loaded (2005) 192
Here Come the Co-eds (1945) 14
Here I Am a Stranger (1939) 76
Hero for a Day (1939) 197, 198
High Time (1960) 14, 41, 50, 86, 130, 171, 192
Higher Education Research Institute (UCLA) 13, 24
Higher Learning (1995) 33, 49, 81, 108, 110
Hinton, David B. 1
H.M. Pulham, Esq. (1941) 198
Hold That Co-ed (1938) 154, 155
Hold That Line (1952) 16, 17, 166
Hollywood Production Code 10–11, 12, 32, 84, 87, 88, 96, 104, 106, 112
Holy Cross Junior College 23
Homophobia 137–38, 155
Homosexuals *see* Gays, lesbians, and bisexuals; Same-sex relationships
Hooking up 106–8
Horowitz, Helen Lefkowitz 7, 53, 64, 72
Horror-suspense films 12, 52, 135
Horse Feathers (1932) 72, 147
Hot Stuff (1929) 106
House Party 2 (1991) 30, 33, 81
Housing on campus 46–52
How Do I Love Thee? (1970) 88
How High (2001) 82
How I Got Into College (1989) 20, 27, 28, 148
How to Be Very, Very Popular (1955) 23, 47, 189
Howard University 21, 82
Howdy Broadway (1929) 9
Huddle (1932) 49, 117, 151
The Human Stain (2003) 21, 97, 120
Husband-hunters 12, 98–102

I Met My Love Again (1938) 72, 84
I Shot Andy Warhol (1996) 114
I Think I Do (1997) 114

Ice Princess (2005) 21
I'll Be Home for Christmas (1998) 69
The Impossible Years (1968) 177
In Good Company (2004) 14
In loco parentis policy 38, 47
Indian-Americans (India) 20, 49–50, 58, 120
Indian Americans (Native Americans) 17, 119–20, 145, 153, 163
Indiana University 116
Inexchange (2006) 106, 107
Inheritance, as reason for going to college 18–20
The Initiation (1984) 133
Interface (1984) 69
The Internet Movie Database 1, 9
Interviews, admissions 27
The Invisible Man (1933) 81
The Iron Major (1943) 177

Jack London (1943) 75
The Jackie Robinson Story (1950) 153
Jim Thorpe—All American (1951) 17, 120, 144, 145, 153, 158
Jobs, student 31–33
John Goldfarb, Please Come Home (1965) 143
Johnny Be Good (1988) 161, 166–67
Johns Hopkins University Medical School 102
Johnson, Owen 53
Joy in the Morning (1965) 59, 60

Kent State University 12, 178, 182
Kicking and Screaming (1995) 63, 96
Killer Me (2001) 31
Killer Party (1986) 74, 136
Kilroy Was Here (1947) 51, 78, 126, 170
King Frat (1979) 131, 135
A Kiss Before Dying (1956) 104
Knute Rockne—All American (1940) 143, 152

The Land of the College Prophets (2005) 32, 73
Last Time Out (1994) 168
The Last Year (2002) 115
The League of Frightened Gentlemen (1937) 46, 195
Learning Curves (2003) 67, 80, 108, 191
Legally Blonde (2000) 140
Legally Blonde 2: Red, White, and Blonde (2003) 140
Lesbians *see* Gays, lesbians, and bisexuals
Let's Go Collegiate (1941) 166
Lianna (1983) 93
Life Begins in College (1937) 7, 44, 120, 154
Little Sister (1992) 38, 42, 57
Living on campus 46–52
Loans, educational 30–31
Local Boy Makes Good (1931) 155

London, Jack 75
Loser (2000) 33, 47, 65, 92, 97
Louisiana (1947) 74, 75
Louisiana State University 149
Love, Honor, and Behave (1938) 105, 152, 186
The Love-Ins (1967) 189
Love Laughs at Andy Hardy (1947) 22
Love Story (1970) 118, 119
Loyalty 150–52

Magazines, student 169, 174
The Magic Garden of Stanley Sweetheart (1970) 97
Major, choosing a 55–58, 201
Make a Million (1935) 76
Maker of Men (1931) 40, 56
The Male Animal (1942) 73, 146, 174, 198
Man of the House (2005) 70, 93
Marriage 12, 36, 78, 98–102, 104–6, 122, 126, 186–87, 191
Marshall University 148
Masculinity *see* Gender
Massachusetts Institute of Technology 80, 117
Maybe It's Love (Eleven Men and a Girl) (1930) 161
Meatcleaver Massacre (Hollywood Meat Cleaver Massacre) (1977) 74
Memories of college days 198–202
Mental illness 38, 188
Mentoring 35–36, 77–82, 150, 201
Miller, Chris 1
Million Dollar Legs (1939) 157, 161
Mind Games (1996) 92
The Mirror Has Two Faces (1996) 77
The Misadventures of Margaret (1998) 92
Mr. Belvedere Goes to College (1949) 18, 19, 31, 40, 43, 170
Mr. Doodle Kicks Off (1938) 20, 41, 56, 147, 161
Mona Lisa Smile (2003) 47, 77, 93, 102
The Monkey's Uncle (1965) 68, 138
Most Precious Thing in Life (1934) 37, 117, 130, 133, 156
Mother Is a Freshman (1949) 42, 55, 85–86, 108
Mother's Day (1980) 198
The Movement 177
The Movies Go to College: Hollywood and the World of the College Life Film (Umphlett) 1
Mugsy's Girls (Delta Pi) (1985) 135
The Muppets Take Manhattan (1984) 190
Murder on the Campus (1933) 32
Musical groups and shows 58, 169, 171–72, 202
Musicals (movies) 9
My Big Fat Greek Wedding (2002) 18, 42
My Lucky Star (1938) 60

Naked in New York (1993) 197
National Lampoon's Animal House (1978) 1, 5, 12, 43, 63, 108, 122, 123, 129, 131, 135, 136, 138, 141, 202
Native Americans 17, 119–20, 145, 153, 163
Necessary Roughness (1991) 91, 149, 167
New Best Friend (2002) 191
New Left 177
New outsider subculture 7–8
New York Minute (2004) 31
New York University 14, 27, 36, 97
Newspapers, campus 169–71, 182, 189, 202
Night and Day (1946) 198
Night into Morning (1951) 64
Night of the Creeps (1986) 133
Night School (1981) 90
1969 (1988) 182
Nobody's Fool (1921) 132
Nobody's Perfect (1989) 111
Northwest Passage (1940) 189
Northwestern University 21
Nostalgia for college years 198–202
Now You See Him, Now You Don't (1972) 62, 68, 73
The Nutty Professor (1996) 74

Ohio State University 9, 149
Old Man Rhythm (1935) 43
Old School (2003) 69, 129, 141
Oleanna (1994) 91
The One and Only (1978) 195
One Minute to Play (1926) 20, 156
One on One (1977) 150, 159, 166
$1,000 a Touchdown (1939) 158, 161
Only 38 (1923) 37
Orange County (2002) 13, 22, 27
Ordinary Sinner (2003) 114
Organizations, campus student 169–74
Orientation programs 39–40, 95, 200
Outsider subculture 6–8
Outta Time (2002) 34
Over the Goal (1937) 45
Overnight Delivery (1998) 85

Palm Springs (CA) 97
Palm Springs Weekend (1963) 97
Parents of college students 2, 20–22, 31, 34, 35–38, 57–58, 156–57, 190–91, 200
Paying for college 30–34, 200
PCU (1994) 40, 63, 141, 175
Penelope (1966) 94
The Perfect Score (2004) 5, 29
Pieces (1983) 90
Pigskin Parade (1936) 7, 175, 195
Pinning 102–4, 131
Plagiarism 69–70
Plain Jane (1916) 31, 116
The Plastic Age (1925) 44, 47, 106, 155
Pledge Night (1988) 132, 133, 134, 136, 139

Pledging in Greek-letter organizations 97, 122–35
Political activism 7–8, 12, 169, 174–83, 202
Pregnancy 11, 102, 104–6, 196
Preppies (1982) 19, 42
The Pride of the Yankees (1942) 16, 128, 132
Primal Rage (1988) 61, 91, 109, 171
The Prince and Me (2004) 31, 47, 102
Princeton University 21, 23, 26, 27, 29, 143
The Private Public (2000) 94, 115
The Prodigy (1999) 69, 81, 131, 133, 136, 139
Production Code 10–11, 12, 32, 84, 87, 88, 96, 104, 106, 112
The Professor of Drama (1903) 9
Professor-student relations: in the classroom 72–77; mentoring 77–82; romantic and sexual 82–94, 201
The Program (1993) 66, 120, 144, 148, 159, 161, 167
Prohibition 161–62
Prozac Nation (2001) 38, 108
Psychic (1992) 91
Puddle Cruiser (1996) 151, 189
Pumpkin (2002) 129, 139, 140

The Quarterback (1926) 144
The Quarterback (1940) 95
Quiz Show (1994) 55

Race and ethnicity 21, 33–34, 49–50, 58, 81–82, 95, 119–21, 127, 128, 129, 146, 153, 64, 174, 182–83
Radcliffe College 116
Raiders of the Lost Ark (1981) 55
Rape 93–94, 108–11, 137
Real Genius (1985) 74
Reality Bites (1994) 192, 193
A Reason to Believe (1995) 77, 110, 175, 190
Rebel subculture 7–8
Recruitment of athletes 149, 157–61, 168
Red Letters (2000) 65, 92
Refuge, college as a 23
Registration for courses 40–41, 55–58, 95, 201
Residences on campus 46–52
Reunions, alumni 198
Revenge of the Nerds (1984) 38, 40, 52, 135, 136
The Revolutionary (1970) 178
Rich and Famous (1981) 187
Rise and Shine (1941) 146
Risky Business (1983) 27, 28
Road Trip (2000) 63, 107
Roadhouses 162, 163
Robinson, Jackie 153
Rockne, Knute 152
Rolled Stockings (1927) 163
Romance and sex 3, 4, 5, 10–11, 12, 22, 35, 36, 53, 55–57, 122; among students 95–121, 176–77, 201; between professors and students 82–94, 201; race, ethnicity, and 119–21; social class and 115–18, 120–21
Roommates 46–52, 187
Rose Bowl (1936) 152
R.P.M. (1970) 178, 180
Rudy (1993) 22, 158
Rush Week (1989) 131, 136
Rushing in Greek-letter organizations 123–29
Rutgers University 143

St. Elmo's Fire (1985) 187, 192
St. Louis Woman (Missouri Nightingale) (1934) 188
Same-sex relationships 36, 93, 112–15, 121
Sarah Lawrence College 21, 37–38
SAT (Scholastic Aptitude Test) 25–30, 53, 146, 200
Saturday's Hero (1951) 43, 78, 79, 127, 150, 155, 158, 188
Saturday's Heroes (1937) 159, 160
Saturday's Millions (1933) 163, 198
Scholarships 31, 33, 34, 172
School Daze (1988) 132, 133, 136, 182
School Ties (1992) 17, 29
Secrets of a Sorority Girl (1945) 41
Senior Prom (1958) 16, 118
The Seniors (1978) 33, 190, 195
Senseless (1998) 33, 71
Servicemen's Readjustment Act of 1944 (G.I. Bill) 51, 59
Seton Hill University 143
Sex Kittens Go to College (1960) 102
Sexism 132, 135–38, 155
Sexual assault 93–94, 108–11, 137
Sexual behavior 10–11, 12, 78–79, 82–94, 101–8, 132–33, 137, 189–90, 201; *see also* Gays, lesbians, and bisexuals; Same-sex relationships
Sexual harassment 82–94
Shapiro, Harold T. 53
Shaw, George Bernard 192
She Loves Me Not (1934) 3, 23, 47, 111, 112, 189
She Wrote the Book (1946) 55
She's All That (1999) 20
She's Working Her Way Through College (1952) 14, 76, 149, 172, 195
Shrieker (1997) 52
Sigma Chi (fraternity) 103
The Silent Scream (1980) 52
The Sin of Harold Diddlebock (Mad Wednesday) (1947) 194–95
Sis Hopkins (1941) 127, 188
'68 (1988) 20, 69, 182
Skull and Bones (Yale University) 128
The Skulls (2000) 128, 133, 135, 139
Slackers (2002) 67
The Slender Thread (1965) 184, 185
A Small Circle of Friends (1980) 37, 41, 170, 181, 190

Small Town Girl (1936) 3, 4
Smart Politics (1948) 185
Smith, Bruce 157
Smith College 36, 96, 187
Smith of Minnesota (1942) 157
Snafu (1945) 47, 48, 170
The Snob (1921) 117
So This Is College (1929) 44, 102, 156
Soak the Rich (1936) 65, 176, 179
Social class 49, 115–18, 120–21, 124–29
Someone to Remember (1943) 50
Son in Law (1993) 36, 37, 41, 42, 63
Son of Flubber (1963) 68, 167
The Sophomore (1929) 31
Sororities *see* Greek-letter organizations
Sorority Babes in the Slimeball Bowl-O-Rama (1988) 129, 133
Sorority Boys (2002) 112, 136, 137, 139
Sorority Girl (1957) 133, 134, 174
Sorority House (1939) 3, 104, 126, 127
Sorority House Massacre II (1990) 52
Spartacus (1960) 151
Spencer's Mountain (1963) 31
The Spirit of Notre Dame (1931) 42, 108, 146, 151
Splatter University (1984) 66
Splendor in the Grass (1961) 20, 190
Splitz (1984) 141
The Sport Parade (1932) 192
Sports 3, 4, 5, 9–10, 16–18, 22–23, 53, 107, 124–25, 143–68, 169, 192–93, 202
Sportsmanship 150, 152
Spring Break (1983) 97
Spring Madness (1938) 61, 191
The Squid and the Whale (2005) 93
The Stand-In (1999) 80
Stanford University 20, 27
State University of New York at Buffalo 123
Stay (2005) 93
Stealing Harvard (2002) 31
The Sterile Cuckoo (1969) 42
Stover at Yale (Johnson) 53
The Strawberry Statement (1970) 181
Strike Me Pink (1936) 67
The Strongest Man in the World (1975) 62, 68, 167
Strongheart (1914) 119
Student-athletes *see* Sports
Student government 169, 174, 183, 202
Student Tour (1934) 149
Students, college 2, 13; age 3, 6–8, 14, 50–51, 85–87, 95; dishonest 64–67; female 14–15, 18, 21–22, 32, 43–44, 58–61, 153–56, 202; gender and 43–44, 153–56, 174–75, 202; married 59–60, 98–102, 104–6; parents and 20–22, 31, 34, 35–38, 57–58, 156–57, 190–91, 200; professors and 72–94; race and ethnicity 21, 33–34, 49–50, 58, 81–82, 95, 119–21, 127, 128, 129, 146, 153, 164, 174, 182–83; serious 58–61; social class 49, 95, 115–18, 120–21, 124–29; weak 62–64
Students for a Democratic Society 177
Students, high school 2, 7, 13, 25–30, 43, 53, 159
Subcultures 6–8
Summertree (1971) 63
Sunny Skies (1930) 9, 45, 49, 95, 147, 156
Superdad (1974) 22, 36
The Sure Thing (1985) 79, 108
Surviving Desire (1991) 74
Sweet Lavender (1920) 116
The Sweetheart of Sigma Chi (1933) 103
Sweetheart of Sigma Chi (1946) 73, 163
Sweetheart of the Campus (1951) 10
Swim Girl, Swim (1927) 155
Swing That Cheer (1938) 151
A Swingin' Affair (1963) 128
The Swinging Cheerleaders (1974) 89, 107, 109, 155, 164, 170
Syracuse University 29

Take Care of My Little Girl (1951) 36, 70, 95, 126, 130, 138, 139
Take Her, She's Mine (1963) 21, 177
Tall Story (1960) 12, 56, 100, 148, 165
Tammy Tell Me True (1961) 87, 88, 101
Teacher's Pet (1958) 86
10 Things I Hate About You (1999) 20, 21
Tennis *see* Sports
Texas Western College (University of Texas at El Paso) 148, 153
That Hagen Girl (1947) 118, 172, 173
That's My Boy (1951) 6, 20, 157
Theatrical productions 169, 172, 173, 174, 202
These Glamour Girls (1939) 116
These Wilder Years (1956) 196
They're Playing with Fire (1984) 91
13 Conversations About One Thing (2001) 65
This Reckless Age (1932) 21
This Side of Heaven (1934) 36, 124
Thorpe, Jim 17, 145, 153, 158
Those Were the Days (At Good Old Siwash) (1940) 104, 124
The Thousand Dollar Husband (1916) 116
3 in the Attic (1968) 107
Threesome (1994) 48, 69, 113
Time Walker (1982) 141
Title IX of the Education Amendments of 1972, 155
Too Many Girls (1940) 22, 100
Top Man (1943) 59, 184
Touchdown (1931) 158
Track *see* Sports
Train Ride (2000) 109
Trick Dribble (2001) 95

Trouble Along the Way (1953) 158
Turnitin 69
Two Minutes to Play (1936) 103, 157

UCLA's Higher Education Research Institute 13
Umphlett, Wiley Lee 1
U.S. News and World Report 25, 123
University of California at Berkeley 20, 21, 75, 177, 178, 181, 182
University of California at Los Angeles 13, 20, 69, 153
University of Kentucky 165
University of Michigan 21, 157, 177, 199
University of Minnesota 157
University of Nevada at Las Vegas 69
University of North Carolina 72
University of Notre Dame 18, 23, 128, 143, 152, 158
University of Pittsburgh 21
University of Southern California 21, 134
University of Texas at El Paso (Texas Western College) 148, 153
University of Washington 21
University of Wisconsin 47, 102
The Unnamable (1988) 135
Up the Creek (1984) 63
The Upside of Anger (2005) 21, 191

Values and sports 150–52
Vamp (1986) 69
Van Wilder (2002) 33, 63, 136, 138, 171, 188
Varsity Blues (1999) 18
Varsity Show (1937) 172, 195
Veterans 51, 59, 125, 162
Vietnam War era 12, 63–64, 124, 125, 170, 174, 178–82, 183, 185

Volunteer work 169, 183–85
Voodoo (1995) 52, 133, 135

The Way We Were (1973) 175, 176
We Are Marshall (2006) 148
We Went to College (1936) 198, 199
Welcome to the Dollhouse (1995) 26
When the Boys Meet the Girls (1965) 23, 24
Where the Boys Are (1960) 78, 97, 98, 107
Where the Boys Are '84 (1984) 97, 98
While Thousands Cheer (1940) 163–64
Wild on the Beach (1965) 51
The Wild Party (1929) 65, 83, 84, 91
Wild, Wild Winter (1966) 16
Win That Girl (1928) 157
The Winning Stroke (1919) 163
Winter Carnival (1939) 198
Witch Academy (1993) 133
Witches' Brew (1980) 65
With Honors (1994) 80
The Wizard of Oz (1939) 3
Words and Music (1929) 9

Yale University 3, 20, 23, 26, 36, 49, 97, 102, 105, 117, 128, 151, 152, 163, 167, 186, 190, 198
A Yank at Oxford (1938) 147
Yes Sir, That's My Baby (1949) 106
Yesterday's Heroes (1940) 197
You Can't Ration Love (1944) 13, 98–99
Young Ideas (1943) 42, 85
The Young Lovers (1964) 63, 104, 105, 107, 187
Young Warriors (1983) 79, 132, 133, 136
Youth on Parade (1942) 13

Zabriskie Point (1970) 178

www.ingramcontent.com/pod-product-compliance
Lightning Source LLC
Chambersburg PA
CBHW032051300426
44116CB00007B/687